Juan Bautista de Anza

A late-nineteenth- or early-twentieth-century portrait said to be of
Juan Bautista de Anza. Courtesy of Palace of the Governors
Photo Archives (NMHM/DCA), 050828.

JUAN BAUTISTA DE ANZA

The King's Governor in New Mexico

Carlos R. Herrera

UNIVERSITY OF OKLAHOMA PRESS : NORMAN

Library of Congress Cataloging-in-Publication Data
Herrera, Carlos R., 1961–
Juan Bautista de Anza: the King's Governor in New Mexico / Carlos R.
Herrera.
        pages   cm
Includes bibliographical references and index.
ISBN 978-0-8061-4644-7 (hardcover: alk. paper)
1. Anza, Juan Bautista de, 1735–1788.
2. New Mexico—History—To 1848.
3. New Mexico—Politics and government—18th century.
4. Governors—New Mexico—Biography.
5. Indians of North America—New Mexico—History—18th century. 6.
Catholic Church—Missions—New Mexico—History—18th century.
7. New Mexico—History—18th century.
8. New Mexico—Biography.
9. Sonora (Mexico: State)—Biography.
I. Title.
II. Title: King's Governor in New Mexico.
F799.H46 2014
978.9'02092—dc23
[B]   2014017089

The paper in this book meets the guidelines for permanence and
durability of the Committee on Production Guidelines for Book
Longevity of the Council on Library Resources, Inc. ∞

1 2 3 4 5 6 7 8 9 10

To my wife, Herminia,
and my son, Jose Carlos

Contents

Contents

Illustrations

Figures

Maps

Acknowledgments

THIS BOOK BEGAN its life as a term paper I wrote for Professor John L. Kessell at the University of New Mexico in the fall of 1993. Through his guidance, those few pages evolved into a Ph.D. dissertation and eventually this book. I am, therefore, grateful to John for being a mentor and a friend. Dr. Rick Hendricks has also been an invaluable force in my academic life. Rick introduced me to the world of paleography at the University of New Mexico's (UNM's) Vargas Project, and he has consistently guided me in the right direction regarding ideas and sources. During my stay at UNM, I was lucky to have met and befriended Dr. Robert Himmerich y Valencia. Whether in the classroom or at his farm at Peñablanca, Bob shared a deep-rooted sense of New Mexico history and of life in general. Along with John and Rick, he taught me the importance of always treating people with respect, kindness, and compassion. For this, I am eternally grateful.

I would like to thank San Diego State University (SDSU) for employing me at a time when jobs were scarce, and also for providing support that allowed me to complete the research and writing needed to publish this book. Likewise, my students at SDSU and Vincent Memorial High School in Calexico, California, deserve thanks for listening to my thoughts regarding history. Please know that I have learned as much from all of you as you have from me.

I am grateful to the University of Oklahoma Press staff, in particular Kathleen Kelly, Bethany R. Mowry, Stephanie Attia, and Amy Hernandez, and to my copy editor Bruce Agnew for making the book publishing experience a smooth ride. Gratitude is owed to Ben Pease for the maps. Likewise, I extend thanks to Shaw Kinsley at the Tubac State Historic Park and

Daniel Kosharek at the Palace of the Governors Photo Archives in Santa Fe, for helping me secure permission to use some of the images and illustrations found in the book. I am particularly grateful to Naomi Torres, superintendent of the Juan Bautista de Anza National Historic Trail, for granting me use of the remarkable artwork of David Rickman and Bill Singleton. If a picture truly is worth a thousand words, then David's and Bill's paintings have done as much as I to share Anza's story with the world.

I am also grateful to my family. My siblings, and their children and grandchildren, have always been a source of inspiration. My parents, Irma Yslava de Herrera and Carlos P. Herrera, gave me life, but more importantly they taught me how to live it well. You have been there for me since the beginning, and I have become the man I am because of you.

My wife and son deserve thanks above all else. Herminia, on so many occasions you have honored me with patience and courage, especially at those times when I seemed consumed by my intellectual self. You are the guiding light of my life, and I love you dearly. And in response to my son Jose Carlos's question, "When is daddy going to finish that book so he can take me to the park?," the answer is "Today, and forevermore." Son, you are the soul of my soul, and I pray that when you get around to reading this book you are as proud of me as I have always been of you. I love you, buddy!

Juan Bautista de Anza

Introduction

S OMETIME LATE IN 1776, Juan Bautista de Anza sat in a Mexico City studio while an artist tried to capture on canvas the nature of this frontiersman from New Spain's far northern territory. For his formal portrait, Anza refused to don the fancy silk dress and powdered wigs of his urban counterparts in central Mexico. Instead, he sported a thick coat and a plumed hat that hinted at his social ranking among the hidalgo officer class to which he belonged in his native province of Sonora. Of Basque heritage, Anza displayed a long dark mane, thick mustache and beard, a prominent nose, and a piercing gaze that expressed the cunning of a hunter, or the constant vigilance of the hunted.[1]

Anza's sitting for a portrait coincided with his arrival in Mexico City as a famous and celebrated man. He had distinguished himself as a soldier on the desert landscape of the far north. As important, he had just completed the second of two expeditions from Sonora to Alta California. Anza's travels to this Pacific coast colony resulted in the founding of present-day San Francisco and cemented his reputation as an explorer and frontiersman. While in Mexico City, Anza toasted his good fortune and success with the viceroy and lobbied for his next assignment within Spain's imperial bureaucracy. He left Mexico City with high hopes for a prosperous future. After a brief assignment as commander of Sonora's military forces, Anza received an appointment to the governor's seat of New Mexico, a position he held from 1777 to 1787. His charge must have been difficult, considering the size of the territory entrusted to his care. In the eighteenth century the province included the present-day state of New Mexico as well as lands in eastern

Arizona, southern Colorado, southwestern Kansas, the Oklahoma Panhandle, and western Texas.

Anza remains one of the most important figures in the history of North America. His life is celebrated on plaques that adorn the walls of buildings in both northern Mexico and the U.S. Southwest. Schools, streets, deserts, and even a somewhat famous hotel in the small border town of Calexico, California, bear his name. And yet, unlike contemporaries such as Thomas Jefferson and George Washington, Anza the man remains obscure to a large portion of the people who share this frontier. Many are unaware that he served as governor of New Mexico for ten years. In large part this is because few of the civic monuments constructed in his honor reference his tenure in New Mexico; instead, they speak mostly to the exploratory and colonizing expeditions he led from Sonora to Alta California in the 1770s.[2] Anza's crossings to the Pacific coast are certainly worthy of intellectual and public discourse, but they represent one chapter in a life that was much more complex and diverse than that of a trailblazer.

Scholars, too, have largely ignored Anza's role as governor of New Mexico. Like an anecdotal thread, his life among the *nuevomexicanos* has weaved in and out of the greater fabric of North American history; Anza's history has remained scattered within the occasional pages of books, journal articles, government publications, and tourist pamphlets. This is unfortunate because Anza, as governor, proved a pivotal figure in Spain's efforts to sustain a Spanish American empire threatened by warring Indians and international rivals. He had come to New Mexico at a time when various indigenous groups all but besieged the colony, hoping to wrest from Pueblo Indians and Spaniards what few resources the high desert of this frontier offered. Through a series of changes made to the colony's administrative, judicial, religious, and defensive institutions, as well as a reorientation of the civic and private landscape the Hispanos (Hispanic New Mexicans) inhabited, Anza contributed to the preservation of New Mexico as a territory and the survival of the larger empire to which it belonged. His role in history assumes greater significance when considered within the context of eighteenth-century Spanish colonialism and—more to the point—the conceptual lens of the "Bourbon Reforms," the efforts of Spain's Bourbon kings to stimulate modernization through a policy that became known as Enlightened Absolutism.

Bourbon New Mexico in the Age of
Enlightened Absolutism

Through the work of academics such as the Benedictine monk Benito Jerónimo Feijóo, ideals of the Enlightenment trickled into Spain and greatly influenced the reform program that Bourbon monarchs implemented across their empire throughout the eighteenth century. From his ivory tower at the University of Oviedo, Feijóo had inspired his countrymen to transform the sociopolitical culture of Spain by infusing it with principles found in the works of John Locke, Montesquieu, Jean-Jacques Rousseau, Thomas Hobbes, and Jacques-Benigne Bossuet. These philosophers had called for the modernization of European societies by attacking long-standing traditions that catered primarily to the noble class. They scorned privilege as the prime qualification for social advancement, rejected religious fanaticism, and preferred the use of reason and scientific inquiry to solve civic problems.[3] The philosophers questioned and offered divergent opinions regarding the purpose of government. Locke and Rousseau insisted that all governments constituted a "social contract" by which leaders acquired the right to rule from the consent of the governed and were held responsible for upholding the well-being of the public. In contrast, Hobbes and Bossuet argued that leaders acquired their right to govern directly from God, and that citizens must preserve the state by maintaining social order and expressing absolute loyalty to their rulers. Although their views differed, these philosophers agreed that the purpose of all governments was to promote social progress and prosperity.

The Bourbon monarchy could not afford to ignore the intellectual dialogue of the Enlightenment if it hoped to preserve Spain's preeminent standing in Europe. Among the Bourbons, Carlos III—also known as Charles III, who ruled from 1759 to 1788—embraced this philosophical revolution and borrowed from it ideas used to create the body of laws referred to as the Bourbon Reforms. These legal measures reconceptualized the social, political, and economic institutions of Spain. With the reforms, the Bourbons increased revenues by imposing new taxes and creating royal monopolies on certain commodities. They used this capital to enhance Spain's military defenses and implemented a ministerial form of government that reinforced their absolute sovereignty and enabled them to be more intrusive in the personal lives of their subjects.

In his vision of this new and modern Spain, Carlos III declared that talent and loyalty to the state should supersede pedigree and privilege as markers for individual merit and promotion within the imperial bureaucracy. This ideal served as a cornerstone of the king's Enlightened Absolutism, and it had its greatest impact on American *criollo* elites—that is, American-born colonials who could claim pure Spanish descent on both their paternal and maternal sides. Colonials generated the bulk of the capital that had kept the empire fiscally solvent since the 1500s, for which they received social and economic privileges. Carlos III argued, however, that some of his Spanish American subjects tended to use their standing in the colonies primarily for personal gain. He considered such activities a threat to his royal supremacy, and he believed that any action that weakened his sovereignty also weakened Spain's ability to defend its colonies. Carlos III, therefore, altered the rules by which his colonial subjects achieved social mobility. He extended the king's favor primarily to those most willing to place the needs of the state before their own.[4] In so doing, Carlos III opened up the world of privilege to many who did not have the social connections or capital to achieve social advancement through birth, marriage, or purchase.

Carlos III's reform policy for advancement within the imperial bureaucracy played well into Juan Bautista de Anza's professional ambitions. As a member of one of Sonora's elite families, Anza was born into the privileged world of Spain's colonial nobility. As a servant of the crown, he understood all too well that preserving the social and economic standing of his family required that he prove himself worthy in the king's eye. In Sonora, men like Anza found ample opportunity to serve the state by contributing to its defense on the hostile frontier and promoting its economic progress. Frontier elites advanced by securing positions within the military and provincial governments. Anza fared well in both arenas, and his successful career can be largely attributed to the fact that he was American-born. As a product of New Spain's northern territory, he understood the challenges that all ethnic groups faced daily in this region of limited resources. He had learned to farm and ranch the land from his European predecessors, but he was as adept at interacting with the desert environment as his indigenous neighbors. This knowledge of frontier terrains and peoples helped to transform the public Anza into an effective military leader and political figure. He gained the king's favor by serving dutifully as a provincial officer and statesman, and it was in New Mexico that he made his greatest impression as an instrument of the Bourbon Reforms.

As grounded as they were in the Age of Reason, however, the Bourbon Reforms did not signal the onset of an era of fully "free" and "self-made" Spaniards. In return for his royal favor, the king demanded that this new generation of bureaucrats produce efficiency in government, increase profit margins, and remain loyal to his will. In reality, then, these measures promoted "enlightened despotism" in an age when Spain had witnessed its grasp of international power weaken as a result of territorial gains made by its competitors in Europe and abroad. The Bourbon Reforms thus proved a reactionary effort to preserve an empire extended beyond its feasible administrative limits, and which had become vulnerable to internal strife and the threat of foreign encroachment.

Implementation of the Bourbon Reforms in the Americas varied from region to region, but included as overall goals an increase in the efficiency of government and revenue and the enhancement of Spain's overseas defenses.[5] To meet these objectives, the Bourbons redefined the boundaries of Spain's colonial viceroyalties; in some cases they created new administrative units to better integrate peripheral provinces into their vast imperial structure. Such was the case with New Mexico. In 1776, the colony, along with other provinces situated in New Spain's northern frontier, was incorporated into a semiautonomous military district known as the *Comandancia General* (General Command). Administrative jurisdiction over the General Command was removed from the viceregal government in Mexico City and placed under the direction of a commandant general. This official held powers similar to that of a viceroy and answered only to the Council of the Indies and the king.

The commandant general's primary concern was to enhance the military posture of the provinces under his charge. New Mexico played a strategic role in this plan, as it represented Spain's first line of frontier defense against warring Indians and European competitors. In its far north, New Spain had always experienced hostility from indigenous peoples, and it was at these American Indians that the operations of the military district were first and foremost directed. Still, rival Europeans represented a further threat to Spain's hold on its North American colonies. Along the Pacific coast, Russian fur trappers had moved as far south as California. In Texas, French traders had made efforts to establish colonies until they were expelled from the territory in the 1760s as a result of the French and Indian War with British colonies. On the Atlantic seaboard, British Americans began to exert a push for independence from England. This they achieved in the final quarter of the eighteenth century; afterwards, they set their sights on the rest of North America. The Bourbons recognized the challenges posed by their European rivals on the continent. The creation of the General Command represented Spain's attempt to protect its American assets and, in so doing, to remain a serious contender for international power and prestige.

To enhance the defensive capabilities of the General Command, the Bourbons ordered a series of inspections of New Spain's northern presidial system in the 1760s and restructured this network of forts and outposts in the following decade. Underutilized garrisons were abandoned, and the remaining presidios were realigned to serve as a shield near, or along, the fortieth parallel. The presidio in New Mexico was allowed to remain at Santa Fe, and in 1780 the first commandant general, Teodoro de Croix, approved Governor Anza's plans for its reconstruction.[6]

The cost of defending an empire, however, strained the resources and economy of Spain. To remain fiscally sound and to enhance Spain's military might, the Bourbons assumed a more active role in directing and controlling the economies of their colonies. The burden of increasing revenues fell on the shoulders of Spanish Americans. Historian John Lynch estimates that economic reforms, such as improved methods of taxation and royal monopolies on key commodities, allowed Spanish monarchs to increase their eighteenth-century overseas income by forty percent. Such economic success, it would seem, came at the expense of alienating sectors of Spain's American population, a price the Bourbons appeared willing to pay to preserve their regal standing amongst the monarchies of Europe. In the process, Lynch notes, "they gained a revenue and lost an empire."[7]

New Mexico's lack of exploitable resources never allowed the colony to evolve into a financial asset for Spain, much less to generate the capital needed to sustain a military front. As such, the colony always functioned on subsidies received from Mexico City. What made New Mexico worth maintaining was its strategic location in New Spain's northern frontier. Situated in one of the most contested territories in all of the Americas, the colony had long served as a defensive buffer zone against Indian attacks and foreign intruders. By the eighteenth century, however, New Spain's regional military had failed to stem a growing tide of Apache and Comanche raids on Spanish settlements throughout New Mexico, Sonora, and Chihuahua. Spanish officials feared that these hostilities would eventually penetrate further south into New Spain's silver-producing region, and possibly threaten sites such as Zacatecas. The General Command had been created in large part to protect this north-central corridor. Within this military district, New Mexico was expected not only to protect itself but also to help defend more economically productive areas to its south.

Beyond the need to help defend Mexico's silver-producing region, the Bourbons also hoped that New Mexico would evolve from the isolated missionary frontier it had been in the seventeenth century into an active contributor to New Spain's general welfare. They wanted New Mexico to be more integrated politically, economically, and socially within the imperial structure. In the north, efforts were thus made to establish more efficient communication and contact between the colony and other provinces such as California and Texas. Spain also tried to curtail potential contraband trade with British American colonies by increasing economic ties between New Mexico and distant territories such as French-controlled Louisiana; it did this by ordering the exploration and establishment of a road network that tied the General Command to the rest of the empire. Anza himself had overseen the opening of a land route between Sonora and Alta California. This Pacific coast colony assumed an important role in Spain's reform plan of the eighteenth century, providing defense against further Russian advances into North America and a friendly coast for the Manila galleons that sailed between the East Indies and the Americas.

New Mexicans contributed to the defense of an empire at the same time that they tried to safeguard the unique nature of their pastoral society. The effort to preserve this culture, in turn, exposed a sharp contrast between Spain's imperial policies and the harsh reality of life on the desert frontier. Nuevomexicano resistance to the ideal of absolutism perhaps best illustrates this dichotomy. The Hispanos opposed enlightened despotism because it marked a sharp distinction between Hapsburg and Bourbon regalism—in short, because it challenged the sense of home rule they had enjoyed in New Mexico since the 1500s. As Harry W. Crosby notes, "The new regime initiated a campaign to return scattered authority to Madrid by reducing the influence of provincial nobles and cutting back on special privileges that had been retained by or granted to particular regions of Spain."[8]

The Bourbons did try to diminish the relative freedom that their subjects in northern New Spain had enjoyed under the previous Hapsburg dynasty. Colonials living in this peripheral frontier, however, considered a certain degree of regional autonomy necessary if they were to preserve their societies. Northerners expressed the view that "too much government" got in the way of survival. Historian Charles R. Cutter supported this view when he wrote, "Central Mexico and the peripheries of the far north differed in many ways. But the fundamental difference was that urban complexity gave way to rural simplicity. . . . In this geographic setting [the far north], physical reality and political ideology confronted one another."[9] Northern societies developed a flexibility of governance that allowed them to survive in a landscape of few natural resources. For New Mexicans, then, regional autonomy represented the freedom to spend more time tending to crops and flocks than maintaining the imperial structure. Mexico City's location far to the south of New Mexico only reinforced this sense of home rule.

Although eighteenth-century New Mexicans tried to preserve autonomy in their lives, Bourbon absolutism did not leave their colony untouched. As governor, Anza represented the spirit of enlightened despotism his king demanded for New Mexico. During his stay at Santa Fe, from 1778 to 1787, he carried out a series of reforms designed to increase royal control over the colony. Spain considered this essential if Anza was to fulfill his general orders of enhancing the defensive posture of the province. The monarchy held Anza responsible for militarizing New Mexico so that it could contribute to the maintenance of empire.

More than once, Hispanos opposed Anza's reform measures and complained about his despotic character and style of administration. They accused him of granting offices to ruthless relatives and friends who exploited residents for personal gain. Anza's superiors, however, allowed him a certain degree of nepotism and cronyism as long as he carried out the reform orders of his charge.

In the realm of administration, Anza made few changes to New Mexico's bureaucracy, and he governed with the same powers held by his predecessors. He did, however, improve communication between his office and that of his subordinates, as well as with superiors in Sonora and Chihuahua. In so doing Anza increased the ties that bound New Mexico to other provinces of the General Command and forced the colony to take a more active role in the process of imperial maintenance.

As with governance, Anza rendered few changes to New Mexico's judicial system. He held traditional powers enjoyed by his predecessors, which made him the most important arbiter in the colony. Hispanos did have access to courts of appeal outside of New Mexico, but few could afford travel expenses to Guadalajara, where jurisdiction of the colony's regular courts (*justicias ordinarias*) had been transferred in 1776. Because of this, many New Mexicans sought justice directly from the commandant general. And although this official assumed control of New Mexico's courts of privilege (*justicias privilegiadas*), rarely did commandants general alter legal judgments made by Anza during his tenure. Apparently they did not have to, for little if any evidence exists to suggest that Anza abused his powers as chief justice of the colony. Anza's superiors seemingly allowed him great latitude in legal matters, thereby reducing the influence that special interest groups—such as military officers and missionaries—exerted over the affairs of the colony. Ultimately, however, the Bourbons granted Anza almost complete authority over the colony's judiciary because as governor he served as an extension of the crown, and all final decisions regarding justice rested with him. On this issue, Cutter concludes that governors in peripheral provinces, such as New Mexico, exerted a great deal of power in judicial matters and were considered the "preeminent judicial representative of the crown at the provincial level."[10]

One of the groups most affected by Anza's reformist administration was the Custody of Saint Francis. During his tenure in New Mexico, Anza imposed the ideal of Bourbon absolutism on the Franciscans by stripping them of traditional privileges and powers they had enjoyed since the 1500s. Of these, the most significant included tribute paid by the Pueblo Indians in the form of goods, and the authority the friars possessed to determine mission assignments.

The attack on religious orders actually predated the Bourbons and found early expression during the reign of Isabel and Fernando, the Catholic Monarchs. In the 1500s, the pope had granted King Fernando administrative control over the Catholic Church in Spain and its empire, a power supposedly legitimized as the *Patronato Real* (royal patronage). During the Bourbon era, Carlos III utilized the ideal of royal patronage to impose enlightened despotism on his imperial church. The king was not antireligious, and his efforts to subdue the regular clergy in America stemmed more from his belief that the clergy had failed to incorporate American Indians into Spanish society. Although the Jesuits in Sonora had played a significant role in his upbringing, Anza agreed that the mission ideal in New Spain's far northern territory had failed. For this reason, he promoted an Indian incorporation policy that gave indigenous peoples little choice regarding their relations with Spain: either they accepted peace and economic trade, or they would feel the might of Spanish arms.

Anza's most successful reforms addressed the problem of militarizing New Mexico. The governor first initiated his defense program in the region of El Paso, where it affected salaried troops and lay citizens alike.[11] Spain had always depended on citizen armies to defend its empire, and it continued to do so well into the eighteenth century. Service in militias under Anza, however, bordered on conscription, for which the nuevomexicanos complained ardently. They argued that forced military service took them away from more important duties such as tending their fields and flocks, which, in turn, threatened the colony with food shortages.

Anza's military reforms also affected the landscape and homes of New Mexico's populace. Proposing a plan that would transform all Spanish settlements in the colony into defensive zones, he initiated a building code that outlined, in detail, specific requirements for the construction or remodeling of homes and towns. Anza's instructions left no doubt that the colony's physical appearance would resemble a military camp designed to achieve the defensive ideal of the Bourbon Reforms.

Professional troops also felt the hand of Anza's administration.[12] In the 1580s, the Hapsburgs initiated the presidial system in the far north for the protection of citizens and New Spain's silver-mining region. By the 1700s, however, the presidios had fallen prey to corrupt officers who exploited troops for personal gain. Like Anza, most of these men came from powerful elite families who controlled local economies and governments; many had acquired their military posts primarily to enhance personal business investments. As presidial captains, these officers controlled the garrison supply system and tended to inflate prices on military equipment and food needed by their men. This form of corruption reduced troops to the condition of indebted peons. To alleviate this problem, King Carlos III ordered that the supply and sale of goods to troops come under the control of a salaried *habilitado,* or paymaster. During his tenure, Anza received praise for attempting to ensure the success of this new system in New Mexico. As the province's military leader, he insisted that professional troops be treated fairly and provided for adequately. Anza seems not to have abused his officer standing in New Mexico, but there does exist some evidence to suggest that he profited from corrupt activities earlier while serving as captain of the Tubac presidio—a post he held from 1760 to 1778—in his home province of Sonora.[13]

Anza's reformist program affected all New Mexico residents, but the defensive ideals required of him were first and foremost designed to defend the province from hostile Indian groups. The question of how to deal with combative Indians had plagued Spain from the moment of contact. In this regard, New Spain achieved limited success in its northern frontier through the use of the mission and the presidio. These institutions of acculturation and submission ultimately failed at establishing a lasting peace between Indians and Spaniards who competed for the limited resources of this arid landscape. As an alternative to these institutions, Anza brought to New Mexico a strategy for peace that had worked for him in Sonora, and which gained him his widest repute as a servant of the crown.[14] Known as "peace by purchase," Anza's plan focused on co-opting or buying off Indians by providing them with goods they desired and which Spain could provide. As it had earlier on the Chichimeca frontier, peace on these terms proved cheaper than war, but it came with a clear caveat—that those Native Americans who maintained a hostile posture towards Spain would suffer the heavy hand of an enhanced and more lethal Spanish military.

Anza's dual approach to peace in New Mexico bore positive fruit in 1779. That year, he conducted a successful campaign in present-day Colorado against Cuerno Verde, a prominent Comanche war chief. Cuerno Verde's death in this campaign greatly enhanced Anza's reputation with the Comanches, a standing he quickly exploited to his advantage among other warring natives. Anza warned hostile Indians that they would experience similar defeats unless they agreed to become allies of Spain. He did promise goods, military aid, and increased trade to groups who chose peace over war. In 1780, Anza made good on this ideal when he cemented an alliance with the Hopis, who had suffered a devastating famine due to a three-year drought.

It took several years for Anza to achieve in the north the strategy of peace by purchase. He had refused to negotiate an alliance with the Comanches until all of the groups of this nation agreed to a united peace. In 1786, they did so, and all parties signed what has been called the "Comanche Peace." For Anza, the treaty represented the high point of his role as an instrument of the Bourbon Reforms and servant of his king. Perhaps more important, it stood as a testament of his views regarding Spanish-Indian relations in the hostile north. Since his childhood in Sonora, Anza had come to believe that human life on the harsh frontier was enhanced when ethnic groups agreed to interact socially and economically rather than on the field of battle.

As a student of the Spanish Borderlands, I applaud and welcome any research that sheds light on the life and times of Juan Bautista de Anza. It is my belief that a comprehensive study of his governorship is long overdue. It is also my hope that this book helps to fill a gap in the history of New Mexico and assigns Anza his due place in the greater story of North America. Anza's life offers insight into the unique Hispanic culture that evolved in New Spain's far northern territory, which continues to captivate the imaginations of those who study it and those who live it. He lived during a time when an environment of want forced all ethnic groups of the desert to interact on a more equal basis if they were to survive in the unforgiving land. It seems relevant, perhaps even prudent, to take a closer look at how Anza answered questions regarding the threat of environmental crisis and increased social tensions that defined his time, which seem to be prevalent around the world today. In this regard, Anza's contribution to the human experience truly was remarkable.

Part I

Anza's Sonora

CHAPTER ONE

Anza's Sonora

I N 1778, JUAN BAUTISTA DE ANZA assumed the office of governor in New Mexico, a post he held for the last nine years of his life and which proved the pinnacle of his military and political career. It was in Sonora, however, in the frontier he called home, that Anza honed the life skills he needed to maneuver successfully through the labyrinth of Spain's imperial bureaucracy, and to secure his place within the pages of Spanish American history. The desert of Anza's youth could be a demanding and cruel teacher, but it always schooled its children on the means of survival in an environment of want. Life's lessons were not lost on Anza, who learned early on that the clash of arms on the arid frontier seemed a necessary evil. Sonorans did not devalue life; in fact they embraced it fully. They understood, however, that one's ability to fight fiercely for the limited resources of this landscape could mean the difference between life and death. This cognition of war and peace served as a common thread that bound all Sonorans to the land and to each other; it was a life view shared by all ethnic groups of the desert.

Anza was reared in this environment of constant war. The daily diet of conflict between ethnic groups that he witnessed as a child gave him insight into the warrior's way. As a frontier soldier, he soon learned how Sonora's landscape influenced the military tactics of the enemy he was expected to hunt down, including guerrilla warfare and raiding. Indians had long conducted raids to acquire supplies, especially during times of crisis when the earth fell short of its promise of food and threatened the people with famine and death. From this tradition of raiding, Anza perhaps learned the most valuable lesson of all: peace, and the resultant preservation of life in the desert, could best be achieved through an exchange of goods rather than bullets. In many ways, Anza's understanding of the interplay between culture and environment made him better suited for New Spain's northern frontier than were Spanish-born newcomers—imported peninsulars who always complained about the harsh setting and unconventional war tactics of the Indians. It is fitting, therefore, that an investigation of the qualities Anza brought to the office of governor in New Mexico be prefaced by an exploration of the physical, ethnic, and political landscape that molded his character in Sonora.

Mother Earth and Her Children

With the exception of the northwestern corner of the province, an arid and barren desert, Anza's Sonora consisted mostly of mountainous terrain with limited sources of water and arable land.[1] This geologic reality made human existence difficult to sustain; it defined life in colonial Sonora as an antagonistic affair in which inhabitants competed for their daily bread. As historians Thomas H. Naylor and Charles W. Polzer have noted, "This was a region of broad, treeless basins with uncertain water and forage; the natives were semi-nomadic, loosely organized, and generally hostile . . . in many ways the north remained a terra incognita, defying conquest and exploitation."[2]

Prior to the coming of Europeans, the Pima, Ópata, and Apache Indians, among others, had developed ecological bonds with the parched landscape of Sonora. Here, the environment determined the nature of indigenous societies and their means of sustenance. The Sonorans engaged in cyclical migrations that took them from one resource space to another. They alternated between nomadic, semisedentary, and settled existences depending on environmental conditions. When water was scarce, Indians moved around in search of game and the natural bounty that mother earth provided; when abundant, they settled on river valleys and cultivated a variety of foods.

Whether as nomadic hunters or settled farmers, Sonora's Indians were tied to specific areas of their environment—as well as to the game and arable lands these spaces provided—at different points in time. Cynthia Radding has described these regions as "distinct zones of production." She argues that the spatial relationship between human groups and the environment determined the evolution of culture in Sonora for both indigenous and

European groups. For her, this process of social ecology "signifies a living and changing complex of relations that developed historically among diverse human populations and with the land they acquired. It refers both to the social structures through which different ethnic communities re-created their cultures and to the political implications of resource allocation in the region."[3]

Without a doubt, the limited resources of northern Sonora determined the nature of the tribal chieftaincies that evolved among indigenous groups of the region. In the northernmost section of province—the *Pimería Alta Trincheras* (rock terraces)—cultural groups followed water sources in search of arable land on which to construct temporary *rancherías* (farming hamlets). At these sites, the Indians cultivated a variety of food products including corn, chili, squash, and beans. Trincheras groups added to their food supply by hunting, gathering, and trade with Indians of today's southern Arizona and northwestern Chihuahua. Further south, in the San Miguel and Bavispe valleys, and along the northern tributaries of the Yaqui and Mayo rivers, *Río Sonora* cultural groups developed urban centers by the thirteenth and fourteenth centuries. These Indians were more settled than their northern counterparts, and their economies and societies were agriculturally based.

All Sonorans competed for the fertile lands and water sources the territory offered. This relationship between mother earth and her children affected relations between groups; it made conflict a constant factor among them. By the sixteenth century, Sonora's Indians also had to compete for limited resources with the developing horse cultures of Arizona and New Mexico. With the adoption of the horse in the 1600s, these nomadic bands, most notably the Apaches, intensified the nature of warfare on the northern frontier and forced the Sonorans to seek alliances with the Spanish newcomers.[4]

As the Spaniards had in Mesoamerica, they came to New Spain's far northern territory in search of precious metals and Indian labor. First encounters were both confusing and disastrous. In the 1530s, Álvar Núñez Cabeza de Vaca had laid a foundation of hope among the Indians he encountered in his travels—a hope that Europeans and Indians could find a way to coexist in the arid deserts of the far north.[5] This ideal was shattered by the slaving activities of Nuño de Guzmán and those Spaniards who believed that the indigenous peoples of the region could best serve them as a labor force. The full-blown exploitation of Sonora's Indians, however, arrived with the settlement of the Mixtón War in the early 1540s and the resultant expansion of New Spain's mining frontier into the far north.[6] The discovery of silver at sites such as Zacatecas proved significant for Sonora, for it was the dream of striking it rich that had first brought Europeans, including Anza's father, to the region.

Ultimately, it was the Spanish crown that assumed responsibility for determining the fate of Sonora's Indians. Since the reign of the Catholic Monarchs Fernando and Isabel in the late fifteenth and early sixteenth centuries, Spain had engaged in a process of transatlantic colonialism designed to expand its frontiers and to bring Native Americans into its empire. Spaniards, however, found it difficult to define the nature of this incorporation. While the likes of Bartolomé de Las Casas cried out for a spiritual conquest of American natives, enterprising colonists demanded access to Indian labor if they were to carry out the process of empire building in the so-called New World. Spanish monarchs found themselves caught in the middle of this Indian debate. They could not avoid the process of evangelization; this, after all, had been one of the main arguments used to justify the conquest and colonization of America.[7] Likewise, the crown could not achieve its imperial designs for the New World without the help of adventuring and ambitious subjects. In the end, the kings of Spain set upon a course of exploitation and conversion. As John L. Kessell noted:

> Plainly then, the natives of America had to be made over both spiritually and physically; they must become not only orthodox but productive as well. Just how this two-fold transformation was to be accomplished, a transformation seemingly based upon the naïve supposition that you could save a man's soul while you were breaking his back, became the burning issue of the day.[8]

The education, conversion, and assimilation of Sonora's Indians into Spanish society became the domain of Jesuit priests. Loyola's black robes had cut an evangelical path along the Sierra Madre Occidental that ultimately brought the Jesuits to New Spain's northwestern territory. From the 1590s to 1767, clerics such as Eusebio Francisco Kino and Juan María de Salvatierra expanded the Christian fold by completing a mission-building program among the natives of Sonora, Sinaloa, and Baja California.[9] The Jesuit missionary empire differed significantly from the ecclesiastical front

Mission San Xavier del Bac, Tucson, Arizona.
Courtesy of Herminia Leon.

attempted by Spain among the more sedentary Pueblo Indians of New Mexico. Among the latter, Franciscan friars utilized Indian labor to construct missions within preexisting Pueblo communities. Although this plan increased ties between Indian and Spaniard, it did little to bring the Pueblos completely into the Christian world. The Indians simply regarded the friars as guests who had come to their homes bearing material goods and religious practices that enhanced their own culture.

In Sonora, the Jesuits employed more practical means to lure natives to Christianity. They rounded up the Indians into artificial mission-communities known as *reducciones,* and nurtured a reciprocal relationship between themselves and those natives willing to accept them. In return for the Indians' allegiance and conversion, the Jesuits offered material goods that the Indians found attractive and practical, including glass beads, tobacco, food products, textiles, metal tools and weapons, and of course domestic livestock. The Jesuits also introduced European systems of agriculture and a market economy that increased the Indians' ability to procure food and supplies. These mechanisms of production and trade proved significant in defining the missions as well as Indian-Jesuit relations.

For the priests, the reducción was like an artist's clean, new canvas, on which they sought to create a living representation of the mission ideal they had brought with them from Europe. The padres themselves were the brushes that made physical contact with the canvas and made images of Christianity come to life on the desert landscape. The Indians were the raw paint transformed into figures of the converted and saved. And of course, there was God, the supreme artist who had made it all possible.

The Indians were more practical. For them, the mission community represented a secure domain that ensured a food supply and made possible the sale of goods to the Spanish military, civilians, and other Indian tribes. Through the concept of *ethnogenesis,* "a term that denotes the birth or rebirth of ethnic identities in different historical moments," Radding argues that European systems of agriculture and the market economy altered the traditional ethnic spaces and identities of Sonora's indigenous peoples. "Opatas, Pimas, and Eudeves survived as ethnic entities well into the nineteenth century, but the political, economic, and social dimensions of their cultural identity were radically changed through their relations with the dominant society and through the internal articulation of their communities."[10]

Kessell and Radding suggest that the European presence in Sonora did not obliterate indigenous cultures. Rather, the Indians tried to preserve their way of life and autonomy by adopting aspects of the social, legal, and economic mechanisms Spain had introduced into the region. Sonora natives who accepted the Jesuits did so because the padres shielded them from excessive labor exploitation and offered them assurance that the Spanish government would protect their legal right to work the land for profit. So long as the Jesuits remained in Sonora, mission Indians enjoyed the ability to transform this economic power into the social capital they needed to define the nature of their ethnic spaces, including land use and cultural identity. This strategy of accommodation, however, backfired on those Native Americans who became increasingly dependent on the missions for their daily bread. The Jesuit expulsion from Sonora in 1767 destroyed the reciprocal relationship between priest and Indian. With the Jesuits gone, and the resultant secularization of mission lands, the Indians were left to the mercy of Spanish colonists who transformed them into a peasant labor force.[11]

Not all native Sonorans accepted the Spaniards. For the most resistant—including the Yaquis, Seris, and Apaches—the story of their interaction with Spain is characterized by recurring periods of ethnic violence. At one point or another, even those natives most affected by Spain's presence in Sonora, such as the Pimas and Ópatas, rebelled. In most if not all of these cases, violence represented a breakdown in the mutual ties that had bound Indian and Spaniard to each other in this environment of limited resources. The native Sonorans took up arms against their Spanish neighbors when gifts and material goods stopped flowing, when demands for labor and loyalty proved excessive, and when Europeans resorted to force by military might in their effort to subjugate indigenous peoples.[12]

The *Reglamento y Ordenanzas* (Regulations and Ordinances) of 1729

Spain's push into Mexico's vast northern territory had unfolded along three geographical corridors: the west coast to Culiacán, Sonora, and later Alta California; the central plateau that ended at New Mexico; and a northeastern route established in earnest in the 1680s to confront French incursions into Texas. To help defend this frontier, Spain established a presidial system that, for all practical purposes, served a role similar to that of the present-day U.S. Border Patrol, which was established more than two hundred years later.

The Spanish border patrol was charged with monitoring and controlling the movement of people between physical spaces. Unlike the U.S. Border Patrol—which attempts to stem the flow of people north from Latin America—the presidios worked to prevent the territorial advancement of Europeans and hostile Indians from the northern fringes of the *Provincias Internas* (Internal Provinces) into southern settlements. Spain's greatest concern regarding the flow of humans across these northern frontiers focused primarily on the raiding practices of the Apaches and Comanches. The Spaniards feared that these raids would not only disrupt the silver production industry at sites such as Zacatecas but also encourage France's continued incursion onto Spanish lands.

In 1719, the threat of French incursions loomed large in the mind of New Mexico's governor, Antonio de Valverde Cosío. He heard rumors that

Frenchmen were supplying muskets and pistols to Pawnee Indians of what is now Nebraska. Determined to discover the truth, Valverde hunted the alleged gunrunners through October but eventually abandoned the trail. The search continued the following summer under the command of Lieutenant Governor Pedro de Villasur. On the twelfth of August, Villasur and his troops—including Pueblo Indian allies—made camp on a grassy Nebraska plain near the confluence of the Platte and Loup rivers. The next day, at first light, violent screams broke the calm of dawn as a large force of Pawnee and Oto Indians fell upon the slumbering Spanish camp. The Spaniards scrambled into formation only to find themselves completely surrounded by natives, some of whom were brandishing European-made firearms. Villasur may have been the first to fall, but within minutes the battle was over and his blood, along with that of forty-three slain Spanish and Pueblo soldiers, began to stain the dusty Nebraska soil. The remaining troops, about fifty-three in all, retreated to Santa Fe. Here, the story of the Villasur expedition assumed an air of mystery when the survivors could not agree whether Frenchmen had aided the Indians during the attack on the Spanish camp. Governor Valverde lamented the loss of his men but continued to push the notion that heretical French Huguenots had lured the Pawnees and Otos to war. In Spain, King Carlos III overlooked Valverde's claims regarding French provocateurs, but he refused to ignore the fact that in one swift thrust, the Santa Fe presidio had lost a full third of its garrison because of the Villasur affair. The king demanded answers; he wanted to know why the presidial system in his North American domain was not working.[13]

In 1722, Viceroy Juan de Acuña, the Marqués de Casafuerte, ordered Brigadier General Pedro de Rivera y Villalón to inspect the condition of Spain's frontier presidios and determine if their defensive capabilities could be enhanced. Rivera toured the Provincias Internas from 1724 to 1728, covering some seven thousand miles on horseback. He concluded that military discipline in the far north was wanting among presidial troops, and that financial abuses by their officers were common.[14] Herbert I. Priestly has pointed out that Rivera expressed great concern about the need to "eliminate the practice of paying presidial troops in merchandise sold by their officers—a system that injured the soldiers and made the officers mere merchants."[15] From its inception, then, New Spain's presidial system had quickly evolved into a moneymaking bureaucracy that enriched local elites of the north but failed in its intended purpose of monitoring human traffic across ethnic spaces. Officials worried that the porous nature of the frontier would further jeopardize peace in the region. They pressed Rivera for answers and for a plan that would enhance Spain's hold on its North American domains.

Rivera's Reglamento y Ordenanzas of 1729 represented Spain's effort to defend land it had already conquered in the Americas and aimed also to fulfill the king's demand that the overall cost of military expenditures in New Spain should be reduced. The plan seemed simple enough; garrisons of the northern frontier would no longer be allowed to function independent of each other, but would be expected to coordinate defensive efforts as well as to consolidate manpower and resources.

Rivera called for a reduction of garrisons—from twenty-three to nineteen—which decreased Spain's military budget for the north from 444,883 to 262,000 pesos, a saving of 182,883 pesos.[16] In addition, Rivera recommended a reduction of troops stationed along the three northern geographical fronts, basing the elimination of personnel on the degree of hostilities in each region. In Texas, where Indian attacks had temporarily subsided, the presidios lost half their forces. Troops serving in the Texas garrisons, however, were exempted from additional cuts in salaries, which dropped elsewhere from 450 to 365 pesos per year.[17]

Rivera's Reglamento also addressed the question of abusive officers. The general had exposed a tradition of corruption by which commanders of presidio garrisons and government officials enriched themselves at the expense of troops. Treasury officers, for example, charged soldiers a fee—the *quite*—for distributing their salaries. Some garrison captains entered into agreements with merchants from central Mexico by which the merchants provided inferior goods to officers, who in turn sold the products to their men at inflated prices. On occasion, captains failed to report vacancies in their garrisons due to death or desertion, but continued to collect salaries for these posts. This practice tended to leave presidios undermanned and deprived widows and children of pensions earned by deceased husbands and fathers.[18] Another widespread form of corruption involved the use of presidial troops as manual labor on farms or ranches owned by officers. Local military authorities deemed such a practice justified—a way for soldiers to pay off debts—and they demanded the freedom to act as they did for having to serve in such a violent and inhospitable landscape.

Officers serving in the north received little or no formal military training for the conditions they would be facing. They believed that the harsh frontier molded the character and abilities they needed to legitimize their place in the elite corps. Some lived at their presidios while others served as absentee officers; the majority surrounded themselves with ardent supporters whose promotions through the ranks were based on loyalty or nepotism. Most officers engaged in economic ventures that complemented their military income. In some provinces, such as New Mexico, governors also served as presidial captains. And although not all officers of the north engaged in questionable activities, enough of them did to bring down upon themselves investigation and reform.

Rivera's Reglamento y Ordenanzas attempted to impose a much-needed air of professionalism on public servants who had a long tradition of malfeasance. In the effort to rule by the ideal of absolutism, the Bourbons supported Rivera's plan to punish and/or replace officers found guilty of using their stations for personal gain.[19]

The Pima Rebellion

Rivera's military reform measures and budget cuts may have impressed his king, but they did little to ease the tension between ethnic groups in the northern frontier. In the 1730s, Spanish colonists in Sonora demanded access to arable lands controlled by the missions, which had primarily served the interests of the indigenous population. As it had in the past, competition for this limited resource ignited the wrath of Sonora's natives. Then, in 1736, the discovery of silver in the region of Arizona lured hordes of would-be miners to the colony. The influx of colonists further strained Sonora's resource base and fueled animosity between groups. Native Sonorans resented the expansion of the silver frontier into their homeland because it included increased demands for land and Indian labor. In response to this new encroachment, the Seris, Yaquis, Lower Pimas, and Apaches conducted separate waves of offensives to keep the Spanish intruders at bay. The shattered peace ran through the 1740s, and in 1751—the year before Anza became a cadet among the troops of Fronteras—the violence reached its zenith when the Upper Pimas of the Pimería Alta took up arms against their Spanish neighbors.[20]

The discord that grew into the Pima rebellion had been roused in the 1740s and involved multiple causes. In the region around Guevavi between

1745 and 1751, measles and smallpox had taken their toll on the Pimas. To reverse a decline in the mission population, presidial troops relocated Indians from their villages to mission reducciones. In 1748, the Jesuit Carlos Roxas suggested that "Christianity and the mission villages would be greatly augmented" if the priests could count on soldiers to help them reduce the indigenous population.[21]

The Jesuits complemented forced relocations in Sonora with efforts to "restrain or temper traditional [Indian] dances, festivities . . . [and their] centuries old tradition of polygamy," according to historians Daniel Matson and Bernard Fontana.[22] This attack on Indian culture enraged the Upper Pima, as did the growing Jesuit reliance on their labor. At Guevavi, Father Joseph Garrucho violated royal decrees that had set at three the maximum number of weekdays Indians were required to work on mission lands. The increased demands for labor resulted in the production of more food—the most obvious feature that had attracted Indians to the missions in the first place. Nevertheless, Pimas chafed under a Jesuit project meant to impose an absolute authority over their lives and complained that the use of force violated the promise of accommodation by which Europeans had agreed to attract Indians to the Catholic faith with gifts of food, protection, and goods.

Garrucho and his brethren cannot be singled out as the sole cause of the 1751 rebellion. The age-old factionalism between ecclesiastical and secular officials also fueled indigenous resentment in Pimería Alta. In an investigation that followed the uprising, the Jesuits blamed Governor Diego Ortiz Parrilla and the native leader of the revolt, Luis Oacpicagigua. It was known in the colony that Ortiz Parrilla hated the Jesuits. Like most colonists, the governor believed the padres had used the mission ideal to control and monopolize the region's most arable lands. Ortiz Parrilla's disdain for the priests manifested itself when he elevated Oacpicagigua, a native of Sáric, to the rank of captain general of all the Pimas without consulting the Jesuits. The governor had granted the promotion to Oacpicagigua in reward for the chief's successful participation in a military campaign against the Seri Indians of Sonora's west coast region.

The Jesuits did not trust Oacpicagigua, whom they criticized as vain and overly ambitious. Nor did the padres trust Governor Ortiz Parrilla. His unilateral dealings with the Pimas led the priests to suspect that he had used his office to protect Oacpicagigua so that Oacpicagigua would turn his people against the missionaries. In the fall of 1751, the resident priest at the mission of Soamca, Father Ignacio Xavier Keller, met with the Pima leader and proceeded to insult him, referring to him as a "Chichimeca dog." Outraged, Oacpicagigua retreated to an isolated canyon near Sáric, where he and his cohorts from the Altar Valley planned the rebellion.

Oacpicagigua and several hundred Pimas initiated their revolt in the region of Tubac and Arivaca on 20 November 1751. One or two days later, news of the uprising reached the Spaniards at Guevavi. Panic ensued. Many Pimas of that mission abandoned Father Garrucho for the surrounding mountains; others fled west to join Luis. Those who remained loyal to the priests gathered what provisions they could and joined in a general exodus. For the remainder of November and through December, the Pima rebels laid down a path of death and destruction in Sonora's northern region. In the end, some one hundred individuals, including Fathers Tomás Tello and Enrique Ruhen, lost their lives. At Guevavi and San Xavier del Bac, Indians ransacked the missions for food and livestock, and they destroyed church property.

Hoping to appease Oacpicagigua, Ortiz Parrilla reached out to him and refused to order an all-out offensive against the warring Pimas. Oacpicagigua rejected the governor's peace offerings. By January 1752, the tide of war had shifted in favor of the Spaniards. On 5 January 1752, the unorganized and undisciplined Pima mob, which now numbered some two thousand, was defeated at Arivaca by a Spanish contingent of eighty-six troops. Oacpicagigua's forces managed to carry out several more skirmishes, but he knew the end had come; he was now ready to talk peace. The Pimas returned to their homes, but only after the Spaniards agreed to grant the rebels amnesty and to remove Fathers Keller, Garrucho, and Jacobo Sedelmeyer from Pimería Alta. On 18 March 1752, Oacpicagigua rode alone to Tubac where Captain José Díaz del Carpio accepted the formal Pima surrender.[23]

The Jesuits' willingness to subject three of their own to temporary exile indicates their readiness to restore the spirit of accommodation in Sonora. The other padres soon returned to their missions in Pimería Alta. Still, tensions between Indian and Spaniard lingered in the aftermath of war, and the missionaries received a lukewarm welcome. Only at Soamca did the local Pimas appear eager to have Father Keller—one of the three priests originally exiled as a condition of peace—reinstated at his mission. The

Indians continued to steal livestock, and at Guevavi the people seemed ill disposed. Spanish officials responded with the assignment of another garrison to northern Sonora under the command of Captain Juan Tomás Belderrain. In 1753, these troops took up permanent residence at the newly established presidio of Tubac. To the south and east of this hostile arena, at Fronteras, sixteen-year-old Juan Bautista de Anza continued his military training under the watchful eye of his brother-in-law.

The forced relocation of entire Indian communities into Spanish colonial spaces seemed a logical and simple enough plan. The Spaniards believed that native Sonorans were easily lured to settlements that promised access to Spanish material and military culture, and that the availability of these resources would encourage them to help defend their European neighbors. In the early 1760s, the Indian population of Pimería Alta had begun to dwindle from disease and increased attacks by Apache bands. Once again, Sonoran officials considered the relocation of indigenous groups to Spanish settlements as a means of defending against these new hostilities. Haunted by memories of the Pima Revolt, however, officials assumed a cautionary posture regarding forced relocations and searched for an alternate solution. The interim governor, José Tienda de Cuervo, decided that the most effective and peaceful way to move Indians within the Spanish colonial arena would be to "invite" rather than force them. In the spring of 1762, the Spaniards asked the Sobaípuris of the San Pedro valley to settle on lands around Tucson, Soamca, and Sonoita. These Indians had resisted forced relocations in the past, but the land the Spaniards now offered were located in the fertile Santa Cruz valley. Lured by the opportunity to increase their food supply, the Sobaípuris accepted the invitation to move and agreed to help defend the region between Tubac and Tucson.[24]

The relocation of the Sobaípuris proved a costly mistake. In their native San Pedro valley, situated across the mountains east of Tubac and Sonoita, these Indians had long served as a buffer against Apache groups who raided into Sonora from the northeast. With the Sobaípuris now living in the heart of Spanish Pimería Alta, the San Pedro valley was left undefended. Nomadic warriors did not wait long to use this northeast corridor to raid Sonoran settlements. The frequency of these attacks increased steadily. More important, the nature of Apache aggressions changed as well. Prior to the 1750s, the Apaches raided primarily to acquire livestock and other goods. By the 1760s, and more so in the 1770s, they began to see warfare as a means by which to stem any further European encroachment onto their lands. In this vision of the warrior's way, humans became the primary target for violence, and the destruction of life an end in itself.[25]

Anza was born into this environment of competing and evolving ethnic spaces. Although he matured among the Spanish community of priests, miners, farmers, and soldiers, he was very much aware of the Indians' presence and their contributions to the social and economic fabric of Sonora. Like all Sonorans, he became aware that the onset of offensive warfare in the 1760s altered the meaning of war for all the children of the desert. The use of violence would no longer simply determine who controlled coveted resources; it would now also resolve the question of who would become the true masters of Anza's Sonora.

CHAPTER TWO

A Child of the Desert, 1736–1755

O N 8 MARCH 1736, JUAN BAUTISTA DE ANZA was held above a
stone baptismal font within the small and dimly lit mission church of
San Ygnacio de Cuguiárachi. Here, the infant received his Christian name
and the sacrament that initiated him into the Catholic fold.[1] Juan had been
born at the frontier presidio of Fronteras where his father, Juan Bautista
de Anza I, served as military captain and his mother, María Rosa Bezerra
Nieto, prayed daily that her husband would return every evening from his
daily patrols against warring Apache Indians.[2]

Located a few miles east of Cuguiárachi, the Fronteras presidio sat
perched atop a rocky hill overlooking a long valley that locals called home.
On the southern stretch of the dale, adobe structures baked in the sun; to
the north, colonists had subdivided the land into a checkerboard layout of
farms and irrigation ditches that fed the earth and produced the hard-won
fruits of their labor. Further to the east, the Sierra Madre Occidental mountain range loomed tall against the desert floor, offering some protection
from raiders who too often relieved *vecinos* (citizens) of their livelihoods
and, on occasion, their lives.

Life at Fronteras was ordinary but never easy. From sunup to sundown
the locals went about their business of tending to crops, ranching cattle,
seeking buried veins of silver, or serving the state as presidial soldiers. Juan
spent his childhood playing among these frontier miners, farmers, and
ranchers. But it was the *soldados de cuera* (leather-armored troops) who
most captured his young imagination. On the presidial grounds, the child
experienced the daily routine of troops mounting horses and riding off into
the desert in search of Spain's enemies. When he came of age at sixteen, the

Soldados de Cuera (leather-jacketed soldiers). *Tuquison,* by Bill Singleton,
from the Anza Trail Illustrations.
Courtesy of National Park Service and Bill Singleton.

young Juan, too, entered the military as a cadet. And for the next fifty-two
years, until his death in 1788, Anza served the Spanish crown as a soldier,
explorer, and statesman.[3]

As an ennobled member of Sonora's Basque community, Anza was
expected to answer his king's calling. In fact, all the men in his family had
lived by a tradition of service to Spain. Years earlier, his maternal grandfa-
ther, Antonio Bezerra Nieto, had been appointed captain of the Janos presidio, which was located east of Fronteras in the territory of Chihuahua.
Bezerra Nieto toured Sonora as a visiting magistrate in 1718. As a result of
his inspection of the colony, he tried to convince local Pima Indians that
they would reap great benefits if they accepted Christianity.[4]

Juan Bautista de Anza the Elder

Long before the heroic career of the young Anza, his father had earned the
family great respect among Sonora's ecclesiastical and secular colonists. Of
Basque origins, Anza I stemmed from a noble family with a genealogical
past that has been traced to the ancient Iberian kingdom of Navarre in the

twelfth century. His ancestors settled in towns and villages that were scattered among the mountain valleys of Guipúzcoa, a Basque province located near the Spanish and French border. His great-great-grandfather, Martín de Anza, made the village of Berastegui his home, but his great-grandfather, Juanes de Anza, chose to settle nearby at the village of Hernani. It was here that the elder Juan's father, Antonio de Anza, firmly planted familial roots. Born on 23 July 1693, Anza I was the second of five siblings who included a priest, a merchant, and his oldest sister, María Esteban, who inherited the family estate at Hernani.[5]

Scholars believed for years that Antonio de Anza had died in New Spain.[6] Donald T. Garate, however, has shown that he in fact lived his entire life at Hernani: "Antonio de Ansa [sic] was born, lived, and died in Hernani where he was a businessman, city councilman, mayor, and financier. From 1689 until his death in 1737 he owned and operated the town pharmacy. He was married to Lucia de Sassoeta of the wealthy and prestigious Sassoeta family of Hernani. They raised five children."[7]

Juan was the only one of Antonio's children to come to New Spain—this he did in 1712—but what is not so clear is his motivation for so doing. Regarding this question, Garate's findings are important for the conclusions they suggest. It is possible that Anza I sailed across the Atlantic in search of economic and social opportunity not available to him at Hernani; this he may have done in light of the fact that his sister was designated heir to their father's estate. Such a decision would not have been uncommon. Since the era of conquest, Iberian nobles who had not inherited familial estates—especially those of the lower nobility, the *hidalgo* class—looked to New Spain for the opportunity it represented. In the New World, the most ambitious and enterprising of these individuals acquired social and economic advancement within the various branches of Spain's imperial government and military.

Anza I would have been especially attracted to New Spain. Here, the Basque community had created an extensive network of merchants, bankers, silver magnates, administrative and church officials who tended to look after their own. Organizations such as the *cofradía de aránzazu,* a confraternity founded in Mexico City in 1670, made capital resources and political influence available to Basque immigrants and American-born Basque colonists. Basque colonists tended to stick together; they intermarried and nurtured an ethnic community they had built within the larger Spanish American empire.[8] Garate does not mention whether Anza I became a member of the cofradía de aránzazu, but he does indicate that Anza II received financial assistance from prominent Basque merchants for his famous expeditions to Alta California in the 1770s.[9]

In New Spain, Anza I followed the silver trail to the far northern territory. In Sonora, between 1718 and 1720, he made a go at silver mining and operated stores at Aguaje, located south of present-day Hermosillo, and at a site south of Arizpe called Tetuachi.[10] To supplement his mercantile and mining enterprises, Anza I embarked upon a frontier military career with the support of his soon-to-be father-in-law, Antonio Bezerra Nieto.

Bezerra Nieto was a respected military captain at the Chihuahua presidio of Janos, and it was probably during his inspection of the Sonora colony in 1718 that he met Juan. Anza I followed Bezerra Nieto to Janos and enlisted in the cavalry. Soon, he achieved promotion to the rank of lieutenant. In the villa of Chihuahua, he also served as *alcalde mayor* (district magistrate) until 1721, at which time he gained appointment as interim captain of the presidio at Fronteras. Prior to his relocation to Sonora, however, Anza I married Bezerra Nieto's daughter, María Rosa.[11]

Anza I's marriage expanded his connections to other Basque elites in the far north, most notably to doña María's father. This familial tie provided Anza greater access to New Spain's administrative bureaucracy and guaranteed him promotion within the ranks of the officer corps. His decision to enter the Spanish American military in the early 1720s proved a watershed in his life—he was at the right place at the right time—as an atmosphere of war loomed over Sonora and Bourbon kings demanded drastic presidial reforms in the northern frontier.

By order of Inspector General Pedro de Rivera, Anza I was appointed to replace the troublesome captain of the Fronteras garrison, Gregorio Álvarez Tuñón y Quirós, in 1726. Tuñón y Quirós had been at odds with the Jesuits over the use of land and Indian labor; he led a faction of colonists who petitioned the crown to have the priests removed from Sonora and to secularize mission lands. Even worse, Tuñón y Quirós was a cheat and a negligent officer. He had been embezzling presidial funds for years, often collecting salaries for troops who had already died. Moreover, he refused to order his men into battle for fear that they might be killed without settling debts they had incurred to him over the years. The captain's disregard for Fronteras's defenses encouraged raiding activities by Indians. As a result,

Rivera concluded that Tuñón y Quirós's malfeasance and neglect had pitted Spaniards against each other and threatened the settlement's existence. He ordered the captain removed from office. Two years later, in 1728, Tuñón y Quirós was dead.[12]

Rivera's intervention at Fronteras helped to settle the strife between the Jesuits and Tuñón y Quirós's ambitious followers. Moreover, the inspector's admiration for the priests led to talk of increasing the number of missionaries in Sonora. In 1728, the crown issued *cédulas* (royal decrees) that called for the assignment of three new priests to northern Pimería Alta; in so doing, it reaffirmed the mission ideal of conversion and education of Indians initiated by Fathers Eusebio Francisco Kino, Agustín Campos, and Luis Xavier Velarde.[13]

Anza I's assignment to the Fronteras presidio took place in 1726 but did not receive royal sanction until 1729. Endorsements for his promotion had to travel through regular channels, and this of course took time. Rivera's recommendation reached the desk of Viceroy Marqués de Casafuerte, who in turn forwarded his own to the king's counselor, José Patiño, in November 1727. The viceroy's letter included an interesting passage by which he suggested that the crown might facilitate the imperial cause in northern New Spain if it did not assign at Fronteras a newly arrived, European-born officer. He claimed that such an individual would find it difficult to adapt to the harsh environment of the northern territory, as well as to the unique nature of the Indians and their nonconventional methods of warfare. Casafuerte based his recommendation of Anza I on the fact that the newly appointed captain had already lived on the northern frontier for most of his fifteen years since coming to New Spain. This experience, Casafuerte decided, made Anza I better suited to fulfill the military duties he had been ordered to assume.[14]

The Jesuits welcomed Anza I's appointment; they considered him their friend and praised him as "a well-known, respected military man of the frontier and a nobleman in every way. The new Commander's name was spoken with reverence, for devotion to God and King was the guiding force of his life."[15] As the new military commander of Fronteras, Anza I made it a point to support the Jesuit mission ideal. In October 1731, the three individuals chosen to resume missionary work among the northern Pimería arrived at Fronteras. Here, Captain Anza made them feel welcome.

Fathers Juan Bautista Grazhoffer, Phelipe Segesser, and Ignacio Xavier Keller faced a difficult task in Pimería Alta. Their respective missions of Guevavi, San Xavier del Bac, and Santa María Soamca had deteriorated greatly and were no longer functional. To make matters worse, the padres had been erroneously led to believe that the Pima Indians welcomed baptism and conversion to the Christian faith and would thus accept them with open arms. The three Jesuits immersed themselves in learning the language and customs of their flock. At the same time, Captain Anza oversaw the construction of new living quarters for the priests at their mission sites. In May 1732, he escorted the padres to Guevavi, where he explained to some one thousand Pimas that the Jesuits had returned to Sonora to minister to their spiritual needs.[16]

Mission activities in Pimería Alta did not go well for the padres. In May 1733, Father Grazhoffer died under a cloud of mystery, which hinted at the possibility that the Indians had poisoned him. One year later, the threat of an Indian revolt brewed as the Pimas abandoned Soamca and Guevavi, fleeing to the surrounding mountains with the livestock and priestly vestments of the Guevavi mission. Anza I led a contingent of troops to Guevavi where he discovered that "the cause of the flight . . . was a rumor that the captain was coming to kill all of the Pimas."[17] Only the negotiating skills of the Jesuits managed to preserve the Guevavi mission front; they convinced the Indians to return to the missions with the stolen goods. Try as they might, however, the padres were unable to develop a permanent hold on the lives of the Indians, and so the missions of Pimería Alta once again faced the possibility of neglect and abandonment. Then, in October 1736, an amazing discovery occurred on a hill some ten miles southwest of Guevavi that altered the history of Pimería Alta forever. Mother earth had given up one of her most prized gifts: silver!

Antonio Siraumea's *Planchas de Plata* (Slabs of Silver)

Antonio Siraumea, a Yaqui Indian living at the newly established *real de minas* (mining camp) *Nuestra Señora de la Limpia Concepción del Agua Caliente* (Our Lady of the Immaculate Conception of Agua Caliente), hoped to strike it rich by prospecting in the rugged, oak-lined canyons of northern Sonora.[18] The Yaqui was not alone in his quest, for others had already established small settlements in the area with similar dreams of immediate wealth. In the early 1730s, for example, the captain of Altar presidio, Bernardo de Urrea, had founded an *estancia* (ranch) at a site he named Arizona, located just north of Agua Caliente. Likewise, Captain Gabriel de Prudhom Heyder Butrón y Muxica had established a mining camp in the vicinity.[19] Ironically, the good fortune of a major silver strike did not present itself to a member of Sonora's military or social elite, but to the humble Yaqui Indian. As Garate recounts, in October 1736, Antonio

> stumbled onto some large chunks (*planchas de plata*) of almost pure silver. Since he was living at Agua Caliente, he returned home and took some of his children back up to the site to help look for more pieces of the precious metal. News of the discovery, of course, spread like wildfire. The first wealth seekers on the scene were residents of Agua Caliente. Francisco de Longoria filed the first, and what appears to be the only legal mining claim at the site of the discovery before the authorities arrived on the scene and put a stop to the digging. Others, illegally and without registering, scooped up the pieces of silver, which were lying on or near the surface of the ground. José Fermín de Almazán discovered a single slab that weighed over one hundred *arrobas,* or roughly one and a quarter tons. . . . Word of the marvelous discovery spread from there all over Sonora. Practically overnight a frenzied silver rush was on.[20]

On 13 November 1736, *Justicia Mayor* (District Officer) Anza I was holding court ninety miles away, at the village of Bacanuchi, when he received word of the silver strike near Urrea's Arizona ranch. As the chief royal official for this region, Anza was responsible for determining the nature of the discovery and deciding how much of the silver belonged to the crown. Initial reports proved confusing. Captain Anza suspected that the find did not include virgin silver but was a buried treasure hoarded by *indios antiguos* (ancient Indians), or possibly a clandestine smelting operation. Defining the nature of the unearthed metal was crucial. If the silver was taken from a natural vein, then by law those individuals who had filed legal claims on the ore had every right to ownership, after the crown's fifth had been deducted. If the find proved to be a buried treasure, or an illegal mining operation, then the crown could claim the entire prize. Captain Anza had no choice but to visit the silver site and unravel the mystery.

After a brief layover at his estancia near Guevavi, Anza set out toward Arizona. He arrived on 20 November and proceeded to name the silver site after his patron saint, San Antonio de Pádua. Here, Anza estimated that some four hundred people were "scratching in the earth, searching for more of the bolas y planchas (balls and slabs)." Anza ordered prospectors to cease their operations immediately and called for a general impounding of all silver extracted, including that which had already been illegally taken away and hoarded. Having posted guards at the site, Anza traveled twelve miles south to Urrea's ranch and began the process of collecting depositions from individuals who had taken part in the now famous silver rush. After surveying Almazán's massive one-and-a-quarter-ton slab of silver, Anza returned to Fronteras to spend the Christmas season with his family.

In ensuing months, the investigation of Sonora's silver strike shifted to Mexico City and into the waiting hands of Ambrosio Melgarejo, the viceroy's *fiscal* (legal adviser). The ambitious adviser seemed determined to have the silver classified as an ancient treasure.[21] This would enable the state to claim the entire find and, he hoped, would place him in good standing with the viceroy. Melgarejo's maneuvering happened to coincide with his efforts to find a space for his son within the state bureaucracy. On 17 September 1737, he petitioned superiors for an official appointment of his son as either an *abogado* (lawyer) in the Audiencia (Supreme Court) de México, or as an *alcalde ordinario de primer voto* (senior magistrate) at any *plaza togada* (superior court) within the Audiencia de Guadalajara.[22]

On 8 June 1737, Viceroy Juan Antonio de Vizarrón y Eguiarreta ordered Captain Anza to conduct another survey of the silver site to determine once and for all the origins of the ore. Anza gathered five of Sonora's leading miners and complied between August and September 1737. In the end, all agreed that the silver had indeed come from natural veins and, therefore, all prospectors had legal right to their claims. Almost a full year had passed since the original discovery, and many of the participants in the boom had grown impatient with the bureaucratic machine that kept them from their prize. The citizens petitioned Captain Anza to lift the embargo. He obliged them, but only after deducting the crown's fifth and expenses incurred during the investigations. In the end, Antonio Siraumea, the Yaqui who had started the rush on Sonora's northern mountains, was granted a claim of 1,440 square feet.[23]

If the Jesuits had not assured Spain's foothold on Sonora's northern frontier, the silver boom of 1736 to 1738 certainly did. The effects of the discovery were immediate, as hopeful prospectors poured into the region. Historian John L. Kessell writes, "Like magnets, the planchas de plata had drawn northward to the very margins of Guevavi all the loose human scraps of a mineral-oriented frontier society. Some of them stayed, planted a few crops in the fertile bottomlands, and let their stock graze the hills. Most prospected."[24]

The Bourbons recognized that silver, would-be miners, and ambitious missionaries represented a reason to continue Spain's imperial expansion in North America, and by 1736, Sonora had all three. The arrival of new colonists in the territory, however, did not result in the emergence of large urban centers. As the silver near Arizona ran out, the mining frontier moved elsewhere, and Spanish settlements in Sonora continued to be isolated islands of human existence. Nevertheless, the temporary increase in population caused by the discovery of silver forced Spain to reinforce established garrisons and to found new ones. In 1741, the Spaniards built a presidio at Terrenate and ordered the Terrenate troops to support Fronteras in the defense of Pimería Alta.[25]

María Rosa Bezerra Nieto de Anza

Sonora's population boom strained Spanish-Indian relations. The Yaquis, Mayos, and Seris sensed that this encroachment represented a serious threat to their traditional resource and cultural spaces; so the Yaquis and Mayos rebelled in 1740, cutting southern Sonora off from the rest of New Spain by June.[26] That same year, the Anza family received news that a band of Apache Indians had taken the life of one of their own. Anza the Elder was dead. Kessell recounts:

> It happened near Soamca. Father Keller, knowing that Apaches had recently scouted the area, cautioned the Captain to be on his guard. Heeding the Jesuit, Anza closed up the ranks of his column as they rode through broken terrain. When they reached open country, however, the danger seemed less and Anza rode on ahead of the column. Hidden by the chaparral, the Apaches lay in ambush. Without warning they were upon him. Before his men got to him, the valiant officer was slain. In an instant the hostiles had claimed their trophy—the crown of Anza's scalp.[27]

Anza's death struck a heavy blow to Spanish Sonora. The captain had done much to protect colonists from aggressive Indians, and the Jesuits always welcomed his support of their missionary cause. Still, those who suffered most from his loss were his wife and children. Doña María's life on the northern frontier must have been difficult even when her husband lived. Reared in a world of warring Europeans and Indians, she was very much aware of the hostile nature of the landscape she called home. Still, the far north was all that she knew. Like so many other military wives who prayed constantly that their husbands might return from military patrols, she accepted the daily reminders of Anza's calling.

Doña María had followed her husband to Fronteras from Janos, and she had stoically set about to create as harmonious and comfortable a home as a desert presidio could offer. In Sonora, Anza I and doña María looked to the needs and social education of their offspring: Francisco, María Margarita, María Manuela, María Gertrudis, Josefa Gregoria, and the young Juan.[28] The Anza children were taught to assume their place among the Basque nobility of Sonora, even though their exposure to Old World Basque culture was limited. Josefa Gregoria was the only Anza sibling to travel to Spain. In 1775, she, her husband Gabriel Antonio de Vildósola, their two daughters, and a grandson relocated to the Vildósola family estate in the village of Elejabeitia, Vizcaya. There, Josefa Gregoria died in 1800.[29]

Doña María's problem of raising her children as a widow was compounded by debts she inherited from her husband. Anza had contracted with the *Hacienda* (Treasury) of Durango to collect *diezmos* (tithes) in Sonora, but as of 1739 he still owed the state a total of 1,010 pesos. On 13 January 1741, *Capellán Bachiller* (chaplain) Juan José de Grijalva wrote to the *señores juezes asesores de diezmos* (treasury assessors for tithes) of Durango to inform them of Anza's death. In his letter, Grijalva requested that Anza's contract to collect tithes in northern Sonora be terminated as of that date. Grijalva also claimed that he had been entrusted with the collection of diezmos for the region of San Juan.[30] Six years later, on 22 April 1746, Grijalva reported to the asesores that doña María—who apparently was now living in the region around Arizpe, at the town of Basochuca—still had not paid off her husband's diezmo debt.[31]

Grijalva wrote to doña María in July 1746. She replied in August. She stated that she had not been able to raise the funds to cover the money owed by Anza, but that she had asked Captain Francisco Xavier de Miranda to assume the debt because he owed her money.[32] In September, Grijalva relayed doña María's plan to the Durango asesores and stated that due to her poor financial situation, he had agreed to let Miranda assume her debt.[33] Miranda was informed of doña María's case, and he agreed to pay.[34] Even so, by 2 February 1747, doña María was still in arrears. Miranda claimed that the governor of Sonora, Agustín Vildósola, had intervened on his behalf and ordered him not to pay the debt.[35] Capellán Grijalva once again contacted the asesores of Durango and requested that he not be held liable for the money owed by doña María.[36]

Whether or not doña María was forced to pay Anza's diezmo debt is unclear. It is possible that Governor Vildósola came to her side. Vildósola, an Old World Basque nobleman, had served as *sargento mayor* (sergeant major) in Sonora and established his household at his hacienda of Santa Bárbara. Vildósola had been a close friend of the Anzas, and the two families achieved kinship ties when Vildósola's son, Gabriel Antonio, married doña María's daughter, Josefa Gregoria.

It is clear that doña María's financial situation in Sonora was not secure, and that Anza's death left her seeking means to supplement his military pension and investments in land and mining. She found support within the Anza and Bezerra Nieto clans, and relatives on both sides of her familial network became caretakers to her children. For young Juan, this brought his relationship with his godfather, Pedro Felipe de Anza, into sharp focus.

Don Pedro Felipe de Anza

Don Pedro Felipe de Anza, a cousin of Anza the Elder, had come to New Spain from his home village of San Sebastián, located a few miles from Hernani, Guipúzcoa. In the New World, he established well-crafted connections with influential Basques. Of these, perhaps the two most important included Manuel de Aldaco—the leading silver banker of the day—and José de la Borda. Borda had been don Pedro's business partner and was considered one of the richest men in New Spain. With Aldaco and Borda's help, don Pedro became a wealthy miner in Taxco and a member of the *Real Sociedad Bascongada de los Amigos del País* (Royal Basque Society of Friends of the Country), an organization established in 1765 with royal sanction and protection from King Carlos III.[37]

As first cousin to Anza the Elder and godfather of Anza the Younger, don

Pedro was expected to render economic and social support to his godson. He had lived with Anza I's family at Janos and Fronteras, and he probably provided some funds for Anza II's upbringing in Sonora after his cousin's death. It is almost certain that don Pedro played a key role in getting New Spain's influential Basque network to fund Anza the Younger's California expeditions of the 1770s. The nature and degree of any direct aid Anza II received from his godfather, however, is not clear.

Juan Bautista de Anza the Younger: The Formative Years, 1740–1755

Anza the Younger lost his father at a critical time in his life. Barely four years old in 1740, the boy was entering into that childhood stage of emerging self-awareness. Juan must have looked to his father for a sense of identity. Sonorans, after all, had declared Anza the Elder a man of virtue and honor, deserving of respect for his defense of the people, for the aid he extended to missionaries, and, of course, for the silver he returned to miners after the famed 1736 "planchas de plata" strike. In death, Anza had been transformed into the archetypal heroic figure that became ingrained in the collective minds of most Spaniards in Sonora. What boy would not want to emulate such a man? For the young Juan, such a calling must have had special meaning because the mythic warrior was not only his father but also his namesake.

Hero or not, Anza the Elder's death deprived his youngest son of a significant social and intellectual role model—a figure the boy needed to help prepare him for the life he was expected to lead, that of nobleman and servant to the crown. To fill the void, Anza the Younger turned to other father figures in Sonora's Spanish community. One individual who may have played an important role in this regard was the Jesuit priest Carlos Roxas. Like Anza II, Father Carlos was American-born, a colonial whose service in Sonora began in 1727 as missionary at Arizpe. The padre eventually rose to the rank of father visitor for the province, an office he held until 1767, at which time the Society of Jesus was expelled from New Spain.

Roxas had baptized Juan in 1736 and officiated at his marriage in 1761. But it was during Anza's formative years—between 1740 and 1752—that Roxas helped to temper the emotions and perceptions of the boy who had lost his father. Contact between child and priest increased when doña María and her children relocated to Basochucha after Anza the Elder's death.[38] Here, Roxas had ample opportunity to call upon Juan because the settlement was within the environs of Arizpe, where the padre lived and worked. It is probable that Roxas assumed an active role in Anza's education, although this aspect of Juan's life remains obscure.

Although Carlos Roxas seemingly helped Anza develop his spiritual and intellectual side, it was Juan's brother-in-law, Captain Gabriel Antonio de Vildósola, who prepared him for a career in the military. In 1752, Vildósola took sixteen-year-old Juan under his wing as a cadet at the presidio of Fronteras. Anza was quick to learn the ways and means of warfare. Like the leather-armored soldados de cuera that he had admired as a child, Juan's military training took place on the field of battle. His classrooms were the sun-drenched scrub deserts of Pimería Alta and the precipitous rock-laden uplands of the Sierra Madre Occidental. Max L. Moorehead emphasized this tradition of on-site military preparation when he described the nature of the average soldier who served in the garrisons of the far north:

> The troops who manned the frontier presidios comprised a unique branch of the armed forces, distinct from Spain's regular soldiers, from the colonial militia, and from the civilians who were occasionally mobilized for military service. On the one hand, their deficiency in military instruction and discipline was such as to appall the regular army officers who inspected their units; on the other, those who were their commanders came to admire their toughness and stamina. They were neither elite troops nor raw recruits, but hard-bitten, home-grown *vaqueros* who were at ease in the saddle, inured to the harsh and lonely terrain in which they served, and accustomed to the cruel and unconventional tactics of Indian warfare.[39]

Anza II was not considered a common recruit. He had been born at a presidio into the officer class and was expected to follow in his father's footsteps as a noble servant of the crown. In this regard, young Anza did not disappoint his superiors. He received his first commission as a lieutenant at Fronteras in 1755, and for the rest of the decade he participated in a series of military operations orchestrated to suppress and prevent indigenous uprisings throughout Sonora.[40] With the days of his youth now behind him, the

nineteen year-old Anza looked to the future and glanced at a life of service that awaited him. Many years later, after distinguishing himself as a
frontier officer and administrator, he eagerly returned to Sonora and to the
memories he cherished as a child of the desert.

CHAPTER THREE

A Servant of the Crown, 1756–1778

HAVING ACQUIRED HIS MILITARY EDUCATION alongside the men he would ultimately call to arms, Anza understood the hard life that awaited desert warriors, and in a very direct sense he considered himself to be one of them. As a young officer, he acquired a reputation for being courageous, not thinking twice before leading his military brothers into battle. Perhaps such daring stemmed from an assumed need to measure up to the legacy of his father, but more likely it spoke to the unbridled ambition of his youth. Either way, Anza's drive to excel as a soldier matched the severe circumstances he and his fellow colonials faced in a Sonora that once again found itself torn apart along ethnic lines.

The Jesuits had continued their efforts to bring the Pimas into the Christian fold, but many natives had lost the faith and cast their lot, instead, with a new generation of rebel leaders bent on ridding their homeland of those imperial-minded Spaniards. In 1756, Pima Indians from the Gila region allied themselves with Pápagos from northwestern Sonora and unleashed a united offensive against the Europeans. The violence in Pimería Alta conjured up memories of the 1751 Pima Revolt, and to a large degree this new round of war represented a continuation of the old. Many of the Pimas who now raided mission sites and Spanish towns were descendants of the old chief, Luis Oacpicagigua.[1]

Throughout the latter half of the 1750s, Anza rode alongside his brother-in-law, Captain Gabriel Antonio de Vildósola, as part of a military force ordered to weed out Pima insurgents from Apache villages and to suppress their renewed hostilities. The experience honed Anza's skills as a soldier and afforded the young lieutenant valuable insight into the nature of

Indian warfare. He had learned that groups such as the Gila Apaches raided to acquire supplies that they needed to survive in a landscape of limited resources. The act of taking material goods from one's enemies, however, also expressed a sense of valor that these nomadic warriors converted into symbolic capital within their immediate and extended social family. Moreover, Sonora's natives engaged in warfare to avenge the killing of a relative; as such, they considered the act of war a moral imperative that preserved their community's sense of self-worth and its place in the hierarchy of power that defined relations between the people and their *inda* (enemy).[2]

Anza must have proven his worth as a soldier during the Pima campaign, for he received high praise from a Jesuit chronicler:

> Legitimate son of his father, the deceased Captain Juan Bautista de Anza, he inherited with the name and surname not only the memorable merits of his father, but also a solid disposition, valor, rapport with his soldiers, and the ability to place himself on their level and to excel them in bearing the hardships and the duties as well as the good fortune of their expeditions. . . . [He had] learned to fear no danger, to trample the barbarians, and to earn for himself the applause of Governor [Juan de] Mendoza, of the province, and of all the garrisons.[3]

But if the 1750s marked a period in Anza's life that was characterized by merit and the acquisition of accolades, the decade that followed presented the aspiring officer some of the greatest trials of his professional life.

In 1760, at the age of twenty-four, Anza received the coveted rank of captain, as well as command of the Tubac presidio. As the primary officer of Sonora's northernmost garrison, he was expected to excel in the role chosen for him since childhood. Optimism ran high among the local populace, who rejoiced that the young captain had come to protect them from Indian raiders. The anticipation of his deeds, however, was almost shattered soon after he assumed his post at Tubac. One day, Anza and a squad of troops set out on patrol in the region of Arivaca. Here they drew arms against a group of hostile Indians. Anza received an arrowhead wound but survived the encounter, and he must have felt that fate had granted him mercy on that day. Soon, however, it bestowed upon him the tragic loss of his mother. María Rosa Bezerra Nieto de Anza died in September of 1760. Juan had his mother's body carried eighteen miles from Tubac to the mission at Guevavi, where she was buried beneath the steps of the altar.[4]

The Presidio of Tubac, by William Ahrendt.
Courtesy of Tubac Presidio State Historic Park.

Having lost both his parents, Anza gave serious thought to starting his own family. A young woman from Arizpe, Ana María Pérez Serrano, had captured his heart. In true military fashion, the dashing captain strategized on how best to capture her affections. Anza maneuvered his way into Ana's life by ingratiating himself with her brother, José Manuel Díaz del Carpio. José had served as a secular priest at Arizpe, but Anza convinced him to assume the role of capellán (chaplain) for the Tubac presidio, where he would provide religious services for the garrison. Reluctantly, Díaz del Carpio agreed to Anza's proposal, but only if he could serve in a visiting capacity, coming periodically to Tubac from Arizpe where he wished to reside.[5] With José at his side, the hopeful bachelor now had an ally in the affairs of the heart. Throughout the course of Juan and Ana's courtship, José served as messenger and intermediary between his sister and the famous captain from Tubac.

Anza's choice of Ana as a companion and wife proved a complicated matter. By law, Juan was required to submit a formal request to his commanding officer in which he stated his desire to marry and identified the intended bride. Anza's ranking military superior, Governor and Captain General Juan de Mendoza, was killed on 27 November 1760 while on campaign against the Seri Indians, a full five months before Anza initiated the marriage petition process. Without Mendoza's consent, Juan faced the possibility that his petition to wed could be rejected by a new commanding officer. He therefore turned to Father Felipe Segesser to help him convince the acting governor, Bernardo de Urrea, that Mendoza had indirectly granted Juan permission to marry before his demise.

The seventy-two-year-old Segesser had not forgotten the support Anza's father had extended to him when the Jesuit arrived in Pimería Alta from his native Switzerland. On 13 May 1761, Segesser wrote a convincing letter of support on behalf of the younger Anza. Mendoza, he wrote, had mentioned on numerous occasions his desire to see Anza wed. Segesser added that the late governor had asked the padre to take it upon himself to arrange Juan's marriage if Anza requested it. The Jesuit concluded that Mendoza, by this request, "had given license for him [Anza] to marry."[6]

Segesser added his letter of support to Anza's marriage petition, along with another written by the priest of Cucurpe, Salvador Ignacio de la Peña. All documents were forwarded to Urrea, who granted Juan permission to marry. On 24 June 1761, Father Carlos Roxas married Captain Anza and Ana María Pérez Serrano at Arizpe in the presence of her brother, Father de la Peña, and Alcalde Mayor Buenaventura de Llenes.[7] Back at Tubac, the Anzas settled into family life, but soon the duties of office consumed Anza's attention.

In Defense of Pimería Alta

The recurring conflict in Sonora weighed heavy on Anza's shoulders, but the stalwart captain took on the responsibility of defending Pimería Alta with characteristic diligence. In 1763, war once again became personal for Anza when the violence took the life of yet another family member. His sister-in-law, Victoria Carrasco, wife of his older brother Francisco, was killed in an Apache attack at Buenavista in the San Luis Valley. In October, after this attack, settlers from the San Luis Valley asked his permission to abandon their homes because of raids. Without the approval of Governor

Juan Claudio de Pineda, Anza acquiesced to the demand, perhaps because the colonists presented their petition along with Victoria Carrasco's corpse. The locals told Anza that Victoria had perished in the most recent attack by the Apaches. Terrified at the prospect of facing a similar fate, the residents of San Luis Valley fled en masse to Tubac and Terrenate, hoping that the presidial garrisons might be better able to protect them.[8]

In 1764, Jesuits and Indians complained to Governor Pineda that refugees from San Luis had begun to squat on mission and indigenous communal lands around Tubac and Terrenate. The governor expressed concern about the potential breakdown of ethnic relations in Pimería Alta and suggested that Anza's decision to allow the San Luis Valley residents to abandon their homes may have been a mistake. One year later, however, Pineda granted titles to farmland surrounding Altar presidio to ten families. At Terrenate, officials did stop José de Olave from conducting arbitrary measurements of land, which he was "awarding . . . indiscriminately to the *vecinos* [residents] without taking into account the area reserved for the presidio and the Pima missions."[9]

Hoping to make amends for the San Luis Valley debacle, Anza submitted a plan to Governor Pineda that involved the relocation of Sobaípuri natives living around Tucson to Buenavista. In 1762, the Sobaípuris had agreed to settle and defend the territory of Tucson in return for access to land. Now, however, they complained to Anza about the inadequate amount of arable land and water at Tucson. Anza argued that the move to the San Luis Valley would make more resources available to the Sobaípuris and ensure their full cooperation in the defense of settlements in the region.

It would appear that Anza's plan to relocate the Sobaípuris came to naught. Jesuits serving in Pimería Alta, especially Father Visitor Manuel Aguirre, opposed the idea on the belief that it represented a diminution of the mission frontier. Aguirre had hoped to see Tucson elevated to mission status, but he knew this required the presence of a substantial indigenous population in the region. Without native souls to cater to, the Jesuits knew they would have to abandon their dream of expanding the mission frontier to Tucson. Aguirre and his brethren took no chances and pleaded their case directly to the governor. Hoping to sway Pineda, they asked that the Sobaípuris be allowed to stay at Tucson and suggested that Pápago Indians would fare better in the San Luis Valley.[10]

Anza's plan also met resistance from the Sobaípuris of Tucson themselves.

From there, the proud and independent-minded leader, Chachalaca, relayed his people's sentiments to Governor Pineda regarding the issue. He stated that the Sobaípuris did not oppose moving to richer lands, but they would decide where and when such a move would occur. Chachalaca made it clear that, for the moment, his people would stay put at Tucson. To convince Pineda that his words were indeed wise, Chachalaca reminded the governor that the Sobaípuris had remained loyal and passive toward Spain when other indigenous groups had openly rebelled. The history lesson proved a veiled threat, but the headstrong Indian got his way. Chachalaca and his people continued to farm the lands around Tucson well into the 1770s.[11]

The Apaches remained a serious threat in northern Sonora well into the 1760s. Eager to defend their homes, Anza and the Indians of Pimería Alta realized that together they would be better able to deal with this common enemy. More and more, indigenous peoples, especially the Pimas and Ópatas, willingly served as military auxiliaries of Spain. At Tubac, Anza openly welcomed Indian allies and adopted a policy that allowed them to share equally in the spoils of war. Moreover, he became convinced that taking warfare to the Apaches through offensive maneuvers was the only way to deal with these hostile Indians. In 1766, for example, he led an offensive against Apaches in the dreaded northeastern region of Sonora. Troops from Terrenate, Fronteras, and Tubac presidios accompanied Anza, along with a contingent of Pima auxiliaries. When Anza's forces returned to Tubac, the captain saw to the equal distribution of all the captured booty— including fifteen Apache women—among his European and Indian troops. The nature of war in Pimería Alta, it seems, had become more egalitarian.[12]

The Marqués de Rubí and the *Reglamento e Instrucciones* of 1772

Anza's successful use of offensive warfare, Indian auxiliaries, and a reward system for service became the cornerstones of his military strategy in New Mexico. While he was still in Sonora, however, his tactics came to the approving attention of Cayetano María Pignatelli Rubí Corbera y San Climent, the Marqués de Rubí. Rubí had crossed the Atlantic in 1764 as part of a team of field marshals ordered to conduct a general reorganization of New Spain's defenses. Rubí toured the northern provinces extensively from 1765 to 1768 with specific instructions to evaluate the effectiveness of Pedro de Rivera's 1729 Reglamento. He was granted powers to implement any military reforms needed to ensure stability in the far north without sacrificing territory. The king deemed Rubí's efforts vital if Spain was to effectively face off against the expansion-minded British, who had been tagged a new threat ever since France had agreed to leave North America as a consequence of the Seven Years War.

The English were not the only Europeans with an eye for territorial expansion on the continent. Along the Pacific, Russian fur trappers had already pressed south from Alaska into California. And of course, contentious Indians continued to threaten Spain's precarious hold on the entire northern region. The Spaniards feared that their inability to subdue the natives would leave them vulnerable to the inevitable invasion of their North American domains by a rival European state. As with Rivera, then, Rubí's role in this new era of military reform focused on Spain's need to secure peace with indigenous peoples.

Like Rivera, Rubí concluded that corruption among presidial officers continued to hamper the effective use of garrisons as a deterrent to Indian raids. In Sonora, however, the inspector suggested that Anza had not abused his rank for personal gain. Anza had received Rubi at Tubac during the Christmas season of 1766, and Rubí wrote positive reports regarding him. Rubí praised him for selling supplies to his men at prices lower than those regulated for the military. Likewise, the inspector was impressed with the level of military training and discipline Tubac's garrison had achieved under Anza's watchful care.[13]

Rubí also submitted a plan for the reform of the presidial system and a military strategy that he believed would enhance the defenses of the northern colonies. His *Reglamento e Instrucciones* (Regulations and Instructions) of 1772 signaled a departure from the "defensive posture" Rivera had outlined in 1729. Rubí called for an initiation of offensive warfare as a means to hunt down and subdue rebellious indigenous groups. Frontier veterans had argued for years that such maneuvers were needed to gain an upper hand against belligerent Indians. As stated, Anza had already initiated such a strategy against the Apaches in northeastern Sonora. Rubí applauded Anza's efforts in this regard and sanctioned the captain's tactics even before the Reglamento of 1772 was issued.[14] In so doing, the Marqués extolled Anza as a model officer on the hostile frontier. In the inspector's eyes, Anza possessed the qualities the Bourbons looked for in their commanders—the type of ingenuity, motivation, and enthusiasm they were willing to reward with promotion. The accolades heaped on Anza, however, did not excuse him from proving fealty to his king. In February 1767, King Carlos III ordered that all Jesuits serving within his realms be rounded up and exiled from the Spanish empire. For Anza, the expulsion of the padres proved one of the greatest tests of his loyalty to the monarchy.

The Jesuit Expulsion: 1767

The Jesuit expulsion of 1767 was one of the most drastic measures taken by the Bourbons to achieve royal absolutism. The padres had been accused of inciting bread riots around Madrid in 1766 and turning the general populace against the king. Carlos III believed the Jesuits harbored an unflinching allegiance to the pope that undermined the ideal of absolutism; even worse, he accused the black robes of plotting against his life. In his imperial eyes the papist-minded priests had to go, they had to be removed from the empire.[15]

Regarding New Spain, the king accused the Jesuits, especially those serving in Baja California, of challenging his authority by attempting to create theocratic societies among the local Indians.[16] Carlos III recognized that such efforts subverted the true essence of Spain's mission program. By making the northern Indians dependent on the missions, the Jesuits had in fact prevented the full transformation of natives into active, tax-paying citizens of the empire. In Sonora, the crown's attack on the Jesuits found favor with many land-hungry colonists who wished only to see the missions secularized. Others, like Anza, questioned the expulsion because it promised to sever the close ties they had nurtured with the Jesuits.

Carlos III issued the Jesuit expulsion decree in February 1767. In July, Sonora's governor, Juan Claudio de Pineda, received the proclamation with orders to proceed with its execution in a highly cautious and secretive manner. Pineda appointed the captain from Altar, Bernardo de Urrea, to oversee the general roundup of Jesuits. However, Pineda ordered all his captains—including Anza at Tubac—to carry out the actual arrests. Pineda feared that incarcerating the Jesuits might set off an uprising among Indians and colonists who had remained loyal to the padres. He figured, however, that Anza might help douse inflamed emotions and prevent conflict; therefore he assigned to Anza the task of informing Father Visitor Carlos Roxas of the king's decree. He hoped Anza's longstanding friendship with the Jesuits might contribute to an orderly expulsion process by calmly exposing the priests to their fate.[17]

On 23 July 1767, Anza broke the seal of the instructions he received from Pineda. He read the king's royal decree and reflected on its meaning. In light of Anza's relationship with the padres, Pineda must have wondered if Anza would refuse to carry out the expulsion decree. This Pineda could not afford. Anza was much liked and respected in the colony, and he might sway the populace against the state on the Jesuit issue. The captain was also young, ambitious, and a faithful servant seeking promotion within the imperial machine. Pineda knew this, and so he played on Anza's sense of obedience by ordering him to complete his charge without any delay. Pineda signed off by stating he had no doubt the captain would see to the king's will with honor and zeal, and that in so doing, he would provide evident proof of his fealty to the crown.

On 25 July 1767, Anza travelled to Arizpe to meet with his friend and confessor. Details of the reunion between Father Roxas and Captain Anza remain a secret, perhaps in part because the clerics were ordered to observe a strict and complete silence regarding their expulsion; they had been forbidden to discuss the matter even among themselves. With stoic resolve, Anza informed Roxas that as head of his order he must sway his brethren to congregate at Arizpe with due haste and with no excuse for delay. The padres were to be relocated to Mátape, and then sent on to the port of Guaymas, where they were to live under house arrest until ships could be made available for their transport to central New Spain.[18]

Anza must have left Arizpe with somber spirits, but he pushed forth to fulfill his charge of gathering and transporting those Jesuits serving in missions along the Río Sonora. By 5 August, he reported to Governor Pineda from one of these missions, perhaps Aconchi:

> My Governor and sir, I have almost completed my commission here and hope to leave for Mátape, where I expect the three missionaries who were unable to accompany me, but who were conducted to this site by the commissioners [I appointed for this task], have arrived. I would have departed by now, but Father Perera's illness, and the need to let him recuperate so he can travel, has detained me.[19]

Nicolás de Perera, a native of Zacatlán, New Spain, had refused to be left behind at Aconchi while his fellow priests suffered the indignity of arrest and exile. He informed Anza that he would gladly follow his brothers as best he could. Anza accommodated Perera by ordering the construction of a stretcher that, rigged to mules, carried the ailing padre to his imprisonment.[20]

Much to Governor Pineda's relief, Anza carried out his orders without incident at the height of the summer. In August 1767, he bid farewell to his lifelong friend, Carlos Roxas, and informed his superior that Carlos III's will had been fulfilled. Although Anza did not question in public the absolutist ideal that underlay the expulsion, he was not so sure that Sonora's Indians would be better off without the black robes. In the end, Anza summed up his feelings about the Jesuit affair when he wrote to the governor, "After all, the king commands it and there may be more to it than we realize. The thoughts of men differ as much as the distance from earth to heaven."[21]

The Jesuit expulsion sparked an intense debate in Sonora between church and state officials regarding the failed assimilation of natives. Franciscan gray robes who replaced the Jesuits blamed military types such as Anza for failing to stem an increase of Apache raids into northern Sonora. The fear of meeting a violent death, the friars claimed, had led many Indians to desert their missions. Likewise, Spanish colonists who had settled in peripheral regions like the San Luis Valley began to abandon their homes and seek shelter at more fortified towns as early as 1768. At Tubac, for example, Indian and Spanish refugees congregated near the presidio in hopes that Anza would, somehow, keep them alive. Anza made no excuses for his inability to defend Pimería Alta. He insisted that increased Apache raids had resulted from Spain's demand that he first deal with warring Seris who were located further south in Sonora.[22]

The Seri Campaign: 1768–1771

Visitor General José de Gálvez, whose inspection tour of New Spain resulted in the creation of the Comandancia General, had ordered the Seri Campaign of 1768. Gálvez feared that the Seris of Cerro Prieto and Tiburón Island would threaten the silver region south of Sonora if their resistance to Spain went unchecked. He thus convinced the king that the Seris would have to be defeated before Apache hostilities in the northern provinces could be confronted. The Seri war consistently pulled Anza and his men away from Tubac and impeded his ability to defend Pimería Alta against the northern marauders. The campaign, however, afforded Anza the opportunity to associate with a company of Catalans recruited in and around the Spanish city of Barcelona, who had been ordered to New Spain specifically to fight the Seris.

The Bluecoats, as the Catalans came to be known, served under the command of Domingo Elizondo. Along with Anza's troops, they focused their maneuvers on the Cerro Prieto, a string of mountains that run one hundred miles north from Guaymas to Pitic. Pitic, located just south of Hermosillo, served as the Spanish headquarters for the Seri war. From here, Anza led sorties to sites such as El Cajón de la Nopalera, where he faced off against a group of Seris armed with nothing but bows and arrows. Five natives were killed during this encounter, and a fifteen-year-old Spanish captive was rescued. This young man had lived among the Indians for nine months. He informed Anza that the natives feared Spanish soldiers most when the latter wore their *cueras* or leather jackets.[23]

Try as they might to flush the natives from their mountain strongholds, the Spaniards botched the Seri campaign. To make matters worse, the author of this Spanish offensive, José de Gálvez, seemed to be losing his grip on reality. The visitor general had traveled to Álamos in 1769 to extend amnesty to Indians who laid down their arms and accepted peace. By September, only a handful of "starving Seris" had surrendered. In October, the road-weary Gálvez suffered a mental breakdown that threatened the northern offensive altogether. In a state of delusion, Gálvez claimed that Saint Francis of Assisi had appeared before him and promised total victory against the Seris. Governor Pineda thought otherwise. He decided that the visitor general must be removed from command for his own good, and for the preservation of order among his confused troops.

By 1770, Spain's war against the Seris had stalled and Spanish forces resorted to guerrilla tactics to gain the upper hand in the mountains. The strategy resulted in few and inconclusive victories. That same year, in March, a smallpox epidemic devastated the Seris, who now threatened to ally themselves with Pápagos, rebel Pimas, and Apaches of Pimería Alta. Governor Pineda ordered Anza back to Tubac to deal these contentious natives a swift and thorough military blow. The captain and his men performed well in subduing the three thousand-strong Pápago nation, with

Anza personally slaying their chief. In May, the Tubac garrison gave chase to an Apache band, killing four and capturing seven children. By June, Anza believed he had restored some semblance of order in the volatile region north and west of Tucson. But then in July, the Apaches attacked Sonoita, killing nineteen settlers, including the Pima leader, Juan María.[24]

Hoping to avenge the Sonoita massacre, Anza requested and received permission from a newly appointed governor, Pedro Corbalán, to recruit Pima allies and continue the offensive.[25] In August, the fortified Spaniards and their Pima allies ambushed an Apache village situated northeast of Tubac. The Apaches scattered, but not before Anza's forces had killed nine of them and wounded many others. That same summer of 1771, several hundred exhausted Seris agreed to lay down their arms and sue for peace. The timing of their surrender could not have been more opportune. The crown had, by now, acknowledged that the Sonora offensive was a lost cause and ordered a cessation of hostilities. The war in Pimería Alta, however, was far from over. Anza returned to Tubac in the fall to take part in the planning of a new offensive against the Apaches.[26]

Anza's accomplishments on the field of battle did not go unrewarded. In April 1770, Governor Pineda and Colonel Elizondo forwarded petitions to Viceroy Marqués de Croix in which they recommended Anza for promotion.[27] Anza himself wrote to the king to request advancement in Sonora's officer corps. To support his case, he included in his petition a memorandum that outlined his service record. As of 1770, Anza had already served seventeen years on the northern frontier, two years as a volunteer cadet, five as a lieutenant at Fronteras, and ten as captain at Tubac. He had participated in fourteen general campaigns against warring Indians, of whom he had killed some 115. Under his leadership, 109 enemies had been taken prisoner and more than 2,500 head of livestock had been captured or retaken. Finally, he had subdued the entire Pápago nation.[28] Anza's meritorious service record impressed the king, who granted him promotion to the rank of captain of the military cavalry by royal order of 2 October 1770.[29]

Anza Condemns the Failed Mission Program

Anza never forgot the tragedy of his father's death at the hands of the Apaches. Even so, he rejected Franciscan claims that Apache raiding had been the major cause of the flight from missions. Anza blamed the failed assimilation of Sonora's Indians on the mission system itself. The Jesuits had enjoyed considerable control over the lives of the Indians, as well as the secular and ecclesiastical administration of the missions. Anza believed that these powers had spawned extensive and negative sentiments among the Spanish populace. Colonials considered the priests and their Indian wards an obstacle to what they most coveted, those highly productive lands they had been denied in favor of a mission ideal that they probably did not believe in. Anza argued that the seclusive nature of the missions had kept natives isolated from Spaniards, and that this strategy of limited and controlled interaction had prevented the desired incorporation of Sonora's Indians into Spanish society. With the Jesuit expulsion, ethnic tensions between Native Americans and Spaniards soon resurfaced, and it was this, Anza believed, that had led many Indians to abandon the missions and to take up arms against Spain yet again.

With the expulsion of 1767, King Carlos III exerted the Bourbons' absolutist policy by placing the financial care of the missions in the hands of secular officials. The Franciscans did not welcome those reforms, which denied them unlimited access to material and capital assets produced by mission lands. They depended on these resources to supplement the annual *sínodos* (subsidies) each friar received, which—by their own calculations—were not enough to meet the needs of the padres. In 1769, the friars complained to Visitor General José de Gálvez that they could not conduct the business of saving souls unless the crown extended to them the paternalism and resources enjoyed by their predecessors. The friars demanded a renewed empowerment, and on 3 June 1769 Gálvez granted their requests on a temporary basis.[30]

Anza disagreed with Gálvez's decision. It is possible that he had wearied of the Jesuit-inspired paternalistic mission ideal. It is more likely, however, that like so many other Sonorans, he hoped the crown would allow colonists to expand their land holdings by secularizing the lands controlled by the missions. Anza himself had already managed to acquire, or hoped to purchase, land in the settlements of Santa Rosa de Corodéguachi, Sicurisuta, Divisadero, Santa Bárbara, Cíbuta, Sásabe, and Sópori.[31]

Aside from any desire for self-enrichment, Anza opposed Franciscan demands for power for more ideological reasons. In 1772, he submitted a report to the viceroy of New Spain, Antonio María Bucareli y Ursúa, in which he offered one of the most scathing criticisms of the Franciscans—

and the mission system—since the friars had replaced the Jesuits in 1768. In his report, Anza outlined his rejection of the reducción as a tool for the incorporation of Indians into the Spanish empire and offered an alternative. He advocated a society where Indians were immersed in European culture.[32] He favored a social policy that increased—rather than limited—the amount of contact between indigenous peoples and Spaniards. Anza recommended that Europeans be allowed to live within Indian settlements, where they were to expose the native people to the Spanish language on a daily basis. Likewise, he encouraged his superiors to consider the creation of language schools for Indian children.[33]

Anza recognized the power of language as a tool for acculturation. Perhaps more important, he had learned early on that the goal of assimilating Native Americans into Spanish society could best be met by improving economic ties between Indians and Spaniards. He understood that native Sonorans desired economic gain through trade with Europeans. This relationship of mutual accommodation had served New Spain well during the exploratory and conquest phase of its imperial expansion into the far north. Since the time of Coronado, Indians had welcomed God's earthly representatives into their homelands so long as missionaries, and the monarchs they served, guaranteed consistent access to European goods and markets, as well as defense of the Indians' lives and lands.[34]

Anza supported expanded economic ties between Indians and Spaniards. He believed Native Americans should be encouraged to seek wage labor in Spanish mines; in so doing, they would be more readily exposed to the Spanish economy and society. Likewise, wage income would increase the Indians' capital assets, which, in turn, would enhance their bargaining stance in trade. Above all else, however, Anza argued that acculturation and assimilation of natives could not occur unless indigenous Sonorans were allowed to own land that they worked for their own benefit. He knew that Indians welcomed a policy that empowered them over the resources they needed for daily survival; they had told him so. Some natives had expressed willingness to share one-third of their harvest with the missions if they were freed from the three days of servitude imposed on them by clerics.[35]

Anza's views regarding the acculturation of Sonora's Indians were controversial for his time. He, after all, was promoting a free market where Spaniard and Indian interacted on an equal basis. Although his stance on Spanish-Indian relations may appear enlightened on the surface, it is

Anza meets with the Pimas.
The Pima, by David Rickman, from the Anza Trail Illustrations.
Courtesy of National Park Service and David Rickman.

more probable that his preference for the ideal of mutual accommodation reflected practical needs. Anza was first and foremost a man of the military—a champion of the Spanish empire who had dedicated his life to its defense. As a professional soldier, he understood the need to utilize native Sonorans as military allies. But the incorporation of Indians into New Spain's defense policy required incentives that lured them into alliance. Through the strategy of "peace by purchase," those natives who helped defend the Spanish American Empire received European-made goods, land, and trade privileges. Those who did not suffered the heavy hand of Spain's military. Enlightened or not, Anza took the strategy of peace by purchase with him to New Mexico. And here he demonstrated that the promise of trade was a more powerful deterrent to war than the most advanced military technology the Spaniards could bring to the field of battle.

The California Expeditions

After the Seri campaign, Anza received orders to explore and establish a land route from Sonora to Alta California. His successful missions to this Pacific coast colony in 1774 and 1776 have been the most celebrated of all his accomplishments. But although his achievements in this regard have been elevated to the realm of legend and myth, for the Bourbons the establishment of a road from Sonora to California was in keeping with their efforts to consolidate this corner of the empire.

Since the early 1700s, Spaniards such as Anza the Elder had dreamed of expanding the Sonora frontier into the region of the Gila and Colorado River valleys, which promised abundant water and arable lands for agriculture and ranching. The Jesuits and Franciscans also envisioned a presence in southern Arizona, where they hoped to bring the word of God to the Gila Pimas, the Quechans, and the Hopis. Both settlers and missionaries considered the region where the Gila and Colorado Rivers converge a springboard to Alta California, which offered an even greater resource base than southern Arizona and plenty of Native Americans deemed in need of spiritual salvation. Spain had long envisioned using California as a safe haven for ocean-weary travelers engaged in the Manila galleon trade.[36] But it was not until the 1760s, at which time Russian fur trappers expanded their activities down the Pacific coast, that the Spanish monarchy assumed a determined attitude to settle Alta California.

After his famed *visita* (visitation), José de Gálvez convinced Carlos III that expanding the imperial frontier into Alta California was the first step needed to defend New Spain from her European competitors. The visitor general identified England as the most dangerous threat to Spain's claims in North America. Throughout the eighteenth century, the British had expressed their imperialist designs on the continent through acts of war. England attempted to gain Spanish holdings along the Atlantic seaboard during the War of the Spanish Succession, which ran from 1700 to 1713. In 1719, during the War of the Quadruple Alliance, the British allied themselves with France, Holland, and Austria in an effort to seize Spanish territories in Italy as well as in America from Florida to New Mexico. England made another grab for Florida in 1739 during the War of Jenkins' Ear, and it finally took possession of Spanish Florida as a result of the Seven Years War, which ended in 1763.[37]

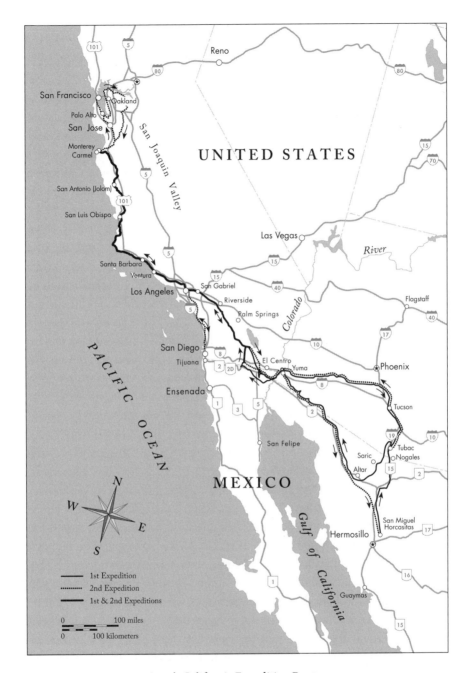

Anza's California Expedition Routes.
From *Anza Trail and the Settling of California,* by Vladimir Guerrero.
Reprinted by permission of Heyday and the cartographer, Ben Pease.

Spain colonized Alta California in 1769 under the secular leadership
of Captain Gaspar de Portolá and the spiritual guidance of *fray* (friar)
Junípero Serra.[38] In ensuing years, Franciscan friars and Spanish troops,
including a contingent of the Bluecoats who had fought alongside Anza in
the Seri war, expanded the California mission frontier as far north as Monterrey.[39] Spain soon discovered that maintaining the Pacific Coast province
would be a difficult task. José de Gálvez had intended to use Baja California
as a base for supplying its sister colony in the north. His plan was thwarted,
however, by the fact that the prevailing winds and tides of *El Mar Pacífico*
were anything but calm. It was not uncommon for Spanish vessels, especially during the winter storm season, to be blown off course while making
their way north along the Pacific coast. Hence, by the early 1770s Gálvez
decided that a land route connecting Sonora and Alta California had to be
established to preserve the latter colony. In 1774, Anza undertook the first of
two expeditions to establish such a road.

On 8 January 1774, Captain Anza and a small contingent of troops,
scouts, friars, and servants set out from Tubac presidio. Counted among the
company's muster role was a Cochimí Indian from the Alta California mission of San Gabriel who had recently traveled to Sonora along the very route
Anza ultimately followed to the Pacific coast.[40] Anza pressed the native,
Sebastián Tarabal, into service and used him as a guide on the rough road
to Alta California. On the ninth of February, the Spaniards arrived at Yuma
and were greeted by Chief Salvador Palma and several thousand Quechans,
whom Anza described as the tallest, most robust, and most naked natives
he had yet met in the Internal Provinces. Anza was quick to note the abun-
dance of water and fertile lands at Yuma, and he must have weighed the
possibility of having Spain establish a mission settlement in the region.[41]
Just west of the Colorado River at Yuma, the Spaniards struggled to find
their way across a formidable stretch of sand dunes that offered no water
and little vegetation for their horses. Anza recognized immediately that he
would have to find a way to skirt these dunes. More important, he realized
that a settlement at Yuma would be necessary if colonists were to survive
this unforgiving stretch of the trail. Beyond the sandy barrier lay the sun-
baked deserts of the present Imperial Valley. Here, within sight of *El Cerro
del Impossible* (Mount Signal), Tarabal directed the company in a more
northwestern direction and led the party through another stretch of desert that now bears Anza's name (Anza-Borrego). Next, the Spaniards from

Tubac worked their way over the San Jacinto Mountains and into the Los Angeles basin. Finally, Anza and company found their way to San Gabriel and ultimately to Monterrey.[42]

The explorers of 1774 returned to Sonora five months and some two thousand miles after their odyssey began. Although Tarabal had been mostly responsible for finding the land route between Pimería Alta and Alta California, it was Anza who received credit for the expedition. Back at Tubac by May, Anza planned to travel to Mexico City to meet with Viceroy Bucareli, who waited with eager anticipation to welcome the celebrated captain and bestow upon him the rank of lieutenant colonel. Anza's trip to the capital was delayed when Deputy Inspector Antonio de Bonilla ordered him to remain in Sonora to help restore order and discipline among the troops of the north.

Commandant Inspector Hugo O'Conor had ordered Bonilla to inspect Sonora's presidios and to implement military reforms outlined in Rubí's Reglamento of 1772. Having traveled from Chihuahua, Bonilla was shocked at the undisciplined rabble he met at Sonora and in particular at Terrenate. He soon learned that Governor Francisco Antonio Crespo had arrested the presidio's captain, José Antonio Vildósola, on suspicion of negligence and corruption. Bonilla considered the charges against Vildósola serious enough, but what dismayed him most was the antagonistic relationship between the captain and his men. Bonilla declared that "the spirit of discord and malevolence ruled at the presidio," and that the troops at Terrenate were ready to mutiny.[43] He concluded his tour of Terrenate by declaring that Captain Vildósola would remain under house arrest, and in the custody of Juan Bautista de Anza.

The assignment thwarted Anza's plans to celebrate his recent Alta California accomplishment with the viceroy in Mexico City. Secretly, Anza also must have felt frustrated at the thought of having to interact with Vildósola personally. Vildósola had fought alongside Anza during the Seri campaign and had married Anza's niece, María Rosa Tato y Anza. But in December 1769, while on leave from the war, Vildósola abandoned María when he discovered that she had committed adultery during his absence and was about seven months pregnant. Since that fateful Christmas season, the Tato and Anza clans had tried desperately to persuade Vildósola to protect their familial honor by agreeing to reunite with María. Because he refused to do so, the Tatos and Anzas turned on Vildósola and used their social connections in Sonora to have him disgraced professionally. In large part, Vildósola's problems at Terrenate, including his arrest on charges of negligence and corruption, had resulted from the vendetta these families had carried out against him between 1769 and 1774.[44]

Anza never publicly acknowledged his niece's infidelity, nor the attacks on Vildósola, but he must have feared that the affair would tarnish his reputation if it became public knowledge. This Anza could not afford. On 8 June 1774, he wrote a letter to Viceroy Bucareli in which he blamed Bonilla for delaying his journey to Mexico City.[45] Outraged, Bucareli demanded that Bonilla release Anza from his charge at Terrenate and be allowed to travel to court. This Anza did in August 1774.[46]

In Mexico City, Bucareli declared Anza a hero of the Spanish empire and promoted him to the rank of lieutenant colonel. Anza dined with Bucareli, and together they discussed plans for a colonizing expedition to Alta California. But while the new lieutenant colonel basked in the glory of his elevated fame, and pondered the logistics of another expedition to California, his enemies in Sonora maneuvered to discredit him and gain favor with the crown. The chief culprits in this malicious endeavor included Governor Francisco Antonio Crespo, Commandant Inspector Hugo O'Conor, and fray Francisco Garcés.

Garcés was a missionary of abundant energy and ambition. Since his appointment to Pimería Alta, after the Jesuit expulsion, he dreamed of establishing a Franciscan evangelical corridor between Sonora and New Mexico. He traveled with Anza to Alta California in 1774, but the two headstrong Spaniards did not see eye-to-eye on which route would best tie the two provinces together. Garcés favored a path that followed the course of the Colorado River north from Yuma, and then west—at about the latitude of the Hopi pueblos—to the Pacific coast. He believed that such a route would allow his brethren to make contact with Hopi Indians who lived in the frontier region between northeastern Arizona and northwestern New Mexico. Garcés claimed that contact with the Hopis would allow the Spaniards to create an imperial web that tied New Mexico, Sonora, and Alta California to each other along spiritual, economic, political, military, and social lines. Viceroy Bucareli entertained Garcés's theory but chose to adopt a wait-and-see policy regarding the Colorado River route.

Governor Crespo agreed with Garcés that the Colorado River route was better suited than Anza's trail for tying Sonora to the Pacific coast.

Crespo harbored personal reasons for siding with the friar; he had hoped the crown would choose him over Anza to lead the colonizing expedition to Alta California. In his quest for fame and possible promotion, Crespo wrote to Viceroy Bucareli and hinted that he would willingly carry out the important mission should King Carlos III command it.[47]

Unlike Crespo and Garcés, Hugo O'Conor's interest in a Sonora-California colonizing expedition stemmed solely from his responsibilities as commandant inspector. The ruddy-faced, red-haired, Dublin-born Irishman had assumed his office in 1771 and was required to carry out military reforms outlined in the Reglamento of 1772. Donald C. Cutter writes:

> His job as a senior military officer assigned to implement a new defensive scheme for the northernmost portion of a far-flung colonial empire was to ensure its security both in the present and in the foreseeable future. . . . Even though O'Conor had no direct connection with the major frontier expansion into the new area of Upper California that was taking place, the troops under his general control were involved in seeking a trail to transport colonists from the relatively settled area of Sonora to the hinterland of what one day would become the Golden State. It was expansion beyond the Rubí plan and caused it [the plan] to have some unforeseen weaknesses. Certainly any ideas of expansion of the frontier were beyond the imagination of O'Conor, whose time and energy were consumed by the constant urgency of holding off the Apache invasion of existing settlements.[48]

O'Conor toured Tubac in 1775 and concluded that its presidial forces were a shambles. Troops lacked discipline, they were poorly equipped, and corruption among certain officers had once again emerged during Anza's absence. Likewise, O'Conor found few words of praise for the settlement's citizen militias. His report on Tubac coincided with another intensive wave of Apache invasions into Pimería Alta. It is thus probable that O'Conor's criticisms of Anza's garrison was intended to shift away from himself any blame for the failure to stem these renewed attacks. More likely, he discredited Tubac's forces to justify the garrison's relocation farther north to Tucson. O'Conor believed that such a move would improve the defensive posture of northern Sonora and complete the presidial line suggested by the Marqués de Rubí in the Reglamento of 1772.[49]

Lieutenant Colonel Anza was not available to defend his old command post against O'Conor's reproach. Neither could he prevent Governor Crespo's and Father Garcés' political maneuvering. He need not have worried, for the king had made his choice: Anza would travel once more to the Pacific coast.

Since his return to Sonora from Mexico City, Anza had kept himself busy at Horcasitas, planning and recruiting colonists for the second expedition to Alta California. On 23 October 1775, Anza rode out from Tubac at the head of 240 men, women, and children, most of them from Sinaloa, in the direction of Tucson. By late November, the party camped at Yuma. Here, Fathers Garcés and Tomás Eixarch arranged with Anza to remain among the Quechans and preach the word of God. Garcés expressed little joy at having to accompany Anza on the second expedition. Viceroy Bucareli, however, informed the independent-minded friar that a route to the Hopis would not be allowed unless the Franciscans first established a mission front among the Indians of the Yuma and Gila River valleys. Garcés succumbed to the viceroy's demands, but he insisted that Father Eixarch be stationed at Yuma while he made his way north towards the Hopi pueblos.

Garcés reached the Hopi settlement of Oraibi in July 1776. The Indians did not make the friar welcome. He was forced to walk back to Sonora, but not before he convinced the Hopis to allow a letter for his brethren in New Mexico to reach the Franciscans stationed at nearby Zuni Pueblo. Although his way had been arduous, Garcés had demonstrated that a land route between Sonora and New Mexico was possible. His exploratory efforts proved another crucial fact: the Hopis would have to be subdued before a Sonora-New Mexico corridor could be established.[50] Anza attempted to fulfill such a task early in his tenure as governor of New Mexico. Late in 1779, he negotiated a new alliance with the Hopis and persuaded many of them to relocate to Indian settlements along the Río Grande and among the Zunis.[51]

While Father Garcés traversed the deserts and mountain ranges of Arizona, Anza retraced the route he and his fellow travelers had explored during the 1774 expedition to Alta California. The Spaniards gathered their strength at Yuma for several days and accepted a bounty of fruits and vegetables offered by their Quechan hosts. Anza reminded the California colonists that these valuable gifts would serve them well as they struggled across the dreaded Colorado desert. He warned them that this section of the trail would be the most treacherous of all, and that they should pack

Anza and Salvador Palma at Yuma.
Arrival at the Yuma Village, by David Rickman, from the Anza Trail Illustrations.
Courtesy of National Park Service and David Rickman.

as much corn and grass as they could carry in order to feed their livestock during the journey.

On 30 November 1775, at seven in the morning, Anza gave the order to break camp, *"Vayan subiendo* [mount up]." The Spaniards filed into formation. By the afternoon they had crossed the Colorado River and made camp on its western bank. In the evening, the Quechan chief Salvador Palma paid Anza a formal visit, wearing a European-styled suit that he had received from Anza, which consisted of long stockings, an embroidered yellow vest, a cape of blue cloth decorated with gold braid, and a black velvet cap adorned with imitation jewels. The proud Quechan chief represented his people well that day, reminding Anza that Spain had agreed to establish a colony at Yuma.

The Spaniards skirted the Colorado River in a southerly direction for several days so as to avoid the sand dunes located west of Yuma. Unexpectedly, the winter season turned inclement and the bitter cold killed a horse and a mule. Colonists also suffered, finding it difficult to sleep during the chilled evenings. One morning, fray Pedro Font awoke to find that the urine in his chamber pot had frozen during the night, and even he must have wondered why God had brought the Spaniards to such an unforgiving land.

On 9 December 1775, the colonists entered the arid Colorado desert. Anza had divided the party into four groups and ordered them to cross the desert at one-day intervals, thus preventing the depletion of water at wells that an advance guard had dug along the trail. Carlos R. Herrera writes that through the tenth, the Spaniards:

> trudged across territory encompassing today's City of Mexicali and crossed the future U.S.-Mexico border somewhere west of Calexico. Anza's lead party reached Santa Rosa de las Raxas (Yuha) the following day. There, the Spaniards dug six wells that produced a decent supply of water for the thirsty travelers and their beasts. A mere seven miles to the south, the Cerro del Impossible (Mount Signal) cast a shadow on the desert floor that served as an omen of ill tidings to come. On December 12, Anza and company rode into the environs of Plaster City, at Coyote Wash, where they were greeted by a cold wind that bit into the flesh of the weary Spaniards. The following day, the group made camp at San Sebastián (Harpers Well), where they encountered a band of hungry and emaciated Indians. On the fourteenth, storm clouds that had been gathering for two days finally burst open and dropped a blanket of snow on the colonists.[52]

The wretched blizzard dampened the colonists' spirits but could not deter them from their quest. On 17 December all four groups reunited at San Sebastian, and in the evening the Spaniards celebrated the desert crossing with music and dance. In coming days, the settlers crossed the Santa Rosa Mountains. By January 1776, the party, which now included three newborns, reached San Gabriel mission. From here, the colonists continued up the Pacific coast to San Francisco Bay and set themselves to building a presidio and settlement. Having fulfilled his charge, Anza returned to Sonora in the fall of 1776. He then traveled to Mexico City, where he received a second hero's welcome and promotion to the rank of colonel.

Crossing the Colorado Desert.
Desert Snow, by David Rickman, from the Anza Trail Illustrations.
Courtesy of National Park Service and David Rickman.

The Yuma Colony and Massacre

The Hopi refusal to accept Christianity forced Spain to rely on Anza's 1776 route for the establishment of a Sonora–Alta California connection. This fact suited Anza and José de Gálvez, both of whom realized that this corridor to the Pacific coast could be maintained only if Spain befriended the Quechans. These Native Americans controlled the territory at the confluence of the Gila and Colorado rivers. Anza had recognized the strategic significance of this region in 1774, and he believed Spain could not sustain a land route between Sonora and Alta California without access to the fertile land at Yuma and the life-giving water of its rivers. He suggested that Spain negotiate an alliance with the Quechans and seek concessions to establish a mission colony at Yuma.

Anza understood that Quechan Chief Salvador Palma held the keys to a successful partnership between Spain and the Quechans. Palma's sway over his people rested on his ability to defend them and make available the material resources they needed to survive in the desert. Anza wooed Palma with gifts; more important, he made it known that the Quechans would continue to receive such offerings in the future should they allow the establishment of a settlement at Yuma. The Spaniards sweetened their offer when Gálvez, in 1776, announced that King Carlos III had agreed to establish economic ties with the Quechans and promised to establish two missions and a garrison near Yuma. The promise of trade and troops sealed the deal for Palma. To cement the newly formed alliance, Gálvez invited the chief and a small contingent of his people to travel to Mexico City, where they would be showered with gifts and welcomed into Spain's imperial and Catholic family.[53]

Anza stood in as godfather to Salvador Palma at Palma's baptism in the cathedral of Mexico City. Palma's initiation into the faith represented the onset of mutual accommodation between Europeans and Indians along the Colorado River. By securing a foothold at Yuma, the Spaniards believed they could now sustain colonists traveling on the Sonora–Alta California land route, and thus transform the Pacific coast colony into a first line of defense against European competitors. The Russian threat had been met, or so it seemed.

The Quechans had done their part, and all that remained was for Spain to fulfill its promise of making goods and military defense available at Yuma. Government officials in New Spain, however, failed to see these pledges through to fruition. Two mission settlements were founded among the Quechans by January 1780; Purísima Concepción was located on the western side of the Colorado River across from Yuma, and San Pedro y San Pablo de Bicuñer was established some ten miles upriver from the first site.

For the Quechans, the prospect of spiritual salvation was not enough; they wanted the gifts of glass beads and tobacco, the cloth, and the European-made wares that had been promised. Instead, Palma and his people encountered a horde of Spaniards who demanded food, land, and obedience. And so, on 17 June 1781, the Quechans attacked. Three days later, one hundred Europeans were either dead or missing. Among those who perished in the summer heat of June was Francisco Garcés. The exasperated Quechans, it seems, had lost all patience waiting for Spain to live up to the ideal of mutual accommodation. In their eyes, the agreement of peace by purchase had been violated; but this time, it was the Spaniards who suffered the consequences of betrayal. Historian David J. Weber described the tension between the Spaniards and the Quechans at Yuma when he wrote:

> Spanish arrogance, failed promises, corporal punishment, and demands for food and arable land had aroused anger throughout the Yuma community, alienating even the cooperative Salvador Palma. For their part, the Franciscans blamed [Teodoro de] Croix for sanctioning a low-budget enterprise and for limiting their control over the temporal lives of the Yumas in violation of custom and law; Croix blamed Anza and the Franciscans for misrepresenting Yuma docility.[54]

It is doubtful that the Yuma Massacre could have been prevented. Because of the tragedy, Spain never again tried to establish permanent settlements in the region. Perhaps it is best to conclude that the disastrous outcome of the Colorado River experiment resulted from poor timing, bad planning, and priorities that forced officials to focus their efforts elsewhere. In 1776, the crown had approved Gálvez's plan to transform New Spain's northern frontier into a military district that would function independent of the viceroy in Mexico City. At the head of the *Comandancia General de las Provincias Internas del Norte de Nueva España* (General Command of the Internal Provinces of Northern New Spain), as this new polity came to be known, Gálvez placed Teodoro de Croix, nephew of ex-viceroy Marqués de Croix. As commandant general, Croix's first priority was to defend the northern provinces. In Sonora, colonists prayed that the newly appointed officer would assume his duties with haste. The northern portion of the colony had once again been consumed by Indian uprisings. Croix had no choice but to address these hostilities before paying any heed to the Yuma project. To subdue the rebellious Seris, Piatos, and the ever-present Western Apaches, he placed Colonel Anza at the head of Sonora's military forces, hoping that the celebrated frontiersman could once again perform military marvels where others had failed.

After his second trip to Mexico City, Anza returned to Sonora and settled in at Horcasitas by May 1777. He soon discovered that the new wave of violence in Pimería Alta had resulted, in large part, from Hugo O'Conor's ill-conceived plan to relocate the Tubac garrison north to Tucson. The crown had approved the transfer of troops late in 1775. Construction of a presidio at Tucson, however, had been seriously botched due to misappropriation of funds and lack of manpower. Pápago Indians, who had been promised fair wages to carry out the actual construction of the presidio, abandoned the site because they had not received payment for services rendered. Even the Ópatas, who had faithfully served as military auxiliaries in Sonora, threatened to sever their ties with Spain because they, too, had not been paid.

Without a garrison, Tubac deteriorated into a shambles and attracted raiders. Under siege, colonists and friars begged officials to reinstate the Tubac garrison at its old presidio and postpone the Yuma project. The people's pleas fell on deaf ears, and the best Anza could to do for them was to reinforce the garrison at Tucson. Anza might have restored order in northern Sonora, given more time. By 19 May 1777, however, the Spanish crown decided that his talents as an officer and statesman were needed in another corner of the Comandancia General. Anza had been appointed to the governorship of New Mexico.[55]

Anza's expeditions to Alta California fulfilled a dream he had inherited from his father, but they also embellished his social capital as a soldier patriot of Spain. It is doubtful that Carlos III would have promoted Anza to the rank of governor if Anza had not first undertaken the Alta California assignment. It is also unlikely that Anza could have achieved the level of success he did in New Mexico if not for the life he had led in Sonora. It was in his home province, after all, that Anza developed the military proficiency and political expertise he needed to survive as governor of contentious New Mexico. In Sonora, he had learned to balance the desires of the crown with the needs of the local populace; his roles in the Jesuit expulsion and his defense of the northern region best illustrated this dynamic. Above all else, it was in Sonora that Anza learned how to confront the issue of Spanish-Indian relations. He understood that in this land of limited resources, violence was a perpetual danger. Still, he never abandoned his belief in alternative strategies for achieving peace between ethnic groups.

Anza carried with him to New Mexico the life lessons he had learned as a frontiersman in Pimería Alta. In New Mexico, he met strong opposition to the absolutist plan he had been ordered to implement in the colony. As he had done in Sonora, however, Anza fulfilled the Bourbon ideal of reform without upsetting the regional nature of Hispano society. He forced New Mexicans to take a more active role in the defense of their homeland. He subordinated the Franciscans to the state, without attacking the religious ideals the colonists held dear. Anza preserved the spirit of accommodation with the Pueblo Indians. Other indigenous groups, such as the Comanches and Apaches, experienced the full force of Spanish arms under Anza's command; but even they came to accept peace on his terms, and without sacrificing their social-cultural spaces. One can argue that on this account, Anza had traveled a long and arduous journey toward solving the Spanish-Indian dilemma that he had first experienced in Sonora. But whether he perceived the culmination of his professional life in New Mexico through the eyes of a soldier or an enlightened individual, Anza always considered himself a child of the desert and a servant of the Spanish crown.

Part II

The King's Government

CHAPTER FOUR

The Social-Militarization of Bourbon New Mexico

B Y JANUARY 1778, Pedro Fermín de Mendinueta had completed almost eleven years of public service for his king in the province of New Mexico.[1] As governor, Mendinueta survived a long and taxing tenure—a term of office characterized by intense warfare between Indian groups hostile to Spain and its Pueblo allies. He proved a willing defender of the realm but was unable to bring a permanent peace to this violent corner of New Spain. Under his rule, colonists endured a constant barrage of raids by Comanches and Apaches bent on depriving Spaniards and Pueblos of their resources and their lives. The wars bore heavy on Mendinueta's spirit and body, and so the governor longed for the relative calm of retirement. As was his right, he petitioned Commandant General Teodoro de Croix to be released of his charge in 1777. Croix granted Mendinueta's request in a letter dated 11 February 1778.[2] Croix's communiqué reflected an urgent tone. In it, he ordered Mendinueta to make immediate arrangements to travel to the villa (chartered town) of Chihuahua to meet his successor, Colonel Juan Bautista de Anza.[3]

Croix expressed concern for Mendinueta's questionable health, but also a desire for a quick and orderly transition of power in New Mexico. To facilitate the change, the commandant general instructed Mendinueta to inform Anza about conditions in the colony. The picture was grim. A severe drought that engulfed the entire northern frontier of New Spain from 1772 to 1776 had forced the Comanches, Apaches, Utes, and Navajos to increase their raiding activities among both Pueblo and Spanish settlements.[4] Mendinueta reported that these Native Americans had also altered the nature of their attacks. They had shifted the focus of their raiding campaigns to include human beings as well as goods and livestock; they "captured women and children (which they held for ransom), [and] destroyed herds (which made it difficult for troops to defend the colony)."[5] During Mendinueta's decade, New Mexico's Spanish population thus suffered the greatest loss of life of the eighteenth century: more than two hundred colonists perished at the hands of raiding Indian bands.[6]

Haunted by memories of the 1680 Pueblo Revolt, Hispanos pondered the possibility that their homeland might fall once more into the waiting hands of *indios enemigos* (Indian enemies). The potential threat for New Mexico vexed Spanish officials, even if they did not hold the remote colony in the same regard as mineral-rich settlements such as Zacatecas and Guanajuato. Still, Croix warned his king that all of northern New Spain would be left open to increased attacks if New Mexico were lost: "If we lose the important barrier of New Mexico, which I pray God may not happen, the Indians would be masters of that immense country and, accustomed to living by robbery, would indubitably approach us."[7]

Carlos III could not afford to lose mining centers such as Zacatecas. He needed the silver produced at these sites to preserve an empire that had suffered significant territorial losses in North America, and which was still recovering from an economic crisis that roused citizens of Madrid to civil disobedience in the 1760s. The king thus determined that New Mexico must stand, and that a strong-willed individual who knew the ways and means of warfare and governance in the hostile north would have to be chosen to save the colony from complete destruction.[8]

Teodoro de Croix did not favor Anza's appointment to New Mexico. The commandant general's choice fell on Pedro de Garibay. Carlos III disagreed.[9] The king believed that Anza had proven his worth as a public servant on the Sonora frontier. His role in the expulsion of the Jesuits demonstrated loyalty to the crown. Likewise, Anza displayed initiative in his expeditions to Alta California. Most important, Anza had manifested the leadership qualities needed to rally troops, Indian allies, and colonists alike in the defense of the empire. For these reasons, Carlos III granted Anza the title of governor and military commander of the province of New Mexico on 19 May 1777.[10] More than a year passed, however, before Anza traveled to the colony to assume his charge. Croix, it seemed, decided that Anza's military skills were still needed against the Indians of his native Sonora.

In the meantime, Francisco Trébol Navarro served as interim governor of New Mexico.

In June 1778, Anza was released from his command in Sonora. He sent word of his new appointment to New Mexico's lieutenant governor, José Antonio de Arrieta, who set about to receive him at El Paso.[11] In the meantime, Anza gathered his family around him at the Spanish settlement of Horcasitas and together they bid farewell to friends and neighbors of their native Sonora. In the heat of June, this celebrated servant of Spain sat high on his mount and set a course upon weathered trails that led him to his new command. On 8 August, he stood before Croix at Chihuahua and took the required oath of office, swearing to defend New Mexico from the enemies of Spain. Between September and November, Anza unleashed his reform program in the region of El Paso, and by December 1778, he assumed his charge at Santa Fe. Here, Anza received from Interim Governor Navarro the *bastón de justicia*—a silver-tipped black cane that symbolized an individual's authority to hold office—and took up residency at the governor's palace.[12]

Anza had accepted his king's challenge to transform New Mexico into a militarized buffer zone, a defensive colony that would assume its place among others of the General Command in the effort to preserve New Spain's far northern territory. Carlos III considered this charge the governor's primary duty: by creating an effective bastion against warring Indians and intruding foreigners, Anza would help Spain consolidate this American frontier and the empire in general. Achieving such a lofty goal would be no easy matter, for it required that Anza impose a series of drastic military and defensive reforms on professional soldiers and civilians alike. This social-militarization program would have a profound impact on the lives of each and every Spanish and Pueblo colonist, who now more than ever would be called upon to help defend their homeland. Anza's efforts to enhance the defensive posture of New Mexico also changed the lives of those indigenous groups that had made war on the colony, including the Comanches, Hopis, Navajos, and Apaches.[13]

The Chihuahua Council of War: July–August, 1778

The plan to militarize the Internal Provinces was conceived at a war council convened by Croix at Chihuahua and attended by key military figures of the far north, including Anza. The commandant general had summoned his officers to help him conceptualize a new defense policy that would replace Spain's failed presidial realignment project. Initiated in 1772 under the direction of Irish-born Hugo O'Conor, the presidial line in 1778 ran some two thousand miles from Texas to California and required the services of four hundred men. The presidios had been sited to better protect the lives of colonials living in the hostile north and to prevent Indian forays from spilling south into New Spain's silver-producing region. The program fell short of its intended goal. Throughout the 1770s, Native Americans raided Spanish and Indian communities at will, shifting their attacks to settlements whose defenses had been weakened by the abandonment of presidios in their vicinity, such as Tubac.[14] In 1775, O'Conor initiated an offensive war against the Apaches of Texas in an effort to stem the tide of these invasions. Although his campaigning bore fruits of temporary peace in 1776, the harvest of reconciliation between Indians and Spaniards soon began to rot. By 1777, northern New Spain was once again a frontier of bloody conflict.

At the Chihuahua War Council, Croix insisted that the new military plan for the far north mirror colonial policies that France had utilized to interact with American Indians.[15] The most important French strategies included trade relations with indigenous groups that upheld peace agreements with European colonists, the use of Indian military allies, and the policy of "peace by purchase." The latter stratagem involved the granting of annual gifts to indigenous peoples who kept the peace.

Anza had long recognized that Spain's defense policy was flawed by its overreliance on armed retaliation against combative Indians. In 1772, he argued that warfare alone would not end raids against Spanish settlements; it actually encouraged attacks. He also understood that Indians "preferred trade to bullets" and that peace in northern New Spain could best be achieved by making Spanish goods available to those natives willing to maintain alliances with Spain.[16] Nevertheless, Anza knew that the appearance of strength through arms represented language nomadic warriors understood and considered when dealing with their enemies. He therefore insisted that the implementation of a policy like peace by purchase had to be preceded by a show of military might. Like most of his colleagues in the far north, he promoted offensive warfare as a springboard to peace by purchase and a step toward mutual accommodation.

Croix took to heart the counsel he received from the military chiefs who gathered around him at Chihuahua, and from July to August 1778 the war council penned a new defense strategy for the Provincias Internas. The first phase of the plan called for a coordinated offensive against the Apaches of Texas and the Comanches of New Mexico's eastern frontier. Anza's role in the operation required him to unleash the full force of Spain's military might on the Comanches. The war council had figured that a resounding victory against these proud Indians would lead the entire Comanche nation to seek an alliance with Spain. It reasoned further that a treaty with the much-feared Comanches would force the eastern Apaches to sue for peace and render aid in the offensive against their western cousins, the Gilas and Mimbreños. Subduing these Native Americans seemed vital if the Spaniards were to maintain order in northern Sonora and, in turn, to preserve the land route Anza had opened between Pimería Alta and Alta California. Toward this end, Croix also encouraged Anza to establish alliances with the Hopis and Navajos of western New Mexico in the hope that they would apply pressure on the Gilas and Mimbreños from the north.[17]

Interwoven within the Chihuahua defense plan was the idea that those Indians willing to uphold the peace would be granted trade incentives and annual gifts. This strategy represented the second and perhaps most important phase of the Chihuahua plan. By replacing war with trade, the Spaniards hoped that the hard-won peace would last for generations and possibly make their culture more appealing to Native Americans. On these issues, Croix insisted that Indians wishing to reconcile themselves with Spain be encouraged to relocate to *establecimientos de paz* (peace camps), where they would receive goods and be exposed to European culture.[18]

Aside from the need to quell warring Indians, the crown sought to restructure the defenses of the General Command in response to the menacing presence in North America of rival European powers. Throughout the eighteenth century, Spain had suffered notable military defeats in the effort to preserve its imperial domains. The capture of Havana by England during the Seven Years War (1760s), for example, had shaken the Bourbons. More than anything else, Spain's rulers feared that if the British continued their incursions into Spanish America, they would ultimately seek to gain dominance over New Spain's silver region. To prevent such a catastrophe, King Carlos III opted to increase the professionalism of his armies. And for this, he turned to Frederick the Great of Prussia for a model of efficient and effective militarism.

Through the efforts of the Irish-born field marshal Alejandro O'Reilly, Spain adopted Prussian military tactics, including a highly disciplined, three-deep line of infantry, light and heavy cavalry, and state-of-the-art artillery. The crown increased troops' wages and insisted that its armies be outfitted with standard uniforms. Above all, Carlos III demanded professionalism and loyalty to the Spanish imperial cause from his soldiers. The king impressed this ideal most notably among his officers, for whom the crown established training academies in Spain.[19]

Spain did not possess the capital resources needed to finance a standing army in the Americas. Instead, it relied on the expertise of carefully selected field marshals who had received standing orders to reorganize defensive mechanisms already in place in the colonies. From these servants, Carlos III demanded an American military capable of sustaining itself and providing defense against all the enemies of Spain. The Marqués de Rubí's Regulations of 1772 outlined the military reforms to be implemented in New Spain's far northern territory. Aside from the presidial realignment program mentioned above, Rubí emphasized the need for increased training of local troops and the use of citizen militias. He agreed with his king that officers serving in the General Command should be loyal to the crown, as well as industrious men of action and talent; Rubí concluded that Anza was just such a man.[20]

Anza in El Paso

As an instrument of Bourbon militarism in New Mexico, Anza first addressed issues of defense in the settlement of El Paso.[21] Since its founding, El Paso had served as New Mexico's lifeline to the heart of Mexico. According to Carlos R. Herrera:

> Spanish El Paso tied New Mexico to the rest of New Spain, and its river crossing served as a point of entry and exit from the colony. By the 1650s, Franciscan friars occupied the region for Spain with several mission settlements that catered mainly to Manso Indians. At El Paso, the friars developed ranches and farms that, with time, proved a haven for travelers coming and going on the Camino Real. By the late 1660s, the Paseños [citizens of El Paso], which now included a small but growing Spanish population, boasted at their thriving community of some 1,000 souls.

Most built their homes on scattered sites around El Paso. They ranched cattle, sheep, and goats, and plowed the earth for its bounty. Paseños counted grapes among their prized crops, and the sweet fruit allowed them to develop a wine and brandy industry that filled mission orders in the colony and wine goblets in southern markets.[22]

Revitalized as a refugee camp that had housed exiled New Mexicans fleeing the Pueblo Revolt, El Paso received a presidio and fifty troops in 1683.[23] Paseños prospered, and by 1766 the villa's population had blossomed to five thousand. That year, the Marqués de Rubí determined that El Paso could count on enough citizens to defend the district with militias. As a result, four civilian units were created and outfitted in El Paso. The settlement, however, lost its professional garrison when troops were transferred to the Nueva Vizcaya settlement of Carrizal sometime after 1772. Government officials in Mexico City agreed to maintain El Paso's *cuarteles* (barracks), which were then used by militias and paid troops traveling to and from the colony. Moreover, officials considered establishing a presidio at Robledo— located just north of El Paso—but this plan was never put into effect.[24]

Throughout the entire colonial period, officials depended heavily on local militias to help defend New Spain's far northern territory. Historically, these militias focused their efforts on three potential threats: revolt by pacified Indians, attacks from hostile nomadic groups, and encroachment on Spanish American domains by foreign powers.[25] In colonies such as New Mexico, citizen armies provided some degree of protection from warring peoples; their effectiveness in this regard, however, was always limited by innate weaknesses. Colonists resented forced service in these units because most of them were not professional soldiers. Many found it difficult to purchase the arms the crown required of them. And draftees often tried to avoid duty in militia companies by petitioning government officials for leave so that they could tend to their farms and families.[26]

Croix granted Anza almost complete freedom to implement any measures he deemed necessary to enhance the military preparedness of militia units serving in the southern district. Through a series of edicts issued in El Paso between September and December 1778, Anza initiated a defense reform program that touched the lives of all settlers in the region. As a first order of business, he requested that Lieutenant Governor José Antonio Arrieta provide him information regarding El Paso's forces, including a list of all men-at-arms in the region who were adequately supplied with uniforms, horses, and riding gear. In addition, Anza ordered militia captains living in El Paso to determine the quantity and condition of arms at their disposal. Anza informed Arrieta that all regular troops and militiamen serving in the El Paso region should be properly outfitted with regulation uniforms and weapons sold to them at cost.[27]

The military chiefs who gathered at Chihuahua in 1778 considered El Paso's militias crucial in the war against the Apaches. These units, however, were unorganized, undermanned, and poorly outfitted. To remedy the shambled state of El Paso's civilian forces, the war council called for the consolidation of the settlement's four militias into three, the first consisting of one hundred troops and the remaining two of fifty each. The military chiefs also planned to assign a squad of seventy Indian auxiliaries to help support these companies. Upon personal inspection, Anza deemed that El Paso's militias could be better managed if they were merged into two companies rather than three; such a reorganization, he argued, would also reduce military expenditures in New Mexico's southern district.[28]

The pitiful state and supply of firearms available in El Paso weighed more heavily on Anza's mind than did the makeup and administration of its militia units. Weapons had already been purchased for the district, but they were poor in quality and expensive; each *escopeta* (musket) had cost fifteen pesos, three reales. It seemed obvious to Anza that gun merchants had secured a tidy profit from the sale of these inferior arms, but there was little he could do about it. Instead, he ordered Lieutenant Governor Arrieta to collect all useless and obsolete muskets and dispose of them in Chihuahua. Croix had graciously agreed to use royal funds to purchase new weapons for troops serving in El Paso's militias. Croix insisted that these guns be distributed free of charge, but he made it clear that militiamen would eventually be expected to return the muskets in as good condition as they had received them.[29]

In addition to weapons, men of the El Paso militias also received horses. Apache and Comanche raiders had severely depleted New Mexico's herds, and in 1775 then Governor Mendinueta warned that the colony could fall if the crown failed to replenish its stock. Mendinueta requested fifteen hundred mounts, and the king approved the order on 14 February 1776. Carlos III's accountants calculated that this herd would cost ten thousand, eight hundred pesos, of which the king agreed to cover nine thousand pesos.

Spanish Camp with Horse and Cattle Herd.
Llano Grande, by Bill Singleton, from the Anza Trail Illustrations.
Courtesy of National Park Service and Bill Singleton.

Private donors picked up the balance, including one thousand pesos from Francisco Oparto of Chihuahua. Marqués de San Miguel de Aguayo supplied one hundred of his own horses to make up the remaining eight hundred pesos.[30]

A limited and scattered supply of horses in the General Command made it difficult to amass a new herd for New Mexico. By May 1777, only 1,047 mounts had been secured. The full complement of 1,500 animals was successfully rounded up in time for the Chihuahua War Council of July 1778. The herd was entrusted to Governor Anza, who oversaw its transport to New Mexico. Of the total, El Paso received 157 horses along with the hopes that these mounts—together with those of the San Elizario presidio—would help strengthen the units serving in the south.[31]

In Sonora, Anza had learned that the availability of horses determined the nature and effectiveness of the defense Spaniards could muster against *indios enemigos*. For New Mexico, he therefore insisted that colonists pay a levy of one *real* each to help maintain the province's horse herd. Almost any measure seemed justified to protect the community's horses, especially because the Hispanos were not the only frontier people who treasured them. Indigenous Americans also considered horses an essential resource in their economy; many believed these animals measured an individual's personal wealth. The intrinsic value of the horse found other forms of expression in the cultural ideals and customs of many Native American tribes. The Apaches, for example, believed that the acquisition of horses through raids represented a rite of passage for boys seeking entrance into the realm of manhood. The Comanches, on the other hand, looked upon their relation with the hoofed beasts as the ultimate expression of their warrior culture. According to Stanley Noyes: "The horse not only symbolized wealth but also represented mobility and military power. In recognition of these benefits, the Comanches named the animal the 'God-dog.' To them it meant the difference between a constant threat of hunger and assurance of plenty, between vulnerability to their enemies and relative security through strength."[32]

Clearly, horses played a key role in the new defense policy for the General Command. Paseños, however, did not welcome the governor's herd tax. Anza tried to appease them on this matter by arguing that they would be allowed to expand trade relations with merchants from Chihuahua in order to raise funds for the required levy.[33] Paseños had managed lucrative gains in southern markets in the 1600s. At the time of the Pueblo Revolt, for example, they cashed in on hungry exiles by selling them beef and corn acquired from Tarahumara Indians living in the territory southeast of El Paso and from the natives of Casas Grandes.[34] Increased violence in the early 1700s killed these financial partnerships and left colonials hoping for a brighter future.

Anza's economic plan for El Paso seemed to promise worthy prospects. He suggested that Paseños manufacture textiles within the district, and that they sell these goods—along with their wines and brandies—in Chihuahua and Sonora. Croix hoped that the expansion of economic ties between El Paso and settlements located in New Mexico's neighboring colonies would appease Paseño concerns regarding Anza's defensive reforms, as well as generate income to support the social-militarization program. To his dismay, however, the commandant general learned that El Paso merchants tended to utilize antiquated business practices he deemed questionable. He insisted that Paseños would have to cease the use of imaginary currencies and establish uniform price schedules before being allowed to expand their interests.[35]

To improve the efficiency of trade, Anza asked El Paso merchants to select an agent with power of attorney to represent their economic interests in southern markets. He also noted that Croix had already approved a plan to establish a safe route between New Mexico and Sonora and promised that he would make troop escorts available to those wishing to engage in the proposed trans-provincial commerce.[36] The lure of increased profits hit its mark among El Paso merchants, and by 30 November 1778 Anza reported to Croix that many of them had agreed to reestablish economic ties with Sonora by the following February.[37]

Before taking his leave of El Paso, the governor addressed one of the most controversial reforms debated at the Chihuahua War Council: the administration and disbursement of soldiers' wages. An unspoken veil of corruption had long marred the tradition by which troops received their salaries in northern New Spain. Presidial captains managed the payout of these funds as well as the sale of garrison supplies to soldiers. These responsibilities had allowed many officers to exploit the men under their command. They sold goods to troops at inflated prices and docked the troops' salaries to cover debts. Officers also fattened their personal coffers by using their men to work on private lands and in their homes. Because of such schemes, many soldiers serving in the northern frontier found themselves in the unsavory position of debt peons. Anza insisted that New Mexico's troops—including those serving in militias—receive adequate pay and have goods sold to them at fair prices. Croix agreed, and so he set militia wages as follows: two reales daily for each man-at-arms, and three for corporals and sergeants. Anza informed Arrieta of the salary schedule and instructed him to safeguard the monies for these wages in a three-lock box, with one key in the possession of the lieutenant governor and the other two in the hands of the militia captains stationed at El Paso.[38]

By the first week of October 1778, Anza had already been at El Paso for one month and was eager to move his family to Santa Fe. Croix, however, had reviewed Anza's reports on El Paso and concluded that the governor's militia reforms could be improved upon; they could be brought closer in line with Rubí's Regulations of 1772. On 11 October, the commandant general forwarded to Anza official praise for his efforts, but also gave him detailed instructions on how to amend his defense plan for the El Paso district.

Croix ordered that each of El Paso's two militia companies consist of forty-two troops and a squadron of thirty Indian auxiliaries, a captain, a lieutenant, an ensign, two sergeants, and six corporals. He made Anza responsible for approving the selection of militia sergeants and for appointing captains to the Indian units. Moreover, Croix insisted that the tradition of conscription end by allowing men to enlist in militias of their own volition.[39] On this matter, the commandant general spoke directly to the king's desire that the means by which his armies were staffed be reformed. In the past, Spain had relied on military selection processes that included forced conscriptions and the use of the *sorteo*; the latter stratagem involved a lottery that determined who would be drafted into the military but had been abandoned in 1776.[40]

Croix ordered that militiamen adopt required uniforms worn by regular troops serving in the General Command. Herrera has written that standard military dress included:

> a short blue *chupa* (jacket) embellished with crimson *vuelta* (stitching), *solapas* (lapels) and a *collarín* (collar) of the same deep red hue, and fastened with white buttons. Soldiers donned blue breeches made of cloth or wool, a black hat, blue cloak, and any minor *prendas* (adornments) correspondent to the individual's rank or station. The commandant general insisted that any individual able to pay for his military wardrobe should do so, with the understanding that the crown would cover such expenses when funds became available.[41]

Having agreed to outfit El Paso's militias, Croix declared that the crown would also provide riding gear and horses for each citizen soldier, including three mounts and a mule. These totals did not match the number of animals normally issued to veteran presidial soldiers, which included six horses, a colt, and a mule per man.[42] The discrepancy in horse allotments perhaps reflected Croix's concern regarding the overall availability of mounts in the General Command and the frequency by which these animals were lost to disease, old age, and theft. To supplement El Paso's supply of horses, Croix thus approved Anza's plan to unite the settlement's herd with that of San Elizario, "as well as the governor's suggestion that an alternating *escolta* (guard) of twenty soldiers and ten Indian auxiliaries be assigned every fifteen days to protect the animals."[43] Croix followed up on these decisions in December 1778, at which time he ordered Lieutenant Governor Arrieta and the captain of San Elizario, Diego Borica, to see to the union of their respective horse herds. Croix added that a guard of forty-five men, rather than Anza's thirty, would be needed to protect the horses.[44]

Croix further burdened Arrieta with the responsibility of controlling gunpowder usage in the El Paso district. He ordered the lieutenant governor to submit an annual request for the powder and see to its proper storage and distribution. Croix calculated that each man-at-arms required five pounds of gunpowder per year. This amount, he figured, should suffice for all of the individual's military needs, including target practice and battle.

Strict controls on the acquisition and distribution of gunpowder reflected Spain's urgent need to cut expenditures without sacrificing military efficiency. José de Gálvez had imposed a royal monopoly on gunpowder in the Internal Provinces in 1768, but in the following decades it was clear that usage on this frontier continued to be wasteful and expensive. Croix declared that the arbitrary supply of gunpowder to servicemen through unidentified individuals would cease, and that the commodity would now be issued through predetermined officers.[45] Croix also insisted that those troops who failed to utilize their allotted quota of gunpowder would be charged for the unused portion through their presidial account. He made Anza responsible for regulating the sale of the explosive in New Mexico and insuring that it was sold to his men at cost.[46]

Croix closed his militia reform instructions of 1778 by outlining specific duties that each company was to observe. He expected civilian units to conduct daily patrols of El Paso and its environs. He ordered that two militia troops be assigned to serve as a personal guard for the lieutenant governor, and as couriers should this officer need to communicate with the presidios or the commandant general. Moreover, Croix demanded that militias help protect El Paso's horses. He granted Arrieta leave to organize citizen troops into scouting and recovery parties whenever Indian raids required that such units seek out thieves and recover stolen horses and mules. Croix allowed European and Indian troops serving in these punitive expeditions to collect bounties from the owners of each animal recaptured—a policy repealed on 9 December 1784 by Croix's successor, José Antonio Rengel.[47] Finally, Croix agreed to offer extra pay for services that went beyond regular militia duties: captains earned twelve *reales* (thirty-four *maravedís*, or about one and one half pesos) daily, lieutenants eight, *alféreces* (ensigns) six, sergeants five, first sergeants four, and the individual militiaman three.

Croix also set extra pay for Indian allies: three daily reales for captains and two for each auxiliary.[48]

With Anza's defense reforms for El Paso amended, Croix believed militia units would be better able to protect the lives and property of its populace. He worried, however, that expecting Paseños to volunteer for militia service could cause social unrest. Opposition to Anza's reforms had already surfaced in El Paso. In October 1778, citizens from the settlement of Los Tiburcios asked to be relieved from militia duty so that they could tend to their farms. Croix would not bend to the pleas of these colonials, and by November he approved Anza's refusal to grant the Los Tiburcios colonists their petition.[49]

Disgruntled Paseños also questioned the demand that they help finance Anza's militia reforms, including the governor's forced levee for the maintenance of El Paso's horse herd. Colonials could not rationalize such economic burdens when they were already being asked to serve in local militias. Croix, however, made it clear that King Carlos III had sanctioned state-mandated taxes and would not tolerate disloyalty from any subject. To appease their worries, the commandant general encouraged Paseños to adopt Anza's suggestions regarding increased sales of wines and brandies in Chihuahua and Sonora markets. Concurrently, however, he agreed to impose a two-percent *alcabala* (sales tax) on all spirits and fruits produced in the region of El Paso.[50] Moreover, he granted Governor Anza the power to determine if tariffs collected at El Paso were indeed needed to help supply the villa's militia units; if not, these funds would then be utilized elsewhere in New Mexico to support the military reform process.[51] Outraged by the notion that their hard-earned pesos would be used to benefit someone besides themselves, Paseños continued to challenge Croix and Anza's tax reforms. It was not until 1781, however, that they prevailed. King Carlos III ruled then that some of the tariffs Croix imposed on the citizens of New Mexico had proven harmful to their prosperity; he thus officially disapproved such levies and eventually repealed them.[52]

King Carlos III justified the repealing of taxes in New Mexico on the notion that the colony was one of the most impoverished provinces in all the General Command. Neither Croix nor Anza contested this point, but both men reasoned that even the poorest New Mexicans could contribute to defensive reform by providing labor for projects such as the relocation of settlements to strategic sites or the maintenance of roads.[53] Moreover, they could build walls and fences. On 4 November 1778, Anza ordered Paseños to erect defensive barriers around their farmland so as to deter Indian raiders. He demanded periodic inspection and repair of these barricades and ordered colonials to maintain them at the specified height of three *varas* (about nine feet). Expecting resistance, Anza ordered two separate public readings of the edict and provided that a copy be made available in El Paso's city hall.[54] The Paseños could not claim ignorance of Anza's decree and, like it or not, they found themselves being held accountable for the defense of their homeland.

Embittered complaints about Anza's barricades soon morphed into public outcries. The Paseños protested to Croix that their vines would fall into neglect if the governor forced them to construct barriers. Moreover, they proclaimed that the amount of time required to complete these public works exposed their precious grapes to animal predators and Indian raiders—the very threats Anza had hoped to expel from the El Paso region. Did the governor not know that armed natives had already established homes a mere musket shot in distance from Spanish settlements? Did he not realize that El Paso's grape farmers could hardly rely on presidial troops to protect their lands since they had been removed to San Elizario? And did Anza not care that the production of their liquors would suffer greatly if he forced them to relocate to fortified settlements?[55]

It is probable that El Paso's hostile posture towards Anza stemmed from an unspoken disdain that Paseños held for the governor. Anza, after all, was not one of them; he was an outsider from Sonora who could not be trusted. Croix approached the social unrest at El Paso with commendable caution. He supported Anza's defensive reforms for the district, but allowed that man-made barriers might not be enough to keep animals or raiding Indians from seeking booty from its settlements. He refused to embarrass Anza by reversing the barrier edict, but acknowledged the potential impact Anza's order would have on El Paso's grape industry. Croix vacillated on the question of barricades to buy time. He knew the Anzas would be leaving El Paso for Santa Fe in December, and he hoped that the governor's absence would help to suppress the smoldering strife in the southern district. To further placate El Paso's residents, Croix shifted the focus of their antagonism away from the issue of barricades and to an idea proposed by the Marqués de Rubí in 1772. Rubí had suggested that El Paso's defenses would be enhanced if a detachment of troops—twenty from the southern district, and thirty from the Santa Fe presidio—were stationed at the campsite of Robledo, which was located about seventy miles north of El Paso.[56] If implemented, Rubí's recommendation promised to minimize the defense burdens Governor Anza had ordered for the district. Paseños welcomed the Robledo plan, and Croix hoped that the idea would help restore civic peace in El Paso.

The Chihuahua War Council had debated Rubí's idea, and Croix believed that a military presence at Robledo could improve communication between New Mexico and Sonora. Gripped by doubt, however, the commandant general ordered Anza to reconnoiter Robledo during his December journey to Santa Fe and determine whether the site was suitable for the proposed campsite. As he waited for Anza's report on Robledo, Croix took steps to ready troops in case the site proved favorable. In March 1779, he informed Lieutenant Governor Arrieta that the captain from San Elizario had already been ordered to make funds available for an escort of militiamen, Indian auxiliaries, and horses that would be stationed at Robledo. Croix asked Arrieta to take command of the party, but only if his health permitted.[57] The lieutenant governor, it seems, had fallen gravely ill; by June it was evident that he was not able to perform the duties of his office. Croix himself had recently suffered a bout of malaria and lead poisoning that left him paralyzed in the arms and hands. Croix received last rites but managed to survive while convalescing at Nombre de Dios, Chihuahua.[58] From here, he ordered Nicolás Soler to march to El Paso as quickly as possible and assume interim command of the settlement. Arrieta was retired to Chihuahua and Soler was made the military subordinate of the captain of San Elizario; on all other matters, he answered to Governor Anza.[59] As for the Robledo detachment, Croix chose to abandon the project on Anza's recommendation. Anza reported that the maintenance of troops at this site was impossible because of the distance that separated the campsite from the Santa Fe presidio. He added that the inordinate number of hostile Indians settled around Robledo, as well as the rugged terrain, would make it difficult for even one hundred men to defend the territory. As an alternative to Robledo, Anza suggested that a squad be placed at the settlement of Socorro, but here, too, Croix decided to postpone any assignments until a later date.[60]

Although Paseños had scorned him at every turn, Anza's social-militarization program did improve El Paso's ability to defend itself against combative Indians. Forty years after the governor had vacated his seat at Santa Fe, New Mexico's southernmost district continued to enjoy an era of relative peace and economic prosperity. Paseños expanded their landholdings and, as a consequence, gained complete control of all commercial activities in the region.[61] El Paso's good fortune, however, had come at a heavy price. Perhaps those most affected by Anza's defense efforts were the indigenous Americans who had persistently made war against their Spanish neighbors. The Comanches of northern and eastern New Mexico were the first tribe to bear the weight of the war policy that Croix and his captains had outlined at Chihuahua during the summer of 1778. For his part, Anza left El Paso with the immediate goal of killing one of the most defiant chiefs of this proud nation; he left to kill Cuerno Verde.

CHAPTER FIVE

Peace by Purchase

J UAN BAUTISTA DE ANZA SETTLED in at Santa Fe during the cold
of December 1778 and began to address reform measures entrusted to
him, deciding that the most pressing charge was to implement the strategy of peace by purchase. The Chihuahua War Council had ordered Anza
to bring combative Indians into alliance with Spain; more to the point, it
asked him to subdue the Comanches and negotiate a trade agreement with
them. Anza understood that any hope of creating an economic pact with
these Native Americans would have to be prefaced with a show of military might. He figured that defeating the Comanches in battle would gain
him the esteem they granted strong warriors, and he knew he would need
this respect to lure the entire Comanche nation into a mutual peace. Such
a treaty might push other indigenous tribes into seeking similar arrangements with Spain, and those who did not would suffer the lethal might of
combined Spanish-Comanche forces. For Governor Anza, then, the future
of New Mexico truly lay in his ability to crush the Comanches on the
field of battle. Such a task, however, seemed daunting considering the violent history that had already come to pass between Spain and these proud
Americans.

Los Comanches

The Comanches first entered the Hispano-Pueblo world in the early 1700s.
They had come to the northern and eastern fringes of New Mexico to
acquire horses—to trade for them, or steal them if need be. Their needs

Comanche Indians, by George Addison.
Courtesy of Palace of the Governors Photo Archives
(NMHM/DCA) 002508.

were great. Driven by an expanding population base, and perhaps the threat of smallpox, the Comanches had split off from their Shoshone relatives of Wyoming in the late 1600s and burst onto the Great Plains to hunt buffalo, antelope, and elk. They flourished on the grasslands, where they soon evolved into great hunters, horse breeders, and warriors. But as the Comanche nation grew, so too did its need to dominate other ethnic groups that shared the frontier. This the Comanches accomplished with the double-edged sword of war and trade.[1]

Comanche males engaged in war to contend for standing among their people. They considered the most successful warriors to be imbued with cherished ideals of character that included honor, courage, and strength. The bravest earned the highest social distinctions and were considered best fit to govern. As chiefs, these men accepted the charge of bringing war to their enemies for a variety of reasons, including not just vengeance for comrades killed in battle but also to achieve economic gain through raiding.

Beginning in the early 1700s, the Comanches attacked New Mexico settlements on a regular basis. These forays intimidated inhabitants and discouraged them from entering the Comanches' hunting grounds. Known as the *Comanchería,* these realms stretched from the Sangre de Cristo Mountains in the west to the plains of Kansas and as far south as Texas. The grasslands offered plenty of game, but the Comanches desired more than buffalo meat and hides. They coveted the tools and horses that could be had from Pueblos and Hispanos. What the New Mexicans would not exchange for goods, the Comanches took by force of arms. War gave them access to goods they did not produce themselves. Moreover, Comanche raids struck terror in the imagination of their prey, thus forcing the enemy to negotiate peace on the Comanches' terms. Spain sealed its first treaty with the Comanches sometime between 1707 and 1712. As a consequence of this agreement, the Indians agreed to cease hostilities in New Mexico in return for permission to trade meat, hides, and other wares within the colony. The Comanche Horse Lords, however, had developed a reputation for violating pacts, suggesting that they could not be trusted. For their part, the Comanches did not assign any ethical value to the act of breaching contracts. In fact, they considered such blatant defiance necessary because it perpetuated the cycle of war that was intrinsic to their social and economic life. The Comanches' ability to translate violence into economic gain allowed them to replace the Apaches—whom they pushed to the south and west—as the masters of the southern plains. By the 1750s, they had built a western American empire that rivaled New Spain's power and wealth in the northern provinces.[2]

Governor Tomás Vélez Cachupín

Perhaps no New Mexico governor before Anza had understood the Comanche Way better than Tomás Vélez Cachupín. Vélez had been stationed at Havana as a cadet before being assigned as captain of the Santa Fe presidio in 1748. He then served two terms as governor of the province: from 1749–59, and again from 1762–66. Vélez gained insight into the Comanches' dual strategy of war and trade through trial and error. Governors before him had responded to raids on the colony with armed retaliation, as well as the enslavement of captured Indians. The Comanches' code of honor demanded that such reprisals be answered with their own acts of vengeance.[3] The Comanche warriors, however, probably welcomed Spanish aggression because it provided a reason to continue the cycle of war that gave them the upper hand in their economic dealings with New Mexicans. In the summer of 1751, Vélez himself granted the Horse Lords economic privileges when he allowed them to attend the trade fair of Taos. In return, he asked that the Comanches promise not to raid the pueblos of Pecos and Galisteo. The Indians agreed, but in November three hundred warriors wearing black war paint attacked Galisteo pueblo anyway. The foray outraged Governor Vélez but confused him as well. It soon dawned on him that the Comanches had perpetrated this violent act simply to engage in the act of war, and not just to acquire goods. Whether he realized it or not, Vélez had come closer than any of his predecessors to understanding how the Comanches used war to define and preserve their collective sense of honor. In response to the attack on Galisteo, Vélez followed the Comanches' example with a calculated strike intended to terrorize the Indians and impress upon them the need to choose peace and trade over violence. The Comanches, Vélez decided, would have to opt for the practical solution of mutual accommodation, or they would die.

With 124 troops at his side, Governor Vélez delivered on the promise of vengeance when his men faced off against a portion of the Comanche band that had raided Galisteo. They tracked the Indians for six days, onto the plains east of the settlement. Within the thicket of a water hole, the natives stood their ground, ready to die to the last man. Vélez placed his men around the site and ordered them to open fire. Near midnight, the troops set torches to the brush that concealed the Indians and continued their assault. From beyond the burning foliage and smoke, Vélez soon heard the cries of women and children, and so he asked his men to stand down. The governor warned the Comanches that he would spare no life if they did not surrender in a timely manner. Fearing death by drowning more than a musket ball, wounded men, women, and children filtered out of the site and gave themselves up to the governor. Of the 145 Indians who had waded into the water hole for refuge, only 49 survived. The remaining 96 Comanches died a warrior's death at the hands of the Spaniards and their Pueblo allies. In the aftermath of battle Vélez released the survivors, but not before he told them they had a choice: to cease their attacks on Spanish settlements and be granted trade concessions, or to continue to experience the armed wrath of his forces. In April of 1752, a Comanche party arrived at Taos to negotiate peace with the governor.[4]

The diplomatic skills Vélez displayed in his dealings with the Comanches allowed Spain to enter into a relationship of mutual accommodation with the Horse Lords of the Plains. The success of this arrangement hinged on several factors, including the fact that Vélez had bested the Indians in war and on their home turf. In so doing, he had proven his courage as a warrior and gained their respect. Vélez had also shown compassion to those not killed in battle and promised the Comanches access to New Mexico's markets if they kept the peace. Perhaps most important, he convinced his own people to respect the Comanches even if they might not like them.

In 1762 Vélez returned to New Mexico to assume a second term as governor. His arrival could not have come at a more opportune time. Since his departure in 1759, Vélez's successors had abandoned the strategy of peace by purchase and reassumed an aggressive posture that left the Comanches no option but to reciprocate in bloody kind. Through his unyielding efforts, the charismatic Vélez managed to restore peace in New Mexico, but only for a brief moment. He left the colony for the last time in 1766 and his replacement, Pedro Fermín de Mendinueta, made it abundantly clear that his administration would be one of war, and not of reconciliation.[5]

Governor Pedro Fermín de Mendinueta

Mendinueta did not share Vélez's diplomatic skills, nor his cautious respect for the Comanches. Instead, the headstrong governor took their attacks on New Mexico personally and never fully realized that among the Horse Lords, violence and war were strictly business. Within months of assuming his command, Governor Mendinueta developed an unwavering mistrust of the Comanches. He believed they were deceitful people whose treachery was matched only by their ruthlessness in war—characteristics, he felt, the Indians had displayed clearly in the summer of 1767. In June of that year, six chiefs arrived at Taos bearing a white flag and apparently seeking to engage in trade with local Hispanos and Pueblos. The gesture of peace was a ruse to lure citizens from the settlement of Ojo Caliente to Taos, thus leaving Ojo Caliente poorly defended and an easy target for raiding. One hundred warriors marched on Ojo Caliente, but to their displeasure they soon learned that the governor had stationed extra troops in the vicinity of the pueblo to protect it from such an attack. Deprived of their prize, the Comanches retreated, promising to return again and again.[6]

The attempted raid on Ojo Caliente initiated a decade-long series of attacks and ripostes that characterized Spanish-Comanche relations during Mendinueta's tenure. In July 1768, Pueblo and Spanish settlements in the region of Taos fell victim to Comanche assaults. In response, Mendinueta led a major offensive against the Colorado division of the Comanche nation. At the head of a company of 496 men, he scoured northern New Mexico from July to August in hope of falling upon a large Indian camp. The Spaniards sighted two warriors during the campaign; both, however, escaped capture and raised the alarm among their people.

The Comanches interpreted Mendinueta's aggression as a threat that had to be answered in kind. So on 26 September, twenty-four warriors from Colorado assaulted Ojo Caliente. The raiders killed one unarmed man but lost twenty-one of their own during the Spanish counterattack that followed. A lone warrior backtracked to Colorado to share news of the failed attack with his people, but two Comanches were captured and taken to Taos for questioning. One of the prisoners had been gravely wounded and lay near death. In his final moments, he requested the sacrament of baptism and encouraged his comrade to do the same. The warrior thanked the priest who had comforted him in his final hour; then the light left his eyes and he slipped into the dark. Those who stood witness over the still-warm corpse felt uplifted by the dying man's gestures, but they turned to the remaining prisoner with scathing eyes and pried him for answers. Having questioned their captive, the Hispanos concluded that the Comanches would soon be back to vent their rage; they retired to their homes and readied themselves for a war they knew they could not avoid.[7]

As expected, the Comanches returned to New Mexico in full battle regalia. They struck at the settlement of Picurís on 10 October 1768 and killed one Indian. At the end of that month, a war party of five hundred warriors surrounded Ojo Caliente. The Comanches tried to penetrate the settlement's central plaza but found it heavily fortified with barricades and armed citizens. They retreated to a nearby hill, from which they set their musket sights on the pueblo and opened fire. The Spaniards answered with volleys of their own, but soon the confrontation reached a stalemate. To gain the upper hand, or simply out of sheer frustration, a group of Indians rushed the pueblo head-on, hoping to break through the barriers. Leading the charge was a man wearing a green-horned headdress that the Spaniards believed denoted an elevated rank among the Comanches. The Hispanos emptied their firearms on the advancing raiders and managed to unhorse three warriors, including the apparent chief.

The sight of their fallen leader enraged the Comanches, who responded by hurling undignified gestures of anger and hate at the enemy. Warriors raced to help recover their comrades, but some of them paid for such bravery with their lives. A lucky few managed to retrieve the bodies of those who had been cut down by Spanish muskets; more importantly, they recovered the green-horned headdress. Three hundred Comanches then retreated to their home base, leaving behind them a wake of burnt-out homes and agricultural fields, slaughtered livestock, and the victims of their assault.[8]

Back in Colorado, the Indians honored the deaths of their warriors, perhaps none more than that of the man who had led the final charge on Ojo Caliente. The tale of the chief with the green-horned headdress spread swiftly and soon became legend. The Spaniards came to know this Comanche leader as *Cuerno Verde* (green horn).

Cuerno Verde

Governor Mendinueta learned from one of the warriors captured during the 26 September raid on Ojo Caliente that Cuerno Verde acquired power among his people on a promise: he had convinced the Comanches that he would help them obtain vengeance for all Spanish atrocities committed against them in the past. Cuerno Verde's charisma was magnetic, but it was his willingness to lead his men into the fray of battle that most inflamed the warrior spirit of his people. The Comanches saw in him the most valued ideal of courage, and they believed that their reputation as a people would somehow be a reflection of his character. The chief's intrepid exploits— especially at Ojo Caliente—earned him the status of "heroic figure" among his people, but also brought into question how the Comanches should respond to his death. Their moral code called for the killing of one enemy for every slain warrior. Cuerno Verde's elevated rank among the people, as well as the valiant nature of his demise, required however that the Comanches seek a more extreme justice. Their vengeance could only be satisfied with an all-out declaration of war against the Spaniards. To this end, the Comanches turned to Cuerno Verde's son and heir, Tabico Narityante.[9]

The responsibility of avenging his father's death magnified the leading role that Narityante—whom the Spaniards also came to know as Cuerno Verde—played in the unbridled warfare that his people unleashed on the Spaniards throughout the 1770s. The need for vengeance, however, can only partially explain why the Comanches increased the frequency of their assaults within New Mexico during this period. Scholars agree that severe drought also influenced Cuerno Verde II's declaration of war on the Hispanos. The environmental crisis began in the early 1770s and reached its most arid peak by mid-decade.[10] Among farming communities such as those of the Pueblos, Spaniards, Navajos, and some Apache bands, nonirrigated lands went thirsty and failed to produce enough food to adequately sustain inhabitants. Pasture grasses and wild plants that animals ate also dried up and caused a reduction in the game the Indians relied on for trade. As a result, Indians such as the Gila Apaches and the once peaceful Navajos began to raid both Pueblo and Spanish settlements for livestock, with the Gilas focusing on the region of Albuquerque and Laguna, while the Navajos attacked sites along the Río Puerco.[11]

The crisis impacted the Comanches in similar fashion. Lack of rainfall strained the supply of buffalo and forced the Horse Lords to seek more resources among their enemies. In the initial years of the drought, the Indians targeted livestock that they, in turn, used to barter for other goods. Time and again, Mendinueta reported that the Comanches seemed more interested in stealing horses from Pueblo and Spanish settlers than in killing the New Mexicans. But as the severity of the drought increased, the Comanches—among others—began taking hostages they then ransomed for needed supplies.[12] As early as 1773, they expanded the extent of their raids into the heart of New Mexico, at Albuquerque and Cochití. Mendinueta responded by launching massive punitive expeditions against the Comanches, Navajos, and all other tribes who dared to raise arms against Spain. What the governor refused to acknowledge was that his policy of unforgiving warfare had pushed the Native Americans to the edge of their cultural limits. By the mid-1770s, New Mexicans found themselves surrounded on all sides by combative Indians. It was within this atmosphere of broken alliances and failed accommodation that Cuerno Verde II unleashed all his rage and fury on the weary Hispanos.

Cuerno Verde II focused his reign of terror on eastern settlements such as Pecos and Galisteo as well as sites in the northern territory near Taos. The intensity of his attacks became legendary and led Mendinueta to request extraordinary powers he felt he needed to defend the colony. The governor tried to force New Mexicans to congregate into compact settlements that were easier to defend than the scattered towns colonials had established in peripheral regions of the province. Ironically, some Hispanos had already abandoned these sites and sought refuge in larger communities such as Taos. Most New Mexicans, however, refused to leave their homes and demanded that Mendinueta seek other means to defend them. The governor did just that. He convinced the natives of Taos to let refugees build homes within their fortified pueblo, insisting that these structures include doorways and windows that faced inward toward the central plaza. Within Taos, the Spaniards also constructed corrals to protect their livestock from raiders. Mendinueta negotiated similar arrangements with other Indian pueblos. At Picurís, the Spaniards built a fortress-like mission to replace one that had been destroyed by the Comanches. Moreover, this new mission was situated closer to other buildings, making it easier to defend during an attack. Mendinueta also called for the construction of a new presidio at Taos, but his request was denied because Spanish officials had demanded a reduction in military expenditures for the whole of New Spain.[13] By 1777, King Carlos III agreed to help resupply New Mexico's horse herd but offered little else. Mendinueta realized that without further royal support he could not expand New Mexico's defenses and would have to continue to employ the offensive war that had already cost hundreds of lives, and which was beginning to lose him the respect of his own people. That same year, the war-weary governor asked to be relieved of his command; he left Santa Fe for the last time in 1778, knowing that audacious chiefs like Cuerno Verde had bested him on the frontier and that the future of New Mexico seemed far from secure. Within the colony, Hispanos now looked to Mendinueta's successor for leadership and the hope that their beleaguered homeland would be spared from the continued ravages of their Native American neighbors.

Juan Bautista de Anza and Cuerno Verde

The inevitable confrontation between Governor Anza and Cuerno Verde brings to light similarities in their personal backgrounds that helped to mold the nature of their characters, as well as qualities they brought to the field of battle. Both men were born into frontier families that had earned social status and prestige by serving their states, and who were expected to answer the call of duty if and when their nations needed them. In this regard, Anza and Cuerno Verde exceeded the expectations of their peers, and perhaps of themselves. As military leaders, they routinely led troops into the fray with little regard for their own personal safety, thus earning them the respect of the men under their command. Likewise, the frontiersmen had contributed to the preservation and expansion of their respective empires, Anza through his California expeditions, and Cuerno Verde by using war to establish a bargaining advantage over his Spanish and Pueblo neighbors. Perhaps most strikingly similar in the lives of Anza and Cuerno Verde were the relationships they experienced with their fathers. Anza the Elder and Cuerno Verde I had distinguished themselves as leaders and military strategists, and they, too, gained high praise from their people. But it was the nature of their deaths that draws the most interesting parallel between them. Apache warriors ended Anza the Elder's life when they ambushed him near the settlement of Soamca, Sonora. Cuerno Verde I fell as a result of a Spanish musket ball at Ojo Caliente. To what degree a sense of hate and vengeance drove Anza and Cuerno Verde II is uncertain, but what seems clear enough is that they felt compelled to preserve the honor of fathers who met their ends at the hands of the enemy and who, as a result, had been mythologized as heroes in the eyes of their communities. The legacy of esteemed service these men bequeathed to their sons may have felt like a daunting burden at times, and yet Anza and Cuerno Verde II embraced the mantle of leadership they inherited from their fathers. When they finally clashed at Colorado in the summer of 1779, Juan and Cuerno Verde II may have wondered if fate had somehow crossed their paths; there they stood face-to-face, as fatherless warriors and as symbols of rival empires determined to exist on the frontier even if this meant that they must first destroy each other. In that climactic battle, Anza destroyed Cuerno Verde.

Governor Anza's Comanche Campaign

Cuerno Verde's defeat at the hands of New Mexican forces in 1779 signified not only a portent of peace, but also the full maturation of Juan Bautista de Anza as a frontier soldier and diplomat. Anza's campaign against the legendary chief brought to bear all the military education Anza had received from Spaniards and Indians during his formative years in Sonora. Against the Comanches, Anza implemented European tactics that had been tested successfully in the far north for years—including the use of indigenous allies and light cavalry. But it was his willingness to act in the manner of an Indian warrior chief that ultimately gave him the upper hand against these rival Americans. Against the Comanches, the seasoned veteran made ample use of Indian strategies of guerrilla warfare, including maneuvers such as traveling by night, using the landscape as cover, swift raids on settlements, confiscation and redistribution of booty among troops, and the taking of captives as hostages or for enslavement. By far the most significant quality Anza demonstrated in the campaign against Cuerno Verde was his unyielding display of courage on the field of battle. Anza knew that the Comanches considered bravery to be one of the most esteemed attributes of character, one that would-be warrior chiefs used to consolidate social and political power among their people. He also discerned that the

Comanches would consider any suggestion of fear on his part, including an early retreat from the battlefield, as a sign of weakness. Anza realized, then, that the defeat of Cuerno Verde would have to be complete and dramatic if he hoped to lure the Comanche nation as a whole to the peace table.

On 15 August 1779, at three o'clock in the afternoon, Anza and six hundred presidial troops, militiamen, and Indian auxiliaries departed from Santa Fe en route to locate and kill Cuerno Verde.[14] Anza avoided traditional routes used by his predecessors when on campaign against the Comanches, paths that led east to Pecos and then north into present-day Colorado, or north-northeast from Santa Fe to Taos. Instead, he ordered his forces to travel north along a route that skirted the west bank of the Río Grande up to the abandoned site of Ojo Caliente, which was reached on the 17th. From here, Anza's forces shifted their line to the northwest and cut a path through the San Juan Mountains, using the upland terrain and its foliage as cover from prying Comanche eyes. On 20 August, the expedition reached the Conejos River in today's southern Colorado, and here they were joined by a contingent of two hundred Ute and Apache Indians seeking to make war on Cuerno Verde.

With the added men, the total number of troops under Anza's command now numbered eight hundred. These forces averaged daily marches of six to twelve leagues. Within days the New Mexicans found themselves fully within Comanche territory, and Anza ordered evening marches to prevent the enemy from sighting the dust cloud his troops' horses raised while on the trail. On the 30th, the war party struggled across the Sierra Almagre—located on the front range of the Colorado Rockies—then altered its course toward the east, making camp at the Santa Rosa River. The following day, Spanish scouts reported that a large Comanche band was on the move a few leagues east of the river. Anza ordered his men to mount and make ready for battle.

On 31 August, at noon, the New Mexican army came upon the Comanche encampment, which consisted of wooden pole frames for some 120 tepees. The Indians, it seems, had begun to set up camp when they caught sight of Anza's forces. The startled people dropped what items they held and fled toward the eastern horizon. Mounted troops gave chase and killed eighteen Comanche warriors, wounded another sixty, and captured more than five hundred horses. They took as prisoners over thirty women and children and confiscated their material possessions. Anza distributed these goods equally among all the men under his charge. That evening, he questioned

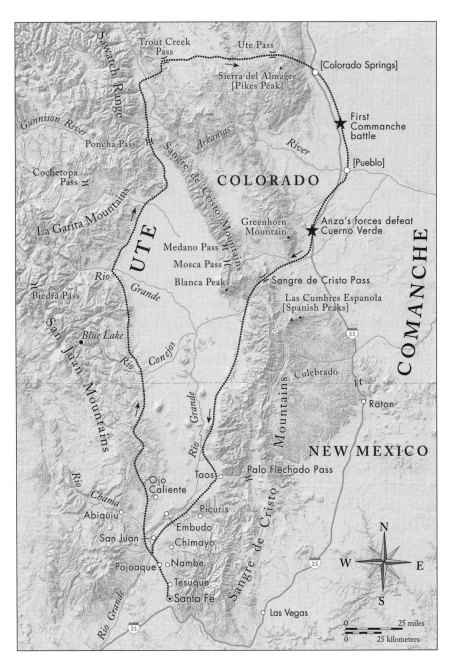

Anza's 1779 Comanche Campaign Route.
Map by Ben Pease, cartographer.

captives and discovered that Cuerno Verde had led a war party into New Mexico some sixteen days earlier. The informants claimed their chief had ordered them to rendezvous at the present site, where the people would celebrate his victory against the hated españoles.

Anza wasted no time. For two days, the company pressed on in a south-southeasterly direction, crossing the Sacramento River in the process. On 2 September, the Spaniards picked up the Comanche trail when they discovered some of the Indians' stray horses. Morale among the Hispanos soared, but only briefly. Soon after they had helped capture the animals, the Utes abandoned the campaign and rode off with their share of the booty. Anza's fortune shifted for the better when, early in the afternoon of this same day, at a site near present-day Greenhorn Mountain, his scouts informed him that Cuerno Verde was coming.

The governor ordered his men to lie in ambush among the foliage of a narrow valley that he knew the Comanches would have to cross. At sunset, the chief and his warriors reached the trap. Anza sounded the attack and, at the head of the central column, led a frontal assault on the enemy. The Indians stood their ground. Then, noticing two companies skirting the sides of the valley in a flanking maneuver, the Comanches whirled their mounts and scattered. Anza's forces managed several kills, but their advance was soon blocked by a marshy gully. As the Spaniards struggled to cross the ravine, Cuerno Verde and his warriors escaped into the night. At eight-thirty in the evening, Anza's companies regrouped near this site and he consulted with his officers. The most experienced men advised the governor to remove his men from the valley because the Comanches were known for attacking at night. Anza would have none of this, and his response proved the most important decision he made in the entire campaign. Anza recorded in his Comanche Campaign diary:

> Judging this as difficult according to the knowledge that I have of other Indians, as well as this proposal might have something of cowardice in it, I replied that the very thing they feared I desired; that they should understand that even in case the encounter had not been decided so much in our favor, we ought for the honor of our arms to wait on the spot until dawn of the following day, and that, until then, it was proper that we should remain under arms. This was done.[15]

Anza's refusal to be perceived as a coward worked to his advantage the following day, when Cuerno Verde and his men did return to press the attack on the waiting Spaniards. The day was 3 September 1779. During the battle, Anza's troops attempted to surround Cuerno Verde and his contingent of fifty warriors. As he had done during their previous encounter, the vigilant chief recognized the flanking maneuver and ordered his men to retreat. Nevertheless, the New Mexicans cut Cuerno Verde and his personal guard off from their main force and trapped them in the very gully that had saved their lives the previous day. Surrounded and outnumbered, Cuerno Verde, his first-born son and heir, four captains, one medicine man, and ten warriors dismounted and used their horses as shields against the onslaught of Spanish muskets. The Comanches returned fire and fought valiantly, but soon their struggle was over, and all of them lay dead in the marshy ravine.

The Hispanos gathered around their victorious chief and together roared a cheer for king and commandant. To impose a sense of closure over the grisly affair, and the campaign in general, Anza proclaimed that the battle site would be named Los Dolores de Santa María Santísima. More important, he had Cuerno Verde's corpse stripped of the green-horned headdress. In so doing, the governor symbolically scalped Cuerno Verde—a ritual common to many warrior groups, representing both the taking of a token from one's slain enemy and the avenging of wrongs committed by this person towards one's own people. By removing Cuerno Verde's crown, and sending it to Commandant General Croix as a trophy of war, Anza intended to erase any vestige of the mythic figure of Cuerno Verde.[16] He hoped that in days to come settlers of the far north would remember the Indian chief as an arrogant and presumptuous man who had led his people into a costly war of hatred and revenge against the nuevomexicanos. The governor most likely also wanted the Hispanos to remember him as the man who had brought peace to their lives by destroying Cuerno Verde. Anza could not have foreseen, however, that the New Mexicans would soon forget.

By 10 September 1779, Anza found himself back at Santa Fe and wasted no time in forwarding his diary to Croix. In the wake of the northwestern campaign, some Comanche chiefs extended offers of peace to the Spaniards. Anza, however, refused to enter into separate agreements with each Indian leader. Instead, he demanded that the Comanche nation as a whole select a representative who would present him with a united indigenous voice. Until then, he warned, peace with the Horse Lords of the Plains could not be guaranteed.

To force the issue of a Comanche alliance, the governor suggested another offensive into present-day Colorado.[17] Croix decided against a second Comanche campaign because Spain had recently declared war on England to drive the British from Louisiana and regain territories lost to England in previous decades, including Gibraltar and Minorca in 1713 and Spanish Florida in 1763. Croix reasoned that hostilities with England might require him to make troops and resources under his command available for the defense of New Spain's northeastern front. As a result, Comanche raids into New Mexico continued even though they had been dramatically reduced in number and severity. For the entire year of 1781, Anza did not mention a single Comanche assault on the colony in his presidial reviews. Of course, it is probable that the Horse Lords refused to enter New Mexico this year due to a smallpox epidemic that struck the colony from February to July.

Anza and the Hopis

If the Spanish-British War of 1779–83 forced Commandant General Croix to shift his attention away from northern New Mexico, it did not prevent him from ordering Anza to see to the next phase of the defense plan outlined by the Chihuahua War Council. The governor thus began to plan how he could best establish an agreement of peace by purchase with the Hopis.

The war council considered an alliance with the Hopis vital for the consolidation of New Mexico's western frontier. It figured they would willingly lend military support against the Gila Apaches if Spain made good on the promise of social and economic aid. Anza understood that the subjugation of the Gilas was needed to establish ties between New Mexico, Sonora, and Alta California. He recognized, however, that securing help from the Hopis for the Gila campaign would be a difficult task because these Native Americans had maintained their virtual independence for generations.

The Spaniards made first contact with the Hopis during the Coronado Expedition in the sixteenth century. They constructed three missions among Hopi pueblos in the seventeenth century, only to see them torn down and their resident missionaries slain during the Pueblo Revolt. The Hopi insurgency of 1680 stood as a rejection of Christianity and an affirmation of the Hopis' autonomy, but it led Spain to declare them apostate Indians. Spanish officials never abandoned hope of subduing this proud nation, and in the 1690s the Hopis begrudgingly acquiesced. They pledged their allegiance to Governor Diego de Vargas, and in return, Vargas agreed not to station priests or troops at Hopi pueblos.

The Franciscans dreamed of bringing the Hopis back to the church, and in 1699 this daunting task seemed close at hand. That year, the Hopi chief Espeleta informed Governor Pedro Rodríguez Cubero that his people would maintain the peace if Spain accepted their right to practice their own religion. The governor refused. In 1700, Espeleta traveled to Santa Fe with another proposal: the Hopis would return to the Christian fold if Rodríguez Cubero limited the Franciscans' visits to Hopi lands to one pueblo, once per year, for six years. The governor again refused, demanding instead that the Hopis submit completely to Spanish rule. In response, most Hopis called for a complete break with Spain. Some threatened to use violence against any of their own people who continued to interact with the enemy. Late in 1700, the Hopis of Awatovi fell as victims of this proposed retaliation.

The inhabitants of Awatovi must have believed their fellow Hopis would not follow through with the warnings because they welcomed fray Juan de Garaycoechea into their homes. Garaycoechea and a fellow friar had come from Zuni Pueblo with high hopes of hearing confessions and baptizing the uninitiated. To their surprise, the padres learned that the Hopis had also entertained the idea of rebuilding the Awatovi mission. The elated friars returned to Zuni and forwarded news of their efforts to Governor Rodríguez Cubero. Meanwhile, word of Awatovi's apparent betrayal spread to other Hopi Pueblos, where dismayed chiefs began to assemble an army of revenge.

The attack began at dawn while the men of Awatovi prepared their subterranean ceremonial structures, or kivas, for a planned ritual. The aggressors fell upon these Hopis first, removing ladders from the kivas and thus eliminating the Awatovis' ability to counterattack. New Mexico historian Marc Simmons has written that the trapped Awatovi males then experienced the unthinkable when their enraged brethren tossed "flaming bundles of sticks" upon them and left the Indians to burn. No one survived the inferno. The belligerent Hopis then vented their wrath on the remaining Awatovi residents, massacring almost the entire population near the ruined Spanish church. Those women and children who survived were taken prisoner, but most of them also soon perished. Unable to decide how best to divide these spoils of war, the Hopis tortured, dismembered, and slaughtered almost all their victims at a site known as Skeleton Mound. The few that remained were distributed among the Hopi pueblos.[18]

The Awatovi massacre may have hindered Spain's effort to subdue the Hopis but did not suppress it completely. For decades the Hopis held steadfast against their Spanish neighbors and made war against other tribes that adopted any vestiges of Christianity. But then, in 1775, some of the Hopis invited the resident friar at Zuni, Silvestre Vélez de Escalante, to their pueblos. A sickly but sincere and well-liked native of Santander, Escalante arrived at Zuni in 1774.[19] From here he visited various Hopi villages with the understanding that he would be allowed to preach freely among the Indians. Much to his dismay, Escalante soon discovered that Hopi chiefs had ordered their people to avoid him at all cost. From this experience, Escalante concluded that the "obstinate Hopi" could only be brought back to the Christian fold by force of arms, and that they desired relations with the Spaniards only during times of crisis or when contact promised to bring them economic gain. Eleanor B. Adams explained Escalante's views regarding the Hopis when she wrote:

> When drought, famine, or active hostilities by their enemies pressed them hard, they would make overtures to the Spanish authorities and religious, leading them to believe that they were on the point of returning to the fold. Then they would prolong the negotiations until the crisis was past, whereupon they returned to their usual intransigent attitude. Their real desire seems to have been to remain on mildly friendly terms with the Spaniards and enjoy the advantages of their trade and protection, but only so long as this could be managed without political or religious ties.[20]

Escalante's journals proved to be a wealth of information for Anza when, in November 1779, he began to plan what he considered the best strategy to establish ties with the Hopis. Anza reported to Croix that the natives were living in dreadful conditions and were in dire need of assistance. For three years, they had suffered a severe drought that diminished their ability to grow enough food for daily needs. Many had abandoned their "adored" pueblos and were forced to make a living by scratching the earth of the surrounding deserts and mountains for any source of sustenance. Some Hopis had sought shelter among the Indians of neighboring tribes, while others were reduced to selling their children into slavery in order to procure food.

Anza ordered the friar serving at Zuni, Andrés García, to communicate to the Hopis his promise of help if the Indians were ready to accept the "true religion" and the dominion of Spain. He offered to relocate them to settlements along the Río Grande and provide them any provisions needed to sustain their lives. Anza advised the Hopis that they would be welcomed at Sandía and that he would make Sabinal pueblo available to them if enough Indians wished to be relocated. Finally, he promised them freedom from any obligations to the missionaries or other Hispanos, including service in the form of labor or the forced rendering of a portion of their harvests.[21]

Anza preferred the relocation of the Hopis to settlements on the Río Grande over the placement of missionaries at their pueblos. He believed the state would find it difficult to provide the capital needed to subsidize friars serving in such remote regions of the colony. This argument appeared legitimate on the surface but probably masked Anza's true feelings regarding the clerics. Since his days in Sonora, Anza had made clear his belief that the missions of the far north had failed to assimilate Indians into Spanish society. Integration, he argued, could be achieved only if Native Americans were given greater access to the social and economic milieu of their European neighbors. The relocation of the Hopis to the heart of New Mexico provided such an environment for interaction, and many of the apostate Indians had already communicated to Anza the desire for such relocations.

Drawing on the lessons he had learned from Escalante—that the Hopis sought contact with the Spaniards only when faced with crisis—Anza argued that the time was right to attempt the assimilation and reconversion of the apostates. He envisioned the relocation of the Hopis to settlements in the heart of the colony that had been abandoned during the Mendinueta era. Anza believed that such integration would give the Indians access to rich farmland along the Río Grande, and that the Hopis would reciprocate by helping to defend New Mexico. He feared that the failure to assimilate the Hopis as soon as possible would lead them to seek shelter and alliance with indigenous groups hostile to Spain, including the Gila Apaches. Should this coalition come to pass, he warned, the Hopis would once again become a formidable adversary. Beyond the need to assimilate the Hopis, Anza also encouraged the establishment of a presidio in the colony's western frontier. He believed a bastion in Hopi country would allow Spain to better defend this corner of the empire and possibly enhance interaction between New Mexico and the expanding colony of Alta California.[22]

By November 1779, Anza received information he believed justified the relocation of the Hopis to Spanish settlements. Fray Andrés García reported the possibility that a band of Hopis had sought shelter among the Navajos to escape the effects of drought. The rumor proved false, but news that pasture and water supplies in Hopi country had been severely diminished was all too real.[23] In a separate report, the alcalde mayor (district magistrate) of Zuni, Pedro Cisneros, corroborated García's account regarding the horrific conditions on the frontier. He claimed that the vast majority of Hopis had deserted their homes and were weathering the winter in the surrounding countryside, surviving on a miserable and insubstantial *atole* (gruel) of grass and herbs. The almost skeletal Hopis who chose to remain at their pueblos refused any aid from the *españoles*, preferring to die as *gentiles* (pagan Indians) before they accepted handouts or advice from any Christian priest.

Not all the starving Hopis wished to die in their homeland, and the entire populace of Walpi accepted Anza's proposal for their relocation. These Indians seemed eager to accept help and shared their sentiment with the governor:

> Where should we go if it does not rain, to the Spaniards? At least they will liberate us from death, as many have died and many more of us will too from hunger. They will make us Christian as you since we have resisted this. Express it [the Hopis' sentiment regarding their relocation] like that to the governor, that we will relocate with the confidence that he will fulfill his promises, and he will agree to be our father as he said he would.[24]

In his effort to render immediate aid to the suffering Indians, Anza requested the state transfer enough *víveres* (provisions) to Zuni so that remaining Hopis might be induced to seek help from the Pueblos. Moreover, he vowed to continue extending protection to the desperate Indians.

Croix insisted that under no circumstance was Anza to relocate the Hopis by force of arms, reminding him of King Carlos III's demand that the pacification of indigenous Americans be conducted with kindness and benevolence, rather than the spilling of human blood. He ordered Anza to visit the Hopis under pretext of reconnoitering a land route between New Mexico and Sonora, a task the Spaniards were in the process of planning anyway. Croix also ordered Anza to offer aid to the Hopis, but in a manner that would not insult their pride or make them feel that assistance was dependent on their subjugation to Spain. If anything, Croix told Anza, the

The Hopi Pueblo of Walpi, by Ben Wittick. Courtesy of Palace of the Governors
Photo Archives (NMHM/DCA) 016350.

relief plan should convince the Hopis of the benefits they stood to reap by
embracing the true faith and vassalage to Spain. Whether they opted for
their relocation or chose to stay at their pueblos, the Hopis' desire to enter
into alliance with Spain had to be voluntary. Should they refuse, the Spanish crown would look upon this with suspicion and possibly regard the
Hopis as enemies of Spain.[25]

In February 1780, Anza ordered fray Andrés García to the western pueblos to recruit Hopis who had willingly accepted relocation. In March, García returned to Santa Fe with a group of seventy-seven Indians and reported
that more Hopis would have accompanied him to the capital if not for the
Navajos, who had "murdered" or imprisoned others seeking aid from the
governor. The Navajos notwithstanding, Anza deemed García's mission a
good omen for his upcoming journey to the west.[26]

Having received news that forty families wished to be relocated to Spanish settlements along the Río Grande, Anza set out for Hopi country at the head of a 126-man contingent on 10 September 1780. Hopi *caciques* (chiefs) welcomed Anza's forces at the settlement of Awatovi on the 22nd but asked that they not force any of their people to abandon their homes. When Anza inquired about the forty families he had come to gather and escort back to New Mexico, the chiefs lamented that a band of Navajos had murdered the men of this party and had taken their wives and children as prisoners. The Navajos, it seems, had lured the families to their settlement with the promise that the starving Hopis would receive shelter and food.

Outraged, Anza demanded an audience with the principal Hopi chief who lived at Oraibi, which was reached on 23 September. The chief embraced Anza, and the two leaders settled in to discuss what the governor could do to end the Hopis' plight. Anza shared his king's desire to see the Hopis returned to the one true God and dominion of Spain, but he emphasized that this choice had to be voluntary. The chief weighed Anza's words carefully and ultimately informed him that the Hopis had always recognized the king of Spain as their lord. The chief said he would not prevent any of his people from returning to the Christian flock, but as for himself, he insisted that he and his followers would remain at Oraibi to die a warrior's death against their sworn enemies. Anza promised the Hopi elder that he would do what he could against the belligerent Utes and Navajos who had recently declared war on the emaciated Hopis. He also offered to improve trade relations between Spaniards and Hopis. Having welcomed the promise of prosperity, the Hopi chief shared a few more words with Anza and then the two battle-wise leaders went their separate ways. The following day, a considerable number of Hopis from Oraibi traveled to the Spanish camp. Here, the Hopis sealed their new alliance with the Spaniards with handshakes, conversation, and of course trade. The celebration lasted all day.[27]

In the end, thirty Indians followed Anza back to New Mexico, bringing the total number of Hopis living among Spaniards and Pueblos to over two hundred. On the surface, this figure appears significant, but it pales in comparison to the number of natives lost between the time Escalante visited the Hopi pueblos and Anza's campaign to bring them relief. In 1775, Escalante had estimated that the Hopi nation held strong at a population of 7,494. By 1780, Anza calculated that a mere 798 Hopi souls remained. In this five-year period, thousands of Hopis had seemingly surrendered their lives to famine or war, or they had fled their homes.[28] In coming years, Croix continued to encourage Anza to seek the complete relocation of the Hopis through non-violent means.[29]

Anza and the Navajos

Having entered into an agreement of mutual accommodation with the Hopis, Anza turned his attention to reestablishing the alliance that Governor Mendinueta had brokered between Spain and the Navajos, but which had since been broken.[30] Anza's efforts in this regard constituted the last phase of the military plan outlined by Croix and his subordinates at the 1778 Chihuahua War Council. This component of the defense initiative called for an all-out offensive against the Gila Apaches, who had been consistently raiding Spanish settlements in the region of northern Sonora for many years. The war council reasoned that the subjugation of the Gilas would not only bring a semblance of peace to this corner of the Spanish empire, but also secure safe passage along the route that Anza had opened between Sonora and Alta California. This trail played a key role in New Spain's efforts to consolidate its northwestern frontier, the expansion of Spain's empire into northern Arizona, and the establishment of ties between New Mexico, Sonora, and California. Moreover, the road promised to help Spain establish a colony at Yuma, where produce and other wares would be made available to supply Alta California colonists. For Spain, the colonization of Alta California had to succeed if Russia's advances into the Northwest Territory were to be contained. All of these lofty ideals, of course, rested on Spain's ability to lure the combative Gila Apaches into a peaceful coexistence. For this to happen, Anza had to find a way to secure military aid from the Navajos who, in turn, would help pressure the Gilas to the peace table.

The crown feared that if Anza failed in his mission with the Navajos, these Indians might ally themselves with the Gila Apaches, thus strengthening the Gilas' ability to resist Spanish arms. King Carlos III, however, did not make Anza's task easy. On the one hand, he expected Anza to persuade the Navajos to fulfill their promise of helping defend the far northern territory. But on the other, the king insisted that Anza establish ties with indigenous peoples through gentle persuasion rather than military might. On 25 March 1781, Commandant General Croix reiterated Carlos III's demands when he asked one Nicolás de la Mathe to visit with the "friendly nations" of the north for the purpose of reaffirming, through peaceful means, their alliances with Spain.[31] Anza understood that such a strategy would prove difficult with the Navajos because these Native Americans, since the defeat of Cuerno Verde, had started attacking the Hopis and raiding into the heart of New Mexico.[32]

Initially, Anza failed to cement a new alliance with the Navajos. Undaunted by this setback, the Spaniards initiated a general offensive against the Gila Apaches in 1784. In March, military detachments sortied into sierras and rancherías north of Sonora, but these forays resulted in few successful maneuvers. A larger campaign that ran from April to May 1784 included five separate divisions of Spanish and Indian troops from Sonora and Nueva Vizcaya, a province comprising much of what today are the Mexican states of Chihuahua and Durango. These combined forces attacked at the heart of the Apachería (Apache territory), focusing their efforts against the Gila and Chiricahua Apaches. Although officials counted numerous victories, the Spanish offensive stalled when a newly appointed commandant general, Felipe de Neve, died in July and command of the Provincias Internas was returned to the viceroy in Mexico City.

Reacting to the onslaught of Spanish arms that had brought death and destruction to their homeland, the Gilas sought refuge and alliance with the Navajos of the north. Together, these Native Americans stormed the Sonora-Nueva Vizcaya frontier, focusing their attacks on the settlements of Tucson and Janos. By the end of 1784, Spanish officials concluded that war with the Apaches would cease only if Governor Anza managed to break the Gila-Navajo alliance. To this end, Anza contacted various Navajo chiefs and informed them that Spain would cease trade relations with them so long as they remained friendly with the Gilas. In addition, he demanded that the Navajos honor the peace agreement they had entered into with Governor Mendinueta; failure to do so would force Spain to refuse them the military aid they desired for defense against their enemies. Finally, Anza hinted that an armed offensive would be initiated against the Navajos if they did not break their ties with the Apaches. To impress this threat upon the Navajos, Interim Commandant General José Antonio Rengel ordered Anza to establish an armed command in the settlement of Laguna.

By the end of 1785, several Navajo bands did break with the Gilas and made good on their promise to help Spain against the Apaches. Still, other Navajos continued to aid the Apaches. In response to renewed Gila attacks into Nueva Vizcaya, the Spaniards settled on a two-point plan: another major offensive to take place in 1786, and a new effort to unite the Navajos under a single leader. In March 1786, at a site called Bado de la Piedra, one month after Anza had successfully concluded the Comanche peace treaty at Pecos, the governor met with five Navajo chiefs and convinced them to choose two individuals who would speak on behalf of their peoples. At this meeting, Anza negotiated a new peace alliance with several of the Navajo groups. In return for military aid and the promise of trade, the Indians swore fealty to Spain and agreed to make available monthly auxiliaries for the ongoing Gila offensive. Moreover, the Navajos agreed to cultivate their lands, where they would live as peaceful and sedentary allies of Spain.[33]

On 5 October 1786, Commandant General Jacobo Ugarte y Loyola congratulated Anza for his successful effort to bring the Navajos into an alliance with Spain. To secure the newly established peace, Ugarte y Loyola suggested that Anza offer formal titles of "general" and "lieutenant" to the two chiefs who would lead the united Navajo nation, and provide them wages in the form of goods. In addition, Ugarte y Loyola promoted new trade relations between the Navajos and Pueblos and encouraged intermarriages between them as a means of incorporating the Navajos into the heart of New Mexico. Finally, Ugarte y Loyola ordered Anza to initiate an immediate offensive against the Gilas, utilizing the Navajos as allies and forcing the Apaches south towards Sonora.[34]

By breaking up the Gila-Navajo alliance, Governor Anza contributed to the pacification of the New Mexico landscape. In coming months and years, the Apaches attacked fewer Spanish settlements within the colony, focusing their raids instead farther south along the Sonora and Nueva Vizcaya frontier. But even here, allied Spanish and Indian forces continued to bring war to the Gila and Mimbreño Apaches. By 1787, the Mimbreño Apaches became the next target of Bourbon militarism. On 10 August, José Antonio Rengel, who had recently been named military chief for New Mexico and Nueva Vizcaya, informed Anza that a rebellious force of 800 Mimbreños had been defeated near the San Buenaventura Valley in Sonora. Rengel reported that 123 of these Indians had been killed.[35] Try as they might, however, the Spaniards never managed a permanent peace with the Apaches. Even the Navajos eventually broke their ties with Spain, ten years after

Anza had convinced them to swear fealty to King Carlos III. In April 1796, they again took up arms against their Spanish neighbors in New Mexico and cemented a new alliance with the Gilas.[36]

The Navajo uprising of 1796 signaled the onset of deteriorating relations between New Mexicans and Native Americans with whom Governor Anza had achieved peace treaties. Between 1803 and 1804, the Navajos repeatedly defeated Spain's efforts to subdue them; but finally, in 1805, they sued for peace and, for what it was worth, agreed to become settled farmers. The Spanish-Comanche alliance, however, proved more resilient and lasted a full generation after Anza defeated Cuerno Verde in battle. For the remainder of the colonial era, it was the Apaches, especially the Gilas, who posed the greatest threat to the peace that Spain desired for the far north. And how could it have been otherwise? The act of war, after all, was as integral a part of the Gila life way as the environment of limited resources that had molded these Americans into a warrior society.

Like his Native American counterparts, Anza, too, had been reared in a culture of violence dictated by a landscape of want. His exploits as a soldier earned him the praise of Spaniards and Indians alike. But like so many frontier warriors of his age, Anza preferred peace to war. If nothing else, then, his contribution to the pacification of contested New Mexico demonstrated that alliances between ethnic groups could be achieved through the ideals of peace by purchase and mutual accommodation. For thirty years after his arrival in New Mexico, Hispanos and Pueblos enjoyed a degree of peace they had not known for decades.

CHAPTER SIX

Defending a Homeland

H ISPANOS HAD GOOD REASON to celebrate. Governor Anza had recently defeated Cuerno Verde in battle and was already entertaining offers of mutual accommodation from other Comanche chiefs. Moreover, he had reached out to the Hopis and Navajos and was poised to cement alliances with both nations. Anza's efforts with the Indians allowed him to secure New Mexico's most contested frontiers and proffer its inhabitants a much-needed respite from war. Peace came with the promise of increased trade and the potential expansion of Spain's imperial domains, but more important it signaled an end of hostilities that had plagued the colony for so many years and had cost hundreds of lives.

Ironically, the atmosphere of calm did not last long; combative arenas were newly drawn within New Mexico. This time around, however, confrontation did not pit New Mexicans against their Native American neighbors; instead, it focused on the relationship between Anza and citizens who had never taken a liking to him. Hispanos had openly scorned Anza from the moment of his arrival in the colony. They accused him of corruption that favored friends and relatives, but mostly they despised the defensive reforms he had initiated at El Paso, and which he now planned to impose on them. New Mexicans opposed Anza's plan to rein them into centralized settlements that were easier to defend against attack, as well as his demands that they take a more active role in the defense of their homeland. The Hispanos had resisted similar proposals made by Governor Mendinueta, and they must have figured that they could muster the same resistance against the Sonoran upstart. They failed to foresee, however, the favorable impression Anza's defeat of Cuerno Verde and his dealings with the Hopis had made on government officials. More than ever, Anza's superiors seemed determined to support his efforts to transform New Mexico into a militarized buffer zone, even if this meant that they would have to marginalize Hispano complaints regarding his seemingly autocratic rule.

The Militarization of New Mexico Towns

In 1772, Governor Mendinueta had made compelling arguments for the forced relocation of Hispanos to centralized towns, proclaiming that the dispersed nature of settlements in New Mexico had made it difficult to effectively defend the colony. On this issue, Mendinueta made a sharp distinction between indigenous pueblos and sites inhabited by Spaniards when he wrote:

> [T]he pueblos of Indians are all grouped together, and for this reason more defensible, while of the Spaniards there is no united settlement, so that to the dispersion of their houses the name of ranches or houses of the field is properly given and not that of Villas and villages. Their being indefensible has caused some of the advantageous frontiers to be abandoned, although I did considerable to maintain them [dispersed Hispano homes]. . . .
>
> No settlement of Spaniards nor Indians can be considered or called the center, but [must be viewed as] frontiers, because they are very remote from one another. This distance, filled in by high sierras and rocky hills, makes easy the entrance of enemies into any of the areas. Incessant care is necessary, which is kept up by reconnoitering the land (an activity which rarely produces the end desired) to see in time if enemies are approaching.[1]

Mendinueta's report to Viceroy Antonio María Bucareli also included his suggestions regarding the realignment of settlements in the colony:

> One of the opportune means which can be taken is to compel settlers of each region who live, as I have said, dispersed, to join and form their pueblos in plazas or streets so that a few men could be able to defend themselves. From this it will follow that they would unite more promptly for their own defense, or give aid to another village. The pueblos placed in this close relationship would be respected by the enemy.[2]

In 1773, Mendinueta again reported that New Mexico would be best served if its settlers were forced to abandon their dispersed communities and relocate to towns enclosed by walls. He added that the Río Arriba was in dire need of troop reinforcements because it was the region most frequently raided by Comanches and Utes. The governor also requested permission to begin construction of a new presidio at Taos, but was informed that the colony would have to make do with the Santa Fe garrison.[3] The aging Mendinueta relinquished his command of New Mexico in 1778, but not before he made one last effort to convince superiors that his ideas for the defense of the province were sound. At the Chihuahua War Council, Mendinueta reiterated the urgency of his proposals and finally found a receptive audience among the assembled body of frontier military officers. At Chihuahua, Commandant General Teodoro de Croix thus ordered incoming Governor Anza to reconnoiter New Mexican settlements and determine whether Mendinueta's proposals were indeed required and feasible.

Other Spaniards had already surveyed various regions of the colony, including the Franciscan missionaries Francisco Atanasio Domínguez and Silvestre Vélez de Escalante. In 1776, the friars traversed the southern Rocky Mountains and the interior basin of western North America in the hope of identifying and establishing a land route between New Mexico and Alta California. In their company came the renowned cartographer Bernardo de Miera y Pacheco, who was employed to chart the missionaries' progress and keep detailed accounts of visited terrains. Domínguez and Escalante failed to fulfill their task, but the mapmaker's work did not go unnoticed.[4] Three years later, Governor Anza beckoned Miera y Pacheco to his quarters and instructed him to produce a map of New Mexico, one that outlined the condition and layout of all Spanish and Pueblo towns.[5]

Miera y Pacheco's 1779 map of New Mexico illustrated the extent of damage inflicted by Native Americans—such as the Comanches—on settlements in the recent past; it emphasized the fact that more communities in the colony lay ruined as a result of such attacks than were occupied by Pueblos or Spaniards. On the legend of the chart, he shared his views regarding the haphazard pattern of settlements that dotted the landscape, and which he believed were vulnerable to raids that had forced so many New Mexicans to abandon their homes. Miera y Pacheco wrote that towns in the colony were extremely ill arranged, with the houses of the settlers of whom they are composed scattered about at a distance from one another. Many evils, disasters, and destruction of towns, caused by the Comanche and Apache enemies who surround said province, killing and abducting many families, have originated from this arrangement in accordance with which they have taken root, each individual building his dwelling on the piece of land granted to him.[6]

The dispersed nature of New Mexico towns—most of which were located on or around the river valleys of the Río Arriba and Río Abajo regions— reflected a pattern of settlement that was determined by the limited availability of water and arable land. These precious resources allowed Hispanos to produce enough food for their own consumption, so they preferred to live close to the fields that gave them their daily bread and fed their beasts of burden. Such land use, however, did not mirror settlement patterns that were common in central Mexico, where the abundant production of food allowed owners the means to live in urban centers and hire stewards to manage their rural estates. With the exception of Santa Fe, New Mexican towns and villages also did not follow the traditional physical layout of cities located farther south, which consisted of a central plaza that was surrounded by a grid system of streets. Since the time of the Iberian Reconquista—the Christian recovery of the Iberian peninsula from the Moors, roughly from the eighth through the fifteenth centuries—Spanish monarchs had preferred this model of urban planning because it allowed settlers to barricade peripheral streets and thus transform the central plaza of a city into a militarized space.[7]

Governor Anza understood the defensive weaknesses inherent in the positioning and layout of communities in New Spain's northern territory. Having studied Miera y Pacheco's map, he may have conjured up memories of the gruesome death of his sister-in-law, Victoria Carrasco, who died at the hands of Apache raiders in 1763. Her death occurred at Buenavista, a Sonora settlement that—like so many New Mexico towns—was located at some distance from a Spanish presidio and, therefore, was difficult to defend. Drawing on the lessons he had learned from this tragic event, as well as from a lifetime of living in presidios, Anza now seemed determined to correct the mistake he felt had cost the life of his relative.

Like his predecessor, Anza knew that forced relocation of citizens to centralized towns would meet with strong resistance and perhaps lead Hispanos to civil disobedience. He opted, instead, to enhance New Mexico's military preparedness by forcing citizens to assume a more active role in the defense of their homeland. In November 1779, he issued a detailed building code that regulated the construction of homes and settlements throughout the colony. Anza's instructions did not call for the abandonment of settlements, but demanded a transformation of existing towns into defensive spaces that were capable of withstanding constant raids by combative Native Americans:

[S]ites [should] be located around a good water supply with a firmness of soil. That all settlements be the same so as to avoid preferential treatment, or resentments, of some sites over others, since the purpose of sites is to provide for the common good and security of civil life. All pueblos should consist of thirty-five to fifty armed families who are to plant seed at the start of the spring to ensure the well-being of all. Homes should have one or two doors with no windows or balconies. Vigas [heavy rafters supporting roofs] should not extend to the exterior of buildings and their ends should be inlaid or concealed. Heads of households will receive all the materials necessary for the construction of ovens and chicken coops, which should be located within sight of homes. Homeowners should build ramparts for their houses, while those for the town should be constructed communally and should be taller than those of homes. Lazy, delinquent, and unemployed citizens shall be provided for by the public who, in turn, will put them to work for the common good. Each pueblo should have one or two corrals for livestock and should be defended against the enemy by building their doors in the direction of town. Ecclesiastical judges should allow colonists to work on religious holidays if needed to ensure completion of a town's construction. Citizens should utilize one third of all materials from abandoned sites for the construction of new ones. All unused buildings should be destroyed to avoid their being used by the enemy. If it is necessary to confiscate land from one who refuses to offer it for the establishment and good of a new town, then he will be persuaded to do so or his case will be forwarded to me [Anza], and his land will be taken nonetheless. All towns of allied Indians should conform to the same building codes. Finally, all new towns should be reinhabited by 1 November 1780.[8]

The Santa Fe Dissidents

The Hispanos did not welcome Anza's building codes, much less the demand that settlements be transformed into militarized spaces. Few colonists, however, openly challenged Governor Anza's decree. Instead, they took their concerns directly to Commandant General Croix, who had recently relocated the capital of the General Command from Chihuahua to Arizpe, Sonora. On 7 May 1780, having fulfilled their morning *oraciones* (prayers), a delegation of twenty-four Santa Fe residents set out for Arizpe, bearing complaints against the headstrong governor. The leaders of this commission included Vicente de Serna, José Miguel de la Peña, Manuel de Armijo, Domingo Romero, Antonio José López, and Cristóbal Vigil. Eager as they were to reach Arizpe, the envoys could not claim to be seasoned travelers. On their journey, they complained about the poor roads they encountered and later claimed to have barely survived death by starvation. The delegates reached the capital over one month after their odyssey began. On 15 June, the haggard emissaries stood before Croix as their spokesperson, Cristóbal Vigil, stated their case against Anza.[9]

The main complaint against Anza involved the Santa Fe neighborhood of Analco. Located south of the Santa Fe River, Analco had been established as a *genízaro* community (a community of Indians—mostly captive plains Indians—who now had settled peacefully in New Mexico) that housed a population of 1,915 by 1779. That year, Anza proposed that Santa Fe's primary administrative and military structures—located at the capital's central plaza and north of the Santa Fe River—would be easier to defend against attack if they were relocated to Analco. To this end, in April 1780, he ordered that buildings in Analco be destroyed or rebuilt to meet the requirements of the new construction codes. The Hispanos complained that such a move would necessitate the destruction of homes for the 274 families that lived at Analco, including the one belonging to Vicente Serna's father, as well as the *capilla* (chapel) of San Miguel.[10]

In addition to expressing their concerns for Analco, the Santa Fe delegates voiced opinions regarding Anza's apparently autocratic administration and the recurring problem of corruption. They warned Croix that state officials were pressing men into militia service against their will and identified Miera y Pacheco as the guiltiest of Anza's subordinates. In addition, they argued that inexperienced troops were ill-treated, terrorized, and could not claim to be the "owners" of their salaries since these were "burned" at the *habilitado's* (paymaster's) presidial store. The emissaries accused paymaster José María Cordero of engaging in questionable commerce throughout the colony and selling goods to servicemen at inflated prices.[11] The Hispanos, however, failed to acknowledge that the corruption for which they scorned Anza had partially fueled their colony's bureaucratic and military machines for generations. Anza did not introduce malfeasance to New Mexico, nor was he the first to try to impose the king's will on its inhabitants. Yet corruption and autocracy were the very charges Cristóbal Vigil and his followers had brought against Anza.

As they filled Croix's ear with the villainous acts of Anza and his cronies, the Santa Fe delegates must have mused over the fact that they had made similar arguments against Anza's predecessor. In the case against Mendinueta, Hispanos convinced Mexico City officials that the governor had overstepped the boundaries of legitimate administration when he demanded that New Mexicans relocate to more defendable settlements, thus forcing them to abandon cultivated fields that fed the people. It was the issue of reduced food production that had led government officials to order Mendinueta to stand down against the Hispanos. And it was this very point that the Santa Fe emissaries hoped would sway Croix in their fight against Anza. In their testimony, however, they conveniently omitted the fact that severe drought throughout the 1770s had actually caused the food crisis they now blamed on Anza. Instead, they insisted that Anza's plan to reconfigure their homes into defensive spaces, as well as the corruption perpetrated by his administrators, were at the root of the food problem because they forced New Mexicans to neglect their crops.

The Santa Fe delegates held Miera y Pacheco largely responsible for the food crisis. He, it seems, had forced settlers to participate in the construction of a *presa* (dam) at a site known as the Cañada del Corral, issuing fines and terrorizing colonists who failed to take part in the project. Townspeople claimed they worked on the dam for one and a half months, being forced to neglect their fields and winter repairs on their homes. As a result, crops went unattended and the hungry citizenry shivered through the frigid months of 1779–80. In Albuquerque, hunger and exposure to the winter elements caused as many as six deaths.

The famine of 1779 did not affect Hispanos alone. In their petition to Croix, the Santa Fe emissaries claimed that the pueblos of Santo Domingo,

Cochití, and Tesuque were ready to take up arms against Anza as a conse-quence of the decreased rations of seed he had offered the Indians. In 1780, the first two settlements received ten *fanegas* (two and a half bushels) of barley and one *almud* (one-half or less of a fanega) of corn. Anza, on the other hand, provided the people of Tesuque one fanega of barley and all the corn harvested from one *milpa* (field). The delegates argued that these native settlements had been driven to the brink of poverty by shortages of food and supplies, and that this crisis was heightened by the fact that the commandant general refused to allow the exchange of goods between Indi-ans and Spaniards. The Pueblos, it seems, had become dependent on trade with their European neighbors to procure their daily needs. Their threat of insurrection, therefore, stemmed from the perception that Governor Anza had violated the principle of peace by purchase and the spirit of mutual accommodation in New Mexico.[12]

The nature of the justice that the citizens of Santa Fe sought from Croix is not clear, but it probably involved their desire to have the commandant general reverse the social-militarization program Anza had unleashed on the colonists. On 21 June 1780, Croix advised Anza of the complaints brought against him. He informed Anza that Cristóbal Vigil had been granted a patient and attentive audience, but that the emissary was asked to lead his party back to New Mexico. The commandant general assured Vigil that he would order Anza not to press charges against the delegates, who apparently had left the colony in violation of an edict that required citizens to obtain permits from the governor to leave or enter the province. Vigil insisted that he and his colleagues had sought consent from Anza prior to their journey, but that Anza, upon hearing that they planned to denounce him before Croix, refused them license to travel. Croix assured Vigil that Hispanos would not be denied the right to seek justice from his office, and that the case against Anza had already been sent to Assessor General Pedro Galindo Navarro for a ruling.[13]

In the end, Croix proclaimed that the capital complex would remain at its original location north of the Santa Fe River and that the Indians of Analco could stay in their barrio.[14] His decision to side with the Hispanos brought to pass an almost prophetic statement made by Mendinueta in 1772, at which time the then-governor offered a dismal view regarding the forced relocation of settlements in New Mexico:

The achievement of this means is impractical to a governor. With regard to the churlish types of settlers accustomed to live apart from each other, as neither fathers nor sons associate with each other, if he wished to force them to congregate, he would make an enemy against himself in each individual and populate the road of this Court with complaints (as they customarily do). It is not foolhardy opinion which persuaded me to the above statement, but experience acquired from cases of less importance, which have happened to my predecessors and to myself. Force not intervening, persuasion does not serve for them. Only a superior and rigid mandate from your Excellency will be adequate to facilitate the consolidation of these settlers.[15]

For the moment, it appeared that the haughty settlers from Santa Fe had achieved a clear victory against the stern and driven Governor Anza. To them, it did not seem to matter that a mere eight months previously, Anza, the man they now wished to discredit and dishonor, had achieved the seemingly impossible task of defeating in battle the notorious Comanche chief Cuerno Verde. Perhaps blinded by an intense desire to be the masters of their own destinies, the Hispanos played down the significance of Anza's accomplishment—that by achieving victory on the northwestern frontier, he delivered to all New Mexicans a renewed hope for peace. With this one strategic and successful campaign, Anza could almost guarantee that the dreaded violence, which had plagued the battered colony for years and touched so many lives, might soon fade into memory. It is of course possible that the colonists welcomed the promise of tranquility Anza had laid at their doorsteps, but that their parochial pride would not allow them to see beyond the fact that Anza was not one of them; he was, after all, a Sonorense.[16] Anza's place of origin seemed to matter little to Carlos III and Croix, and both king and commandant general acknowledged that he had achieved a peace in New Mexico that few believed possible. For this reason, Anza's superiors continued to support the social-militarization program he had initiated in the colony. Like it or not, the Hispanos were forced to live with the stubborn outsider and his reformist tendencies for another seven years.

Spanish-British War of 1779–1783

Up until 1780, the defensive reform measures Anza introduced in New Mexico focused primarily on protecting the colony from warring Indians. Cuero Verde's death, as well as the potential peace Anza had produced in the far north, allowed Spain to shift its primary focus of frontier defense away from combative Comanches and Apaches and toward the threat of British incursions farther into North America. England had become a contender for international power in the 1600s, and it first challenged Spain in North America in 1670, with the establishment of Charleston in the Carolina territory. For the next one hundred years the British made repeated attempts to seize Spanish settlements in Florida. With the onset of the American Revolution in 1776, England began to move on Louisiana and its port city of New Orleans. Spain eyed the American revolutionaries with suspicion; it considered them a potential rival, but mostly Spanish officials worried that the British American colonists' push for independence would influence Spanish Americans to do the same. Nevertheless, Spain secretly smuggled arms and capital to the rebels, as well as intelligence that kept them informed of British troop movements.[17] Moreover, Spain followed up its support of the American Revolution by declaring war on England in 1779.

The Spanish-British War signaled Spain's efforts to prevent British incursions into Louisiana—which it had acquired in 1762—and Florida, as well as to expel England from settlements Spain had established in Central America.[18] New Mexicans probably did not have to fear that the war with England would spill over into their colony. Nevertheless, they were expected to be ready should such a threat come to pass. In 1779, José de Gálvez warned Commandant General Croix that English subjects might be creating alliances with Indian groups that lived east of New Mexico. In response, Carlos III ordered his American subjects to cease all direct communication with British citizens until Spain could execute an acceptable peace with the court of London. In February 1780, Governor Anza posted in public a notarized copy of the king's royal decree. In so doing, Anza closed New Mexico's borders not only to potential enemies but also to Hispanos hoping to engage in trade in the colony's eastern frontier.[19]

The economic ramifications of such wartime restrictions did not go unnoticed among the New Mexico populace. Moreover, continued warfare drained Spain's treasury and forced the king to demand that his subjects shoulder the economic burden of paying for the conflict. On 17 August 1780, Carlos III called on all his Spanish American subjects to make a one-time donation for the defense of the empire. Hispanos were not exempted from contributing to the war effort, but they did not feel the impact of this decree until 1781. Croix asked Governor Anza to use personal discretion regarding the best means to secure the required war funds in New Mexico, but insisted that all free subjects of European ancestry be required to contribute two pesos; castas (people of mixed race) were required to donate one peso (a musket cost about fifteen pesos). The commandant general advised Anza to impress upon the Santa Fe garrison the important ends to which the funds would be used and to assure troops that the fees they were asked to render would not impoverish them.[20] On 16 January 1783, Croix informed Anza that each soldier's portion of the 247 pesos collected from the Santa Fe presidial company would be deducted from his annual *situado* (a soldier's annual stipend), and that honors and distinctions would be granted to all who contributed.[21]

Croix asked New Mexico's Indians to donate one peso to the war fund, and ordered the Franciscans to aid local officials in the collection of this revenue. Croix insisted, however, that due to their impoverished state the Indians should be allowed to contribute to the war effort with the fruits of their harvests rather than in currency.[22] Anza requested that the Zunis, Pecos, and Hopis be exempted from paying into the war fund because of the extreme poverty these groups had experienced in the previous three years. Croix approved Anza's petition on 22 January 1783.[23] By May of that year, the king decided that his American subjects had contributed enough money to help defend the empire, so he ordered a suspension of his decree. Of the war funds collected, New Mexico's contribution totaled 3,677 pesos, of which 233 pesos existed in the form of seed.

Spain and England agreed on a peace in 1783. Still, newly appointed Commandant General Felipe de Neve ordered the monies collected in New Mexico for the war effort to be deposited in the treasury office at Chihuahua.[24] In so doing, Neve upheld Croix's order deducting funds from the annual stipend for the Santa Fe garrison. On 13 March 1784, Anza posted a royal edict throughout the colony that extended the king's official gratitude to all nuevomexicanos who had shared their bounty for the defense of New

Spain.²⁵ Those Hispanos who read the decree must have walked away with ironic smiles, for they knew that the king had taken their money for a war that seemed a thousand miles away.

The Santa Fe Presidio

Although Anza's defense program had a significant impact on the lives of New Mexico's lay population, it certainly did not neglect the colony's professional troops. In fact, historian Marc Simmons has suggested that the Bourbon effort to secure New Spain's northern frontier during the last half of the eighteenth century resulted in a "proliferation of new laws affecting all phases of the military organization."²⁶ For New Mexico, the crown demanded that the colony's presidio and garrison defenses be brought into line with the "professionalism" expressed in Rubí's Reglamento of 1772. During Anza's tenure, Spanish officials targeted several areas of New Mexico's military for reform, including the reconstruction of the Santa Fe presidio and the age-old problems of garrison finances and corruption.

Governor Mendinueta had tried to convince his king that New Mexico needed additional presidios to defend the colony, and he believed that a bastion at Taos would reduce the number of Indian attacks from the north. Likewise, he argued that a garrison at Robledo would help secure the El Paso district. Anza disagreed. A presidio at Robledo, Anza thought, would draw funds away from the Santa Fe garrison and make it more difficult to defend the northern frontier, which was hard pressed by the mighty Comanches. Anza believed that the militia reforms he had enacted in the colony would adequately allow citizens of El Paso to support the local presidio in the defense of the southern district. In 1779, however, he recommended the establishment of a fort on the colony's western frontier, figuring that a presidio in this territory would lend much-needed economic and military support to the newly allied Hopis. Spanish officials considered these suggestions to be at odds with the presidial-line strategy outlined in Rubí's Reglamento, and were aware that the construction of new presidios would place a heavy burden on the royal treasury. It is also likely that the defeat of Cuerno Verde in 1779, and the potential peace agreement that Governor Anza was already negotiating with the Comanches, convinced Madrid that additional forts for New Mexico were not needed. Instead, King Carlos III settled for the reconstruction of the Santa Fe presidio.

Anza received orders to initiate renovations on the Santa Fe presidio early in 1780. The project promised to enhance the process of mustering troops because it eliminated the tradition of having presidial soldiers live at home rather than in a military compound. By May, officers and troops had pledged a total of 2,175 pesos for the barracks. Although these funds represented only a portion of the capital needed to complete the presidio, Anza set about to recruit citizens for its construction. Croix applauded the donations made by the Santa Fe garrison and agreed to let Anza offer wages to workers, so long as he distributed these in the form of goods purchased at current and fair prices.[27]

In January 1781, the military engineer for the General Command, Gerónimo de la Rocha y Figueroa, forwarded to Anza a copy of detailed instructions that outlined requirements for the construction of presidios. In his plan, de la Rocha addressed many subjects, including the height and thickness of buildings and defensive walls and the recommended materials for production of mortar and adobes.[28] Construction of the Santa Fe presidio, however, was put off for most of the 1780s because of insufficient funds, lack of manpower, and issues of bureaucracy. Anza's successor, Fernando de la Concha, requested permission to resume building in November 1787. The following January, he received a favorable response, along with two thousand pesos and a promise of another one hundred pesos from Commandant General Jacobo Ugarte y Loyola. Still, the Spaniards found it difficult to raise the needed capital for the presidio, a problem compounded by the fact that control of the General Command had again reverted to the viceregal bureaucracy of Mexico City, which meant that the required approval for funds was delayed. To make matters worse, the timber needed for construction was not harvested until November 1788. And a year later, heavy rains destroyed some eighty thousand adobe bricks that had already been produced for the project. These setbacks notwithstanding, the presidio was finished at a cost of 8,708 pesos by October 1791, at which time the Santa Fe garrison moved into its new home.[29]

Garrison Finances and Corruption

Although officials found it difficult to achieve effective fiscal administration for the Santa Fe presidio project, they insisted that the financial obligations of garrisons conform strictly to the reform measures outlined in the Reglamento of 1772. Rubí had believed that appointing fort paymasters would resolve the corruption associated with salaries and supplies because it would remove corrupt officers from the garrison supply system. As early as 1780, government officials declared that military officers, and merchants, would not be permitted to collect debts owed to them by presidial troops if these arrears had been incurred through unethical activities. Croix assured these businessmen that soldiers would be obliged to satisfy allowable economic obligations, but only after they had built up assets in their *fondo de retención* (mustering-out pension reserve) and had purchased required military supplies. The goal here was to ensure that troops did not deplete the money from their pension funds before they retired from the military.[30]

The provision of pensions for troops had been instituted in Spain in 1761 and in New Spain in 1775. Of these funds, the most important for soldiers serving in the far north included the fondo de retención, the *fondo de inválidos* (disabled fund), and the *monte pío militar* (a pension for widows and orphans of men who died while in service). In 1778, Croix suggested a substantial increase in the amount of money deducted monthly from troop salaries in order to increase the value of retirement subsidies. Although it is not certain whether the king acted because of Croix's recommendation, he agreed in 1781 to support the collection and payment of presidial pensions until further notice.[31] The crown, however, did not issue a uniform schedule of monthly dues for military annuities until 1816.[32]

As with the issue of troop finances in New Mexico, Spanish officials also focused much attention on the office of the habilitado, or paymaster. In 1780, Anza received a copy of instructions that outlined, in exacting detail, the duties of the paymaster, including the collection and distribution of the annual stipend assigned to the Santa Fe garrison. As a primary responsibility, the crown held this officer liable for serving as an accountant for presidial troops. In this capacity, the paymaster collected salaries for the garrison from the *ramo de guerra* (military department) in Chihuahua, which he then transferred to New Mexico and distributed.

In cooperation with the presidial captain—in New Mexico the governor served as commander of the Santa Fe garrison—the paymaster also kept accurate records regarding the supplies needed by soldiers and their families. In Chihuahua, he purchased goods and sold them to troops upon his return to New Mexico. The crown made it clear that the paymaster must sell these wares at fair and current prices and add only a two-percent charge to cover his expenses. To ensure that the paymaster did not overcharge for provisions, the crown demanded that this officer post a list of goods and their purchase price in the most public place of the presidio.[33]

The crown excluded presidial commanders from direct involvement in the collection and distribution of salaries and the sale of wares to troops, but it expected commanding officers to keep watch over the activities of the paymaster. Failure to do so could result in serious punishment, including the assumption of debts of any man in the garrison if these liabilities resulted from the commander's neglecting his duty to monitor the paymaster.[34] For Anza, this issue became all too real when the 1780 delegation from Santa Fe traveled to Arizpe to denounce him in Croix's presence. The emissaries claimed that the local paymaster, José María Cordero, had abused his office by engaging in questionable commerce throughout New Mexico. The instructions for stipends granted presidial troops the right to banish a corrupt paymaster and elect a new officer. On 19 July 1780, one month after the citizens of Santa Fe presented their accusation, Croix instructed Anza to initiate the process of removing Cordero from office if his garrison wished it. Croix, it seems, forwarded this order in response to a letter he had received from Anza dated 26 May 1780, in which Anza requested Cordero's replacement.[35] What is not clear, however, is whether Anza had sought to banish the paymaster in response to the accusations brought against him by the Santa Fe delegation. Anza's motivation, of course, may have stemmed from Cordero's abuse of his charge.

As of 20 January 1781, Cordero had not been dismissed from his post at Santa Fe. That day, Croix ordered Anza to fire Cordero and see to the election of an interim paymaster. In addition, he demanded that Cordero liquidate all the garrison accounts under his care and remove himself to Chihuahua, where he would receive news of his new appointment.[36] Cordero did not leave New Mexico until August 1781, at which time he traveled to Chihuahua as ordered.[37] It is probable that Governor Anza refused to release Cordero from his post because, early in 1781, a smallpox epidemic struck the colony that left the Santa Fe garrison weakened by the number of troops who had fallen ill with the virus.[38] The pestilence subsided in June, and the following month Anza's troops elected José Maldonado as their new paymaster.[39]

Marc Simmons has written that most paymasters at Santa Fe lacked accounting knowledge and were usually "ignorant" of the commercial skills they needed to fulfill their jobs. Because of this, financial records for the presidio routinely proved confusing. To make matters worse, Chihuahua merchants normally sold goods to paymasters at inflated prices. Early in the 1780s, Croix addressed these problems by hiring private contractors from the merchants guild of Chihuahua to purchase and deliver supplies to the northern presidios. And in 1786, Croix's successor as commandant general, Jacobo Ugarte y Loyola, gave Francisco Guizarnótegui a license to provision the Santa Fe presidio. Paymaster Maldonado's role in this new supply system required him to travel to Chihuahua to retrieve the goods that Guizarnótegui had purchased for New Mexico.[40] Maldonado's responsibility differed from that of his predecessors, who negotiated prices at Chihuahua, purchased goods, delivered them to New Mexico, and sold the wares to troops.

Maldonado proved an inept paymaster who rarely delivered supplies for the Santa Fe garrison in a timely manner. His shortcomings, however, can be largely attributed to forces outside of his control, as well as to Guizarnótegui's disreputable business practices. In 1786, for example, the newly enacted Ordinances of Intendants—economic regulations enforced by colonial officials appointed by the king and charged with the administration of several provinces in Spain's overseas territories—prevented Commandant General Ugarte y Loyola from providing Guizarnótegui adequate funds to purchase commodities required for Santa Fe. To cover his costs, Guizarnótegui borrowed money and tacked the interest onto the overall fee he charged the state. Hampered by a lack of capital, Guizarnótegui purchased commodities of inferior quality and sold them at Santa Fe at unfair prices. Moreover, he routinely overcharged for freightage.[41]

In 1786, Anza complained that Guizarnótegui's dealings had placed an unacceptable burden on his troops.[42] The following year, Anza suggested that the problem of supplying Santa Fe could be resolved if the contract system were eliminated, and if his garrison could elect a paymaster with fully restored powers to purchase and deliver required presidial goods. For reasons unknown, the Santa Fe troops requested that José Maldonado stay on as paymaster with the authority to represent their interests in Chihuahua.[43] Ugarte y Loyola conceded the request sometime in 1788, perhaps because that same year Apaches attacked Guizarnótegui's mule train as it made its way to New Mexico laden with some fifteen hundred pesos worth of supplies earmarked for the Santa Fe garrison. Two years later, Guizarnótegui officially lost the contract to supply New Mexico.[44] And with Maldonado's appointment, Spanish officials made the post of paymaster a permanent feature of the Santa Fe garrison for the remainder of the colonial era.

The New Mexico–Sonora Road

As a product of the hostile north, Anza recognized that the desire for peace in the General Command required more than increased supplies of guns and bullets, reform of militias and troop finances, or the reconstruction of the Santa Fe presidio. He knew that New Mexicans needed to improve their economic standing if they were to participate willingly in the social-militarization program he had undertaken in the province. But Anza soon learned that economic prosperity in New Mexico was as difficult to come by as it was in all other regions of the Internal Provinces. And here lay the crux of his problem, because Hispanos routinely complained that his demands for defensive reform interfered with their ability to expand their financial interests. Anza knew all too well that this argument was grounded in reality, for in Sonora he, too, had experienced the challenge of trying to find balance between his business and military lives. It had been such experiences in Sonora that led Anza to support a fiscal policy for New Mexico that would allow the Hispanos to establish commercial ties with colonists from other regions.

Anza firmly believed that the creation of new markets for New Mexican goods would improve the Hispanos' and Pueblos' attitudes regarding the defense of their homeland. Why would it not? Increased profits, after all, were something worth fighting for. Commandant General Croix shared Anza's views on this matter, and he ordered Anza to open a land route between New Mexico and Sonora in the hope of increasing trade between the two colonies. Moreover, the commandant general granted Anza the power to utilize military forces to ensure the success of this venture.[45]

Spanish officials had sought to increase ties between New Mexico and Sonora prior to 1780. In a 1749 visit to the colony, fray Miguel de Menchero had traversed its far western realms, exploring the region of the Río San Francisco. The friar's efforts convinced officials that a route between Zuni and Pimería Alta was possible.[46] In 1775, Governor Mendinueta, too, argued that a route between New Mexico and Sonora was possible, but noted that such a feat would depend on subjugation of both the Gila and Mimbres

Apaches.[47] Finally, Anza's Franciscan nemesis in Sonora, Francisco Garcés, had proven that a land route could connect the colonies when he traveled from Pimería Alta to Hopi lands in 1776.[48]

Croix and Anza had discussed the idea of a New Mexico–Sonora road at the Chihuahua War Council of 1778, at which time the commandant general ordered Anza to make this matter his primary charge upon assuming his post as governor at Santa Fe. Anza, however, decided to delay the venture until he had first defeated Cuerno Verde in battle. During his stay at El Paso, Anza did begin to recruit citizens willing to participate in the transprovincial trade he hoped would improve New Mexico's economic standing. Anza's early efforts apparently paid off, for on 9 November 1778, Croix applauded Anza's commitment to the project and congratulated those citizens of El Paso who had agreed to engage in trade between the provinces. Anza passed Croix's praises on to Lieutenant Governor Arrieta and ordered him to ready troops from El Paso to serve as an escort for those citizens who would be traveling to Sonora.[49]

Perhaps because of the threat posed by Gila and Mimbres Apaches, as Mendinueta had reported, Croix and Anza decided not to attempt the establishment of a road between New Mexico and Sonora in the region of the Río San Francisco. Instead, they settled on an alternate route that followed the Camino Real south from Albuquerque to the northern terminus of the dreaded Jornada del Muerto, a site the Spaniards knew as San Cristóbal. From here, Anza planned to travel southwest across the Mimbres Mountain range, through the Gila wilderness, to the Sonora site of Las Nutrias, and finally south to Arizpe.[50]

The excitement and anticipation of the New Mexico–Sonora Road project began to sour late in 1779. In November, Anza requested the money needed to pay those troops, militiamen, settlers, and Indian auxiliaries who had agreed to follow him across the inhospitable deserts of New Mexico. Because Spain had recently declared war on England, Croix informed Anza that the royal treasury was already strained to its limits and that funds would not be forthcoming. News that King Carlos III had reneged on the issue of money shook Hispanos' hopes yet again; it chipped away at their confidence in the New Mexico–Sonora project, as well as their confidence in Anza. To make matters worse, Anza claimed, the Santa Fe delegation that had traveled to Arizpe to denounce him had once again begun to spread the malicious spirit of civil disobedience among the provincial populace. On 26 May 1780, Governor Anza reported that morale among the colonists set to accompany him to Sonora had plummeted. Croix offered words of encouragement, and the newly heartened Anza agreed to fulfill the expedition so much desired by his king.

Anza initiated the New Mexico–Sonora expedition on 9 November 1780. He chose to travel in the fall season not only so his contingent of 151 men could accompany the annual *cordón* (caravan) from Albuquerque to San Cristóbal, but also because the Apaches tended to cease their raiding activities during the winter months. Although Anza's decision may have granted the nuevomexicanos a safer journey, it did little to protect the voyagers from the wintry conditions that plagued them throughout their odyssey. In his journal, Anza complained about heavy snows—as thick as three varas (about nine feet) at some sites—that impeded their progress. Worse, the lack of water along some stretches made travel in New Mexico's southwestern frontier most difficult. Three days after leaving the Sierra de San Cristóbal behind, the party shifted its line southwest towards the Mimbres Mountains. The upland terrain proved a formidable barrier, with few watering holes. Unwilling to expose his thirsty troops to an arid landscape he knew little about, Anza altered his course due south. Anza's forces skirted the eastern face of the Mimbres Mountains. At the range's southernmost point they turned southwest and marched in the direction of Janos, Chihuahua. On 6 December, the party reached a section of the Camino Real that connected Sonora to Nueva Vizcaya. From here, at a site just north of Janos, Anza ordered his men to travel west in the direction of Las Nutrias, which was reached on the 13th. Five days later, Anza and company ended their voyage at Arizpe.

At the capital, the frustrated Anza reported that the route between New Mexico and Sonora had eluded him.[51] Nevertheless, he and Croix focused on the positive outcomes of the expedition. From the start, Croix considered the founding of a New Mexico–Sonora route the primary objective of the campaign, but not the only one. He insisted that during their travels, Anza and his forces also seek out Apache bands and "assail and destroy the enemy [by] falling upon them with blood and fire."[52] As such, the expedition proved to be as much a military offensive against the Mimbres Apaches as an effort at exploration. To help Anza achieve this aspect of his mission, Croix ordered two smaller contingents—one from Nueva Vizcaya and the other from Sonora—to rendezvous with Anza at the Mimbres Mountains and escort the New Mexico forces to Las Nutrias. Croix encouraged the outright killing of Apache men, offering to pay troops twenty pesos for each Indian warrior slain during active duty. As evidence of these kills, he requested that the ears or heads of the dead be delivered to him at Arizpe as well as any captured Indians.[53]

The three armed forces failed to meet at Mimbres, but they fared better as Indian fighters. Anza reported that on 28 November 1780 his men had attacked an Apache camp, where they killed three Indian *gandules* (warriors), three women, and managed to capture two hundred head of livestock. The leader of the Sonora forces, José Antonio Vildósola, claimed his troops managed a total of eight kills, eighteen Indians captured, and forty head of livestock taken. For the Nueva Vizcaya group, Francisco Martínez accounted for six slain warriors, eleven women and children taken prisoner, and seventy-five head of livestock captured.[54]

Anza's failed attempt to establish a New Mexico–Sonora route cast a shadow on his exemplary service record. Upon his return to Santa Fe, he faced off with a populace that focused more on his shortcomings than his recent accomplishments with the Comanches and Hopis. Anza did not try to hide his disappointment, and he would not lie down to those who besmirched his character. The Franciscans in particular became targets of his scorn when they, like the Santa Fe delegates of 1780, denounced him as a tyrannical and despotic ruler. Mostly, however, Anza refused to be deterred from the task of implementing in New Mexico the defense measures expected of him. For the remainder of his tenure Anza continued to serve his king well as governor. The defensive reforms he forced upon Hispanos and Pueblos alike, as well as his successful dealings with indigenous Americans, generated a peace that proved fleeting, but which did allow Spain to hold on to its North American domains for a moment longer.

At the dawn of the nineteenth century, Hispanos and Pueblos again found themselves at odds with their enemies of old. Now, however, a new ethnic face had appeared on the desert frontier bearing the veiled mask of North American imperialism—pioneers and adventurers from the new United States of America. To confront the dual threats of Indian raiding and Anglo American entrepreneurs, nuevomexicanos fell back on the defensive ideals Anza had imposed upon them in the 1780s. In 1808, officials called for the creation of three new citizen militias to help the Santa Fe garrison defend the colony. Two years later, however, the flames of revolution spread throughout Spanish America, and the funds needed to finance New Mexico's military machine dried up. Although the war for independence did not find expression in the colony, New Mexicans made efforts to obtain financial assistance from the Spanish Cortes (National Assembly) that claimed to govern in the king's name. In 1812, New Mexico's delegate to the legislature in Cadiz, Pedro Bautista de Pino, laid before his colleagues an exposition that described his colony's precarious existence. Pino wrote that defense of the province required the creation of new presidios and economic aid for militia troops. Pino's most profound remarks regarding New Mexico included his view that the threat of hostile Native Americans would cease with the promotion of free trade between Indians and Spaniards. Whether he realized it or not, Pino's defense strategy for his homeland mirrored the social militarism that Juan Bautista de Anza had brought to the Hispanos thirty years earlier.[55]

CHAPTER SEVEN

Administrative and Judicial Reforms

UNDER THE HAPSBURG DYNASTY, enterprising men like Juan de Oñate and Diego de Vargas assumed the governorship of New Mexico—Oñate from 1598 to 1610 and Vargas from 1691 to 1697—with the expectation that they would be allowed to use their authority to reap economic profits. If for no other reason, these men justified seeking lucrative returns for having to serve Spain in a land that Vargas once described as being "remote beyond compare."[1] In contrast, the Bourbon kings scorned the entrepreneurial spirit of administrators who had ruled New Mexico under the Hapsburgs. They believed that this laissez-faire approach to government undermined the model of governance they had introduced to Spain in 1700, which granted the monarchy absolute authority to rule. The Bourbons believed that administrative power at the provincial level should be centralized in the figure of the governor. It was this official, after all, who directly represented the crown at the rim of the Bourbon bureaucratic wheel. The Bourbons argued, however, that governors were mere agents of their royal will and should not use their position for personal gain.[2]

With Anza, personal skill and loyalty to the king became the cornerstones of good government in New Mexico, and the governor was expected to rule solely for the benefit of the monarchy. To achieve the ideal of absolute government in the colony, King Carlos III charged Anza with the task of initiating reforms that were intended to increase the power of the state over its citizenry. In this regard, Anza fared well in the realms of ecclesiastical and military reforms; during his tenure he did minimize or abolish privileges that the Hapsburgs had gifted to clerics and presidial officers willing to serve in the remote colony. His efforts to bring New Mexico's administrative and judicial systems closer in line with the ideal of absolutism, however, proved less effective.

Government and judicial reforms in New Mexico were intended to increase the efficiency of the state. It is no wonder then that the most significant modifications Anza managed within New Mexico's bureaucracy involved the process of communication, both within the province and with Arizpe, the new seat of government for the General Command. By reforming the means by which New Mexico interacted with neighboring colonies, the Bourbons were determined to bring the province closer into the absolutist world they envisioned. The Bourbons wanted New Mexicans to become more active and better-connected members of the empire. What they could not foresee, however, was that Hispanos embraced the parochial view of life and empire that was made possible by the geographical distance that separated them from Mexico City. New Mexicans were comfortable with the provincial seclusion that had allowed them to enjoy a degree of home rule since the 1500s, and which for all practical purposes had made them the true masters of the province. The last thing Hispanos wanted from the seemingly despotic Anza was a government that threatened their sense of administrative autonomy. But in large part, King Carlos III had assigned Anza to New Mexico for this very purpose. He intended to use Anza as an instrument of absolutism—as a vehicle by which to impose his royal will on the colony's European community.

Anza accused New Mexicans of being the most significant obstacle in his efforts to implement administrative and judicial reforms within the colony. He soon learned, however, that Hispanos' opposition to the political ideal of absolutism was also rooted in their historical sense of self, and in the fact that they considered him an outsider. New Mexicans could not fathom the possibility that this native of Sonora province might understand the tradition of political culture they had lived by for almost two centuries, which had shielded them to a large extent from the intruding nature of New Spain's viceregal bureaucracy. Historian Marc Simmons spoke to the insular nature of New Mexico's civil government prior to 1776 when he wrote: "Because the population of the province was relatively small and the number of settlements few, the organs of political administration remained essentially simple. Even in the first half of the eighteenth century, government in New Mexico was characterized by its lack of complexity."[3] New

Mexico's model of uncomplicated government, however, did not correspond well with the Bourbon ideal of imperial absolutism. The Bourbons considered excessive regional autonomy to be antithetical to the centralized and efficient state, and so they attacked the notion of "simple" government. In so doing, they hoped to strengthen the crown's power and ability to rule and hence to solidify Spain's standing in the international political arena.

Bourbon Absolutism in Historical Perspective

Beginning in 1701 with the reign of the first Bourbon king, Felipe V, the Bourbons based their political philosophy for governance on tenets of despotism espoused by individuals such as Thomas Hobbes and Jacques Bossuet. These intellectuals had tried to justify the superiority of the state over its citizenry by claiming that kings ruled by divine right. By adopting these views, the Bourbons appeared to champion the transformation of Spain's political machine into a modern and centralized government. Beneath the surface of this enlightened despotism, however, the dynasty proved reactionary. The Bourbons' effort to achieve royal absolutism was fueled by their need to consolidate an empire that had come under attack by foreign powers and warring Indians, and to preserve a dynastic rule questioned by the very subjects the monarchy claimed to represent.

Many Iberians, most notably the aristocracy, challenged the notion that a king was absolute in his power to rule over them. Under the Hapsburgs, nobles had helped the crown govern through representative bodies such as royal councils and regional Cortes. Aristocrats thus argued that they and their kings benefited from this cooperative system of governance, for it justified the existence of the crown and granted elites access to committees that managed the administrative needs of the empire. Grandees from peripheral regions of Spain, such as Aragón, believed that kings served to preserve the cooperative relationship between monarchs and nobles so that both could fulfill their obligations of representing the populace. In 1724, Spanish nobles attempted to restore the corporate monarchy of pre-Bourbon days when King Felipe V abdicated his throne in favor of his son, Luis. Luis, however, died from smallpox a few months after his ascension to the throne, and his death set off a dynastic crisis. Felipe's second wife, Elizabeth Farnese, convinced her husband to reclaim the crown in hopes that she might rule Spain. Spanish nobles challenged Felipe's right to rule again, and they wondered if the Bourbon dynasty would be short-lived.[4]

Felipe V survived the attack on his sovereignty, but it had become clear to him that the mechanism of monarchy would have to be reformed if the Bourbons were to continue to rule the Spanish empire. Felipe and his French advisers thus set out to concentrate the power to govern completely within the figure of the king. Beginning with the restored Felipe V, the Bourbons achieved this by resorting to a ministerial form of monarchy. Under this new system, the king handpicked ministers who administered specific departments and controlled bureaucratic legions that conducted the day-to-day business of government. The key to this arrangement was grounded in the notion that the ministers answered only to the king, and not to the prevailing interests of Spanish nobles. The Bourbons also curbed attacks on their rule by limiting powers once enjoyed by regional Cortes. Moreover, they neutralized Spain's menacing nobility by initiating a system of promotion within the government that was based on service and merit rather than social standing. All government employees had to display talent and demonstrate loyalty to the state if they hoped to keep their jobs. And it was through such measures that the ideal of the absolute and centralized state reached its peak with King Carlos III.[5]

Carlos III surrounded himself with ambitious but able ministers who ruled Spain in his name. In 1776, for example, he appointed the loyal and talented José de Gálvez chief minister of the Council of the Indies, making the former inspector general one of the most powerful men in the Spanish empire. It was Gálvez who had conceived the plan to "amputate" New Spain's northern provinces from the viceroyalty in Mexico City, and to transform the region into an autonomous military district. Gálvez insisted that a commandant general who answered directly to him and the king should govern this polity. Gálvez believed that streamlining the chain of command for this region would enhance the king's power to rule the Provincias Internas and reinforce royal absolutism in all of New Spain.[6]

King Carlos III and Gálvez deemed the creation of the General Command vital for reasons beyond the desire to export Bourbon despotism to New Spain. The crown considered the district significant for one very practical reason: defense of a growing empire against warring Indians and European interlopers. In the first six decades of the 1700s, Spain had extended its hold on the North American continent by adding new lands to its imperial realms and colonizing previously unsettled domains. In 1762, France ceded the Louisiana territory to Spain as a result of the Seven Years War. Seven years later, the Spaniards finally moved into Alta California, some 227 years after Juan Rodríguez Cabrillo first claimed the region for Spain.[7] The Bourbons welcomed territorial gains, but they understood that with expansion came the need to consolidate and defend their imperial frontiers against foreigners.

Spain had contended with France for the region of Texas since the late 1600s.[8] The French eviction from North America in 1762, however, left Spain alone to face the more aggressive British and British Americans. At the same time, Russia had begun to escalate its presence along the Pacific Northwest. But unlike the amiable reception granted to Vitus Bering in the 1740s, Spain cast a cautious eye at the fur trappers Empress Catherine II (Catherine the Great) had unleashed on the very shores of Alta California in the late 1770s. Like Spain, Russia had suffered economic crisis as a result of its involvement in the Seven Years War. To counteract her losses, Catherine expanded the absolutist program initiated by Peter the Great, which was designed to strengthen the Romanov dynasty and increase its imperial domains. Russia's push into Alta California thus represented Catherine's effort to improve her country's economy by allowing her subjects to seek new opportunities in foreign lands.[9]

England and Russia's presence in North America served as a warning to the reactionary Bourbons; it was a sign that Spain's imperial influence was waning on the continent and a foreshadowing of her territorial losses of the 1800s. Still, from 1750 to 1780 the threat of European antagonists in New Spain's northern territory paled in comparison to what truly worried Spanish officials—the cycle of violence between warring Native Americans and Spanish colonials. In his effort to subdue the contentious Comanches and Apaches, Carlos III resolved to increase his power over the administrative and military components of governance. Through Gálvez's plan for the creation of the General Command, and the appointment of Teodoro de Croix as the district's first commandant general, the Bourbons thus assumed a more direct involvement in the defense of that region.

Bourbon Absolutism and the General Command

In August 1778, Croix informed Anza that he was forwarding documents outlining the administrative reorganization of the Internal Provinces.[10] Changes in the process of governance focused on the centralization of power within the figure of the commandant general. As stated, this agent served as the direct representative of the king, and his most pressing responsibility included the transformation of the General Command into a defensive buffer zone.[11]

Administrative power in the Provincias Internas emanated outwards from Commandant General Croix. To help him govern, the commandant general was granted the right to employ assistants appointed directly by the king. Of these, the most important included an *asesor general* (chief legal adviser) and a *secretario de cámara y gobierno* (secretary). Lawyer Pedro Galindo Navarro served as Croix's asesor general, and his jurisdiction included both civil and criminal cases. The job of managing correspondence between Croix and his subordinates fell to Antonio de Bonilla. Bonilla had served as adjutant inspector of presidios under Hugo O'Conor and was well versed in the chain of command that existed in the northern provinces.[12]

In theory, the structure of the General Command was designed to promote efficient government. Visually, the polity could be described as a spoked wheel. As the hub of this administrative circle, Croix contacted and issued orders to his governors through his secretary. Governors represented the outer rim of Spain's imperial circle, and they assumed charge over provincial officials who included a lieutenant governor, *alcaldes* (local and district officials), and all military officers. On paper, the administrative mechanism for each colony in the Internal Provinces represented a mirror image of the General Command, which, in turn, reflected the structure of the centralized Bourbon Empire. In New Mexico, Governor Anza served as an administrative and military extension of the commandant general and ultimately the king.

Try as it might, however, Spain found it difficult to achieve the streamlined bureaucracy its monarchs desired for the General Command. The region's limited resources continued to make the north dependent on provinces farther south for supplies; and this, in turn, allowed viceroys in Mexico City to meddle in the affairs of the frontier district. The size of the

General Command, which extended some eighteen hundred miles from California to Texas, also hampered the administrative process, so much so that Croix suggested early in his tenure that the district be divided into two separate polities, each with its own administrative leader.[13] Geographical expanse was not the only problem. Croix argued that infighting and rivalries between Spanish officials posed a greater threat to the proper functioning of the General Command. In this regard, he reserved his most scathing criticisms for New Spain's viceroy, Antonio María Bucareli, and Commandant Inspector Hugo O'Conor.

Both viceroy and inspector harbored personal grudges against Croix. O'Conor held the commandant general in the highest disdain, believing that the European dandy was unfit to govern in the hostile and burning deserts of the far north. O'Conor's contempt for Croix masked an internal bitterness at not having received the office of commandant general for himself. On 22 July 1777, he vented his frustration in a report he forwarded to Croix, in which he described the conditions of the north. In his account, O'Conor cloaked the resentment he felt for Croix in a sarcastic introduction addressed to the "tenderfoot" commandant:

> I was well aware that such a report was a necessary result of the change of command, particularly for a leader such as Your Lordship who has not seen the lands of which it is comprised, even though you may possess fully as much information as given by someone with the most perfect theory. . . .
>
> Thus confirmed, from what I can expect of Your Lordship's acceptance, I should refrain from giving my judgment on a matter concerning which my opinion is so little esteemed and even more so from reporting what I think practicable for the gradual continuation of my successful ideas, as I am certain those of Your Lordship are contrary and different in everything, perhaps because in carrying them out you expect better results, and I will certainly rejoice in them because I desire the advancement of the service and Your Lordship's gratification.[14]

Croix considered O'Conor a serious rival, and he must have sighed in relief when King Carlos III reassigned the red-bearded inspector to the governorship of Guatemala in 1777.[15] Of his two adversaries, however, Croix judged Bucareli the greater obstacle regarding Spain's plan to enhance the defensive posture of the Internal Provinces. The viceroy had deemed the creation of the General Command a personal affront to his ability to govern the north, regardless of the fact that his predecessors also found it difficult to administer the region from the distant capital of New Spain. And although Croix was not responsible for the political embarrassment associated with having the northern territory amputated from the jurisdiction of Mexico City, Bucareli threatened to resign his commission. Only through the king's intervention was Bucareli placated. Still, the viceroy attended his bruised ego by venting his political frustrations on the commandant general.

Croix accused Bucareli of delaying the transportation of pertinent documents that would educate the commandant general about the conditions in the Internal Provinces. Even worse, he charged the viceroy with filing false reports regarding the defenses of the north and the seriousness of the Indian wars. Military officers of the region, such as Anza, had claimed that these armed conflicts threatened Spain's hold on the territory.[16] In letters to Carlos III, Croix expressed his concerns regarding this matter, suggesting that the greatest enemies of Spain's imperial policy for the General Command were not warring Indians but servants of the crown intoxicated by greed for personal advancement.[17]

Political dueling between key players forced Croix to depend heavily on local officials and military leaders in the north to fulfill his charge within the General Command. Although he had originally opposed Anza's appointment as governor of New Mexico, Croix came to regard Anza as the most reliable and esteemed of subordinates in the district.[18] Anza won Croix's favor while still serving as military governor of Sonora. From here, he had kept the commandant general abreast of raids conducted by indigenous groups on European and Indian settlements and identified various sectors of the colony as main targets for attack.[19] Croix welcomed Anza's reports from Sonora, for they supported his suspicion that O'Conor's presidial reforms had not enhanced the defensive posture of the Internal Provinces.[20] It is possible, of course, that Anza's indirect criticisms of O'Conor stemmed from his own dislike of the commandant inspector, who had reproached him in 1775 for the supposed shambled state of affairs of the Tubac garrison. If such was the case, then Anza's harsh judgment regarding O'Conor's failed effort to reform the presidial line of the far north may have been a calculated move designed to advance his own career. Anza, it appeared, had learned to play the political game.

Administrative Reforms in Anza's New Mexico

Carlos III expected Anza to implement royal absolutism in New Mexico. And while Carlos granted him extraordinary powers to achieve this ideal, including partial authority over the church, it was clear that the king planned to make Anza as much a subject as an instrument of Spanish enlightened despotism. The office of governor thus became the target of a government reform plan aimed at increasing the power of the crown in New Mexico. The decree that granted Anza his appointment to the colony made it clear that the governor was first and foremost a servant of the king, and it emphasized the king's right to remove him from office according to royal discretion. Moreover, it granted Anza a term of five years, *más o menos*. This "more or less" clause in his appointment instructed Anza that the extension of his commission, or his removal from office, would depend on his ability to fulfill the king's will in New Mexico.[21] The point hit home with Anza, who appeared unwilling throughout his tenure in the colony to use the office of governor for personal gain.

The titles granted to Anza also hinted at the nature of the absolutist order Carlos III desired for New Mexico. In the past, aspirants to the highest office in the colony received the appellations of "governor" and "captain general." The latter designation carried with it complete jurisdiction in all military matters. Since the time of Juan de Oñate, many New Mexican governors had deemed it necessary to expand the rights and powers inherent within the captaincy generalship if the process of conquest and pacification of Indians was to be achieved. The inspection tours of Pedro de Rivera and the Marqués de Rubí, however, showed that this tradition tended to lead to abusive behavior and outright corruption. In 1768, Carlos III therefore decided that New Mexico's governors would be deprived of the title of captain general: Pedro Fermín de Mendinueta was the last officer to hold this designation in the colony.[22]

Anza would not enjoy the military status and prestige associated with a captaincy generalship. Instead, the king conferred upon him the rank of *commandante de armas* (commandant of the armed forces). In so doing, Carlos III determined that Anza would serve as New Mexico's military leader but, in this capacity, would remain subordinate to Commandant General Croix. Carlos III's message was strong and clear; the king would no longer tolerate corruption from his New Mexico governors. Ironically, although the king did not grant Anza the title of captain general, he nonetheless bestowed upon him the same military powers as those held by his predecessors:

> I require of the above-mentioned, my Viceroy of New Spain, of the tribunals of the kingdom and the rest of the judges and justices of it, that they protect you, and observe all the honors, benefits, preeminences, immunities, rights and prerogatives which touch you and which your predecessors above-mentioned have had and ought to have enjoyed, notwithstanding the suppression of the denomination of Captain General which was given them before, because my wish being that with the title of Commander of the Armed Forces you may enjoy the same powers which they did unaltered.[23]

The realignment of command in the Internal Provinces and the re-designation of titles for the governor of New Mexico thus proved a symbolic gesture designed to reinforce the ideal of royal absolutism. As governor and commander, Anza was expected to use what military means he needed to enhance the defensive posture of New Mexico, but at the same time not forget his place within Spain's imperial hierarchy, much less his role as a loyal servant of the crown.

One final aspect of Anza's appointment to New Mexico further attested to the Bourbon effort at implementing royal absolutism in the colony: Anza's salary. In New Mexico, the governor received two thousand pesos a year for serving as political chief of the province. In accordance with the Reglamento of 1772, another two thousand pesos were added to cover his wages as military commander. As of that year, the governor's combined income was thus set at four thousand pesos.

The two thousand pesos designated for executive services were supposed to be taxed, as per a schedule on salaries set in 1632, to cover the *media annata* (half-annate). This tariff totaled one thousand pesos, and corresponded to half of the governor's administrative income for the first year of his commission. In the past, the media annata represented the crown's desire to produce royal income by selling the office of governor to interested parties. The funds received from the tax were intended to help support Spain's European war efforts of the 1600s, but in America it was also collected to recoup monies colonial officials accumulated during their tenure through corrupt activities.[24] With the Bourbon reform plan, the tariff also came to symbolize the monarchy's push to gain more direct control of officials employed on the periphery of empire.

The use of the media annata as a mechanism for control involved the belief that by granting itself dominion over the salaries of its bureaucratic subjects, the Spanish crown also acquired greater ability to manipulate them for its benefit. In New Mexico, however, governors always found it difficult to survive financially solely on the salary they received as political chief of the colony. This problem made the temptation of supplementing one's income through corrupt means very powerful, especially in New Mexico's normally deficient economy. For these reasons, collection of the media annata was rarely enforced in the province. This laxity, however, was supposed to change with Anza's installment at Santa Fe. The king determined that, as governor, Anza would have to set the example for administrative and fiscal reform in the colony.

According to the Reglamento of 1772, Anza was required to serve as administrative and military leader of New Mexico. In these capacities, he was to enjoy the assigned salaries for both offices. This matter of salaries was brought to the attention of Croix during Anza's swearing-in ceremony, which took place at Chihuahua on 24 August 1778. The commandant general stated that the newly appointed governor was eligible for the full annual income of four thousand pesos. Confusion arose, however, about whether the media annata would be applied to Anza's combined salaries, or if he would pay only on his wages as political chief. Croix concluded that the final decision on this matter should rest with of the king.[25]

It is unclear whether the issues regarding Anza's salary and his payment of the media annata were ever resolved during his tenure as governor. More than a decade later, in 1799, the question on the tariff was finally settled by royal decree. For the remainder of the colonial period, New Mexico's governors were held liable for paying the media annata on their earnings as the colony's chief administrative officer. The Bourbons, it would seem, got their money and their absolutism.[26]

As per the payment schedule of 1632, all appointed officials serving in New Spain, including ecclesiastics, were subject to the media annata.[27] Perhaps because of the colony's poor economy, only the governor was held liable for the tariff in New Mexico. Lesser appointed or elected officials and the Franciscans were exempted from paying the tax.[28] Exclusion from taxation had been common in New Mexico since the time of Juan de Oñate, who convinced the crown that settlers would benefit greatly if the dreaded *alcabala* (sales tax) was not enforced in the province.

The Bourbons, however, demanded reductions in the cost of bureaucracy, and on occasion they targeted certain employee salaries for fiscal reform. During Anza's tenure, for example, the king issued an order that cut in half the wages of specific state servants. This *cédula* (decree) of 1787 focused on individuals who held temporary government jobs that required a royal license. The crown originally intended for the order to apply to naval officers who, on occasion, abandoned their commissions but still demanded full payment of salaries as outlined in their contracts. In New Mexico, the Bourbons designed the decree of 1787 to affect only those individuals who performed services for the state on a contract basis. Such personnel included tax farmers who collected ecclesiastical and other government revenues. Aside from reducing their salaries, the decree did not allow these employees to request income during periods in which they renegotiated their contracts with the state.

The Bourbons issued the salary decree of 1787 to reduce crown expenditures, but also to improve the efficiency of government. In the order, King Carlos III insisted that public servants who failed to meet the responsibilities of their licenses put a strain on royal coffers and forced other employees to fulfill their jobs. The Bourbons considered such practices unjust and ordered Anza to ensure the implementation of the cédula in New Mexico.[29]

In the first three and one-half years of his administration, Governor Anza dedicated most of his attention toward the restoration of peace in New Mexico. Defense notwithstanding, Anza also worked diligently to realize the efficient government demanded by his king. The task proved a challenge, especially since the jurisdiction of government in New Mexico stretched from the environs of Taos in the north to El Paso in the south. Moreover, the governor's administrative responsibilities were numerous and widespread. He supervised the day-to-day activities of immediate subordinates such as alcaldes. These officials represented the governor in the various *jurisdicciones* (districts) of the colony and kept the public abreast of royal decrees and gubernatorial *bandos* (edicts) that citizens were expected to obey. They supervised *teniente alcaldes* (lieutenant mag-

istrates), who carried out the state's business at the local level, administered justice, and made efforts to improve the economy of their respective
jurisdictions.

Anza's powers were not limited to European settlements, for he also
served as the primary agent between Spain and the local governments of
all Pueblo Indian communities. He was head of New Mexico's *hacienda*
(treasury), responsible for the proper collection of taxes and promotion
of improvements in the colony's economy. He oversaw the administrative
functions of the church. And finally, Anza was held accountable for the
colony's meager infrastructure, including the maintenance of *casas reales*
(public buildings), *cuarteles* (troop barracks), frontier outposts, the Santa Fe
presidio, supply depots, roads, and the postal service.[30]

Anza received extreme powers to implement any measures he deemed
necessary for the general welfare of the province, including the selection
of his bureaucratic subordinates. With the exception of the lieutenant governor, the governor appointed magistrates and defined the jurisdictional
boundaries these officials presided over. He supervised the founding of new
settlements, the relocation of those already established, and was empowered to move entire communities to meet the defensive needs of the colony.
Anza controlled the assignment of land and water rights outside the villa of
Santa Fe, and he regulated travel to and from New Mexico. Of all the governor's powers, these last most affected every citizen in the province because
they allowed the governor to intrude into the public and private lives of all
nuevomexicanos.

As stated, Anza demonstrated the intrusive nature of his administration in 1780, when he ordered Santa Fe residents to relocate their community to the south side of the Santa Fe River. And although Croix sided
with the Hispanos on this issue by allowing the settlement of Santa Fe to
stand unaltered, he did not try to prevent Anza from making other inroads
into the private lives of New Mexicans. On 31 May 1782, for example, Anza
announced his intention to conduct a *visita general* (general inspection) of
the colony. Through this review, the crown expected Anza to gather what
information he needed to best achieve a "better administration of justice
and other ends which are a benefit to the royal service."[31] Anza instructed
españoles and *indios* alike to prepare to share with him grievances they
might have against any officials of their communities. He promised to listen

to all legitimate complaints, as well as to rectify any infractions of justice committed by subordinates, but he also used his visita to examine the military preparedness of the local populace.

Anza set out on his tour of New Mexico from Santa Fe on 1 July 1782. By 27 August he was back in the capital, where he set pen to paper and laid out his impressions of the colony. In his report to Croix, Anza painted a dismal picture regarding the defenselessness of settlers in the province. He concluded that in both urban and rural settlements, the populace could not help defend New Mexico because most citizens did not possess military arms. Anza considered this state of affairs confusing in light of the fact that nuevomexicanos had found themselves under siege by the Apaches and Comanches for most of the 1770s. He expressed little surprise at the fearless audacity with which these *indios bárbaros* (non-Christian Indians) had carried out their raids on the colony; New Mexicans, after all, were barely able to resist a belligerent enemy who swarmed the province bearing better implements of war.

Anza refused to accept the poor military state of the inhabitants he was asked to defend and, like it or not, he was determined to force New Mexicans into a state of martial readiness. He ordered all colonists to arm themselves within two weeks after the completion of his general inspection. The governor realized, however, that many citizens could not afford the purchase of firearms. Still, he demanded that the poorest individuals procure at least one bow and twenty-five arrows for the defense of the province. Unwilling to leave the fulfillment of this edict in the hands of the headstrong colonists, Anza ordered his local officials to conduct inspections of settlements every four months to ensure the proper maintenance of weapons. He drove his stern message home by warning nuevomexicanos that any person not complying with his decree would find himself incarcerated for two months in the Santa Fe jail.[32]

In 1778, Croix had allowed Anza to force a similar arms edict on the settlers of El Paso.[33] By affirming these decrees, the commandant general gave Anza a valuable administrative victory over the Hispanos, in contrast to the setback he experienced when trying to coerce the colonists of Santa Fe to relocate their community in 1780. More important, by imposing his weapons mandate on New Mexicans, Anza bridged the distinct powers he held as administrative and military head of the province. His successful implementation of the decree symbolized his increased control of the state and the people.

Judicial Reforms

The state's intrusion into the lives of nuevomexicanos also found expression in New Mexico's legal system. Governors had enjoyed a great degree of power in this realm, and this tradition of authority continued with Anza. In fact, Bourbon officials saw little need to overhaul New Mexico's judicial branch, but they did demand improved efficiency in the implementation of justice in the colony.[34] It was therefore fitting that the most significant legal reform Anza attempted in New Mexico involved the transferring of judicial jurisdiction from the Audiencia de Guadalajara (Supreme Tribunal of Guadalajara) to the General Command. The commandant general was granted authority over *justicias privilegiadas.* These special-interest courts heard cases that involved *fueros,* which were privileges the crown granted to both military and church personnel. Viceroys and audiencias of New Spain had managed these tribunals prior to the creation of the General Command. Losing control of these courts, however, cost these officials revenue that the courts generated from cases involving troops and ecclesiastics in the region. Neither viceroys nor audiencia judges in Mexico City or Guadalajara welcomed the loss of these important colonial institutions. Moreover, they suffered the unspoken embarrassment over losing some of their powers to the northern provinces.

Carlos III paid little attention to the sentiments of Spanish American bureaucrats who put personal gain ahead of the royal will. Moreover, he recognized that the distance that separated Guadalajara from northern settlements nurtured a sluggish legal system. Carlos therefore considered establishing an independent audiencia for the General Command.[35] This plan never materialized and he settled instead for the transfer of authority over justicias privilegiadas to the commandant general. This reform represented a direct manifestation of royal absolutism through the figure of the commandant general. By granting this officer authority over military and ecclesiastical privileges in the Internal Provinces, the crown gained greater control of the church and military in the region.

Because military reform and defense were the commandant general's primary concern, however, the king refused to overburden him with excessive legal responsibilities. For this reason, the crown decided that the Audiencia de Guadalajara would continue to handle legal appeals in civil and criminal cases of an ordinary nature, cases that normally originated at the provincial level in *justicias ordinarias* (regular courts). By February 1782, Anza began forwarding appeal cases not dealing with church matters to the Audiencia de Guadalajara, and those of an ecclesiastical nature to Arizpe. Croix stressed that judicial reforms were needed so as to avoid any "prejudice, damage, or injury" that might prevent the commandant general from achieving the military responsibilities of his charge.[36] This rationale prevailed even after authority of the General Command had been returned to the hands of New Spain's viceregal government in 1785.

Viceroy Bernardo de Gálvez affirmed the judicial reforms of 1782, as well as the defensive role of the district, when he wrote to Commandant General Jacobo Ugarte y Loyola: "So that Your Lordship might dedicate all his attention to war operations, you will as of now have nothing to do whatsoever with contentious affairs of justice, leaving them entirely to the charge of the intendants [colonial officials appointed by the king and granted jurisdiction over several provinces in New Spain and Spain's other overseas territories] and governors of the provinces."[37] Gálvez's order that governors assume complete control of the legal system in New Mexico did not signal a judicial innovation. As stated, these officers had controlled the colony's judiciary since its founding in 1598. According to historian Charles R. Cutter, this legacy of authority stemmed from a legal tradition he refers to as the *arbitrio judicial* (judicial will). In essence, the arbitrio judicial represented the power of Spanish American officials to determine the nature of the sentence issued at the conclusion of a legal case. The crown considered this practice acceptable, especially on the periphery of empire where colonies like New Mexico normally lacked trained legal professionals and were separated from the judicial infrastructure of urban audiencias by immense geographical distances.

The remoteness of New Spain's northernmost provinces dictated that the legal culture there be an organic process so that justice in these regions would suit the peculiar needs of colonists. The legal principle of *derecho vulgar* (roughly translated as local justice) allowed officials to modify existing laws for this purpose. Magistrates thus enjoyed a degree of flexibility to define not only the nature of punishments and rewards, but also to determine how the legal system would function in their respective colonies. Cutter argues that most of the governors who served in New Spain's northern provinces had little or no training in the law, and therefore their application of justice tended to be based on judicial decisions made by their predecessors.[38]

The less formal nature of the legal system in northern New Spain did not allow outright corruption or misinterpretation of Spanish laws. Officials throughout the empire were expected to apply justice by referring, as closely as local situations permitted, to various legal codes utilized throughout the empire. For New Spain, these codified bodies of laws included royal decrees, municipal charters, judicial notions of Roman and canon law spelled out in the thirteenth-century *Siete Partidas* attributed to Alfonso X of Castile, and a legal code published in 1681 that applied specifically to the Americas, known as the *Recopilación de las Leyes de los Reynos de Indias* (Compilation of the Laws of the Kingdoms of the Indies).[39]

Although the customs of arbitrio judicial and derecho vulgar allowed magistrates to modify laws and determine the outcome of cases, the goal of Spanish justice was always the same—*equidad*. This principle defined the very nature of Spain's legal culture and involved the attempt to provide justice for all parties in any given case. Unlike its northern European counterparts, Spain's judiciary did not function to identify clear winners and losers in courtroom battles. Rather, the judicial system was a mechanism aimed primarily at preserving the well-being of a community. From this viewpoint, the true essence of justice focused on the need to achieve compromise and reestablish a sense of harmony between plaintiffs and defendants.[40]

By the time Anza accepted the governorship of New Mexico, communal tranquility had become the cornerstone of Bourbon judicial philosophy. The Bourbons considered public order essential if the centralized state they envisioned was to be preserved. In the General Command, where officials were constantly challenged to defend the violent frontier, the customs of arbitrio judicial, derecho vulgar, and equidad found their greatest expression. The crown expected governors to utilize these legal traditions not only for the implementation of justice but also to weed out individualism and prevent any challenges to royal absolutism. In a sense, as New Mexico's chief justice, Anza assumed the role of an inquisitor. "In short, he became the accusing party, the court investigator, and the judge," according to Cutter.[41]

Commandant General Croix welcomed the reforms that placed the brunt of judicial responsibilities in the hands of his governors. In 1780, for example, he upheld the tradition of arbitrio judicial for New Mexico when he ordered Anza to continue to implement the most adequate forms of punishments needed to combat crime and preserve the common good in the colony.[42] Croix had wanted to know what measures the governor used to combat crime on the king's highways, and more specifically whether or not the *Real Tribunal de la Acordada* had ever operated in the colony.[43] This institution, a rural police force and court that dealt specifically with banditry in New Spain, never formally existed in New Mexico. Instead, governors in the province dealt directly with such lawless behavior. It is not clear whether Anza ever responded to Croix's request, but the question regarding the acordada was settled in 1783. That year a new commandant general, Felipe de Neve, notified Anza that the acordada would not be allowed in the Internal Provinces. Hence, the governor should continue to confront highwaymen as he saw fit.[44]

It is unlikely that Anza received any formal training in the law. Nevertheless, he was very much aware of the legal codes at his disposal and he regularly referred to the Recopilación de Leyes when seeking some sense of judicial protocol. More often than not, however, Anza used the customs of arbitrio judicial and derecho vulgar to determine the best means of achieving equidad in New Mexico. In 1782, for example, the alcalde mayor of Albuquerque, Juan Francisco Baca, informed Anza that the people of Tomé demanded justice from the settlers of Belén, whom they accused of monopolizing the timber and pastureland of the region. The representatives from Tomé, Marcos Sánchez and Juan Maya, claimed that local officials had not observed laws that regulated the harvesting of timber; they were thus unable to determine who was responsible for the near depletion of cottonwood trees in the region. Likewise, Sánchez and Maya argued that José Antonio Padilla and Bernardo Lucero had acquired permits to cut timber, but the people of Belén had impeded their right to do so because they wished to control this industry in order to increase the amount of pastureland available for their livestock.

In an effort to achieve equidad and reestablish harmony between the conflicting parties, Anza ordered the people of Belén to cease the harvesting of cottonwoods unless they purchased the required permits. Likewise, he demanded that the Belén colonists prevent their animals from grazing on other people's pasturage. Regarding this issue, the governor excused only those individuals who had no knowledge that their livestock had trespassed onto a neighbor's land. Through his decision, Anza satisfied the people of Tomé by ensuring that they would have greater access to timber. And although the Belén colonists appeared to have been punished for illegal activities, they were nonetheless given the means by which to see to the needs of their animals. To ensure that public order and the common good were preserved, Anza ordered local officials to keep adequate records of all economic activities in the region, and he set fines for violations of his judgment. First offenders were required to pay twenty-five *pesos de la tierra* (in the form of goods) and serve a twelve-day stay in prison. Anza concluded that the state would reserve the right to determine adequate punishment for subsequent violations.[45]

The confrontation between the people of Tomé and Belén illustrates the process by which Governor Anza took an active role in defining and directing the personal lives of New Mexicans. In such instances, the people sought and welcomed the intrusiveness of the state, for it was this institution that transcended the social and economic rifts that occasionally pitted one group of Hispanos against another. On other occasions, however, legal battles brought individuals and communities face-to-face with the state itself. Such cases normally involved the alleged misconduct of one or several local officials and abuse of the powers granted to them by the crown. In 1783, for example, the people of Las Truchas presented Anza with a petition by which they sought to have their lieutenant alcalde, José Sánchez, and the alcalde mayor of their jurisdicción, José Campo Redondo, removed from office. Originally, the people had directed their case to Campo Redondo for justice regarding several allegations of wrongdoing by Sánchez. The people of Las Truchas turned to Anza only after they concluded that Sánchez had bribed Campo Redondo, who had judged in Sánchez's favor.[46]

The most serious charges brought against Sánchez included extortion, obstruction of justice, and alleged sexual advances toward a girl from Las Truchas. He also was accused of forcing young men to learn how to gamble, only to rob them of goods and capital by cheating them at card games. Some plaintiffs claimed that Sánchez forced them to buy gambling licenses to give his activities a sense of legitimacy. Others complained that the alcalde demanded payment of goods and money to represent them in future legal matters, but that such services were never provided. One individual, Reyes

González, testified that Sánchez had insulted him, accusing his daughter of being less than virtuous.

Campo Redondo gave Sánchez an opportunity to respond to the allegations. In a scathing response, Sánchez stated that his accusers were liars and opportunists who could not possibly prove their case against him because "no matter how many pearls one might feed an animal, the beast will always produce only lard." After taking a second round of testimony, the alcalde mayor stalled on a judgment for four months. It was then that the people of Las Truchas took their case directly to Anza. They accused Campo Redondo of impeding the judicial process by intimidating some of the plaintiffs and demanding that they drop their claims against Sánchez. Likewise, their petition stated that Campo Redondo had offered to represent Sanchez should the case ever be brought before Anza, and that Campo Redondo had accepted bribes from Sánchez for this very purpose.

In the Las Truchas petition to Anza, Cristóbal Frésquez claimed Sánchez had lured a daughter-in-law living under Frésquez's care to an abandoned house, where he proceeded to make sexual advances toward her. Frésquez expressed the deepest concern for his relative and for his family's honor, which he felt was stained when his wife rampaged through the streets of Las Truchas hysterically screaming that she had discovered Sanchez engaged in his licentious and obscene transgressions.

For Anza, the Sánchez-Campo Redondo affair represented a complete breakdown in the accepted relationship between the state and the people. To settle the matter, he appointed a militia captain, Salvador García Noriega, to serve as *juez comisionado* (delegated judge) in the case. Anza ordered García Noriega to take testimony from all parties but to limit his investigation to the allegations of gambling licenses, bribery, and sexual misconduct by a subordinate. García Noriega ruled that the people of Las Truchas could not prove their case against Sánchez and that perhaps they had conspired and presented false testimony to rid their community of the hated official. Anza passed judgment in favor of Sánchez and Campo Redondo. Furthermore, he declared that Las Truchas had acted maliciously. He ordered all parties involved to observe silence regarding the case and warned that any person caught discussing the matter in public or private would suffer a fine of one hundred pesos and serve two months in the Santa Fe jail. The people of Las Truchas agreed to obey Anza, but did so only with a deep sense of reluctance.

The judgments passed in the Belén-Tomé and the Las Truchas-Sánchez cases serve as examples of two different strategies Anza employed to preserve the communal well-being of New Mexico. In the former, he achieved a sense of justice by weighing the social and economic needs of all parties involved. Of the two instances, however, Anza considered the latter case much more serious because it involved a direct attack on the Bourbon state. His judgment against Las Truchas illustrated an unbending need to preserve the reputation of the government and empire, even if this meant sacrificing the legal ideals of compromise and equidad. The process and means by which these disputes were settled also suggest that, from a juridical perspective, Anza did not act as a reformer. If anything, his role as chief justice in both cases reinforced a style of jurisprudence practiced in the colony for centuries: a tradition of custom and empowerment that, in essence, made governors the law in New Mexico. With Anza, however, the symbolic and actual implementation of Spanish law in the colony did not play to his personal interests, but to those of his king. Anza's actions as New Mexico's primary government and legal administrator demonstrated the fact that he served Spain as an instrument of Bourbon reformism and absolutism.

CHAPTER EIGHT

Communication Reforms

S PANISH OFFICIALS RECOGNIZED that enlightened despotism might work in New Mexico if Governor Anza managed to reform the process by which he disseminated state communiqués to the general populace. This goal seemed appropriate considering the 327 miles that separated the colony's two major cities, Santa Fe in the northern territory and El Paso the southern. Anza reserved most of his bureaucratic attention for districts located in the north, leaving those in the south in the hands of his lieutenant governor. According to Marc Simmons, the lieutenant governorship had fallen into disuse in New Mexico for most of the eighteenth century. It was not until Spain formally adopted the Reglamento of 1772 that this position was reinstated in the colony.[1] José Antonio de Arrieta held the post when Anza first became governor in 1778. Illness forced Arrieta into retirement in 1779, but he remained at El Paso, where he occasionally performed official duties for the state. Nicolás Soler then served as lieutenant governor until 1785, at which time Eugenio Fernández assumed the office.[2]

Anza and Fernández developed a cordial working relationship, and together they set about to achieve as efficient a government as their respective jurisdictions allowed, and as the Bourbons demanded. Their effort in this regard is perhaps best illustrated by the method of communication Anza eventually utilized in the mid-1780s to convey state business to his subordinates and the general populace—a complex, intensely detailed system that specified types of mail, routes, requirements for dissemination of different types of government documents, and confidential timetables aimed at avoiding Indian or bandit attacks.

Reform of the mail service in the General Command began with Teodoro de Croix in the late 1770s. Like Anza, Croix believed that efficient communication was the key to achieving Bourbon absolutism in the Internal Provinces, and he demanded efficiency in the process by which government employees exchanged state correspondence. But he soon learned that the distribution of mail had always been a sluggish process in the far north; he routinely complained about the time it took for communiqués to reach him and for his orders to be forwarded to his governors. More important, Croix realized that the efficient government demanded by his king could not be achieved unless he overhauled the process of communication in the far north.

As an example of the mail system's weaknesses, Croix pointed to the slow dissemination of the proclamation designating Arizpe as the capital of the General Command. Croix chose Arizpe in January 1780, and so informed Anza. But it took two years for Croix to receive royal confirmation of the decision, on 12 February 1782. That day, Arizpe was also elevated to the status of "city" and designated as the seat of the newly created Bishopric of Sonora. It took more than another year for Anza to receive official notification of this action, on 25 June 1783. And it was not until 6 March 1784 that Anza reported to Croix that the people of New Mexico had been informed of these administrative changes.[3] It thus took four years for news of Arizpe's new status to pass from Croix to Spain, back to Croix, and then on to Anza and the people of New Mexico.

The problem was hardly new. Prior to 1763, private contractors had charged a fee for collecting and transporting official mail throughout most of New Spain. That year, these entrepreneurs became appointed and salaried government employees under a newly created royal postal service. Although a postmaster general stationed at Durango oversaw the activities of post offices in Saltillo, Chihuahua, and the Real de San Antonio de la Huerta, this mail system did not extend as far north as New Mexico. Croix's plan of 1779 initiated a mail service that included branch offices at all major settlements extending from the Texas coast, at Bahía del Espíritu Santo, to Arizpe. Early in the 1780s, a branch office was established in El Paso. Still, Santa Fe was denied such a convenience because of its location far to the north and the problem of providing couriers protection from Indian attacks. Anza and the Hispanos of the Río Arriba region thus relied on traditional methods of collection and transport of correspondence. These included the annual caravan that traveled south from Albuquerque to Chihuahua and special couriers the governor was allowed to utilize to carry important state papers to Croix when needed.[4]

By 1781, Croix realized that the transport of official mail leaving New Mexico for royal offices in New Spain and overseas continued to be mishandled.[5] He complained that Anza's reports were always delayed and that local officials abused the postal service by having the state pay postage on their personal mail. Croix reminded Anza that the royal treasury would cover fees for government dispatches into the 1780s, but that state employees in the General Command would have to settle expenses for private letters.[6] To this end, Croix demanded that Anza and his subordinates identify state papers more clearly so that the crown would not have to cover postage on personal mail.

On occasion, the distinction between personal and official letters was not obvious. In 1782, for example, Croix questioned Tomás Roybal's petition to secure a disability pension for having served in New Mexico's military. Croix did not question whether Roybal deserved state support—which he eventually received in 1784—but whether Roybal's request was private or official in nature. Croix, it seems, decided that Roybal's petition represented personal mail even though its subject matter involved government business. In keeping with a viceregal order issued in 1781—that citizens cover expenses for letters in which they were seeking services from the state—Croix asked Anza to charge Roybal postage for his pension request.[7]

By forcing subordinates to distinguish between official and personal letters, and by requiring citizens to cover the costs of postage, Croix hoped to improve the efficiency of the mail service in the General Command and reduce government spending. To this end, he also dictated the process by which state papers should be handled and formatted. In July 1782, he ordered Anza to prepare all documents dealing with a specific issue as a single *pliego* (parcel of letters), including a cover letter describing the nature of the correspondence, and to seal the package before forwarding it.[8] In December of the same year, he asked Anza to limit the length of his messages to one page during wartime. Croix's reasoning was simple; he believed that abridged communiqués would decrease the time Anza dedicated to his bureaucratic duties and free him to attend to the defense of New Mexico.

Likewise, shorter notes meant reduced royal expenditures on paper, which tended to cost two-thirds more during wartime.[9]

By the end of 1782, a disgruntled Croix again complained about the handling and costs of mail received from New Mexico. He scorned Anza for forwarding reports in rough draft form and without required signatures. Because of this, he told Anza to resume the previous format for writing messages as well as the former method of transporting documents to the capital.[10] It is possible of course that Croix reversed his correspondence-reform orders of 1782 because the war with England was winding down and eventually ended with the Peace of Versailles on 3 September 1783.

Early in 1783, Croix received promotion to the viceroyalty of the Kingdom of Peru. His successor, Felipe de Neve, continued the effort to reform the process of communication between New Mexico and Arizpe. Neve, a staunch *Andaluz*, had already served as governor of Baja and Alta California as well as commandant inspector of presidios. He had learned that mail couriers employed in the far north were not observing official *portes* (fees) charged for the transport of documents. Instead, these couriers demanded fees in excess of those outlined by a royal order of 1777—set at three reales per letter—and may have been transporting mail for some individuals without asking for payment. Neve argued that such practices placed a financial burden on the state. On the one hand, monies from royal coffers had to be used to cover overcharges for the delivery of mail. On the other, the royal treasury in Spain was deprived of income generated by postage revenue. In December 1783, Neve ordered Anza to ensure that couriers observe the decree of 1777.[11] In addition, he demanded that all mail from New Mexico be registered and postage fees paid before the mail left the colony, as outlined in Croix's reform plan of 1779.[12]

Of greater concern to Neve was the time it took to receive and deliver documents to and from New Mexico. Like Croix before him, Neve complained that up to one year would elapse before news of events from the colony reached his desk at Arizpe. In turn, delayed communication hampered the commandant general's ability to inform Anza of royal orders or of tidings regarding the empire. Neve, for example, was unable to notify Anza of the peace concluded between Spain and England in 1783 until 17 March 1784, a full seven months after the Versailles treaty had been signed.[13]

Neve had earned a reputation as a firm and authoritative administrator while serving in California.[14] Even as he complained about the sluggish mail service of the General Command, he understood that delayed communication with New Mexico resulted from distances that separated Santa Fe from the nearest post office in El Paso. To makes matters worse, couriers who delivered documents to and from the colony faced the constant threat of Indian attacks and banditry. For these reasons, on 18 December 1783 the commandant general ordered Anza to initiate the least cumbersome and most effective means of exchanging correspondence between Santa Fe and Arizpe.[15]

Anza implemented Neve's order with characteristic zeal, and his efforts at mail reform soon paid off. In many state papers he issued from Santa Fe, Anza included specific instructions on how documents were to be handled and forwarded from one settlement to another. District officials and their subordinates normally posted edicts and decrees on public buildings, where literate settlers could read them at their leisure. Anza, however, considered some edicts to be extremely important, and he ordered these read out loud at public gatherings so that no citizen could claim ignorance of the document, including those who could not read. Regarding the latter type of communiqué, the governor made it a habit of requiring local officials to sign his orders as recognition that the king's will had been made public.[16] This official then forwarded the document to his colleague in a neighboring settlement, where the process was repeated. Ultimately, signed edicts and decrees were returned to Santa Fe and placed in the government archive there.

To ensure that edicts and decrees reached all New Mexico citizens, Anza indicated on the margins of documents the exact *cordillera* (chain) of settlements state papers were to follow. He normally forwarded notices to the alcalde mayor of each *cabecera* (principal town of a district), where it became the responsibility of that officer to post the governor's orders in each community of his jurisdiction. For the Río Arriba, edicts and decrees were transported from Santa Fe to Santa Cruz de la Cañada, then to San Jerónimo de Taos, and back to the capital. Officials then forwarded documents to the Queres district, and from here they traveled to settlements in the Albuquerque region. From Albuquerque correspondence moved west to Ácoma, Laguna, and Zuni. Finally, state papers were relayed to the lieutenant governor, who saw to their distribution in the environs of El Paso.[17]

Deliveries of documents to El Paso required special attention because of the threat of Indian attacks. As a solution, Neve had proposed that a squad from the Santa Fe presidio and a group of citizens transport New Mexico's mail every two to four months along specific routes designated by the governor. Neve suggested that couriers travel at night, without livestock or commercial goods that encouraged attacks. Should this plan fail, Neve suggested that Anza limit the number of people carrying documents to two or three. This, he believed, would reduce the *polvo* (dust) and tracks produced by horses and detected by Indians and bandits.

Regardless of the system the governor chose, Neve insisted that schedules for the transport of mail be scattered to prevent undesirables from acquiring knowledge of the timetables used for deliveries. He empowered Anza to use armed presidial detachments as couriers when these troops traveled on campaign. Finally, the commandant general ordered Anza to coordinate the mail system with the lieutenant governor at El Paso, but by no means to relay his plans to Neve in writing. Neve, it seems, feared that the blueprints for communication in the far north would fall into the wrong hands.[18]

Governor Anza's method of collecting and transporting correspondence within New Mexico served as the foundation of the colony's mail service for the remainder of the colonial era.[19] The communicative process was altered somewhat after 1783, but in the last five years of Anza's tenure these changes proved minor. In 1785, for example, Neve's successor, José Antonio Rengel, ordered Anza to ensure that all employees under his charge utilize official paper bearing the seal of the state, which consisted of the Bourbon coat of arms.[20] Spanish kings had actually initiated this practice in the seventeenth century, and it represented the crown's desire to generate revenue throughout the empire by selling paper to government personnel. The fact that this tradition was not enforced in New Mexico until the eighteenth century spoke to the colony's isolation and also to the slowness by which the king's will found its way to remote corners of the Spanish empire.

The state monopolized the sale of stamped paper in America, but in New Mexico this commodity was always scarce. Rengel's decree of 1785 thus presented Anza with a dilemma. Time and again, Anza reminded his superiors that paper bearing the royal seal was rare in his jurisdiction. Anza dealt with this problem by making use of *testigos de asistencia* (attending witnesses) who cosigned and verified his correspondence. This practice was normally reserved for legal cases in which a notary was not available to sign documents. Anza, however, made use of such witnesses for other types of communiqués.[21] By so doing, he adhered to an edict issued in New Spain on 27 October 1783.[22] This proclamation allowed administrators to conduct state business on unstamped paper in cases of emergency. Anza considered the lack of this resource in his jurisdiction a constant crisis and regularly made do without royal paper. His superiors had no choice but to grant him some leeway in this aspect of his administrative duties. Even Viceroy Bernardo de Gálvez, who took control of the General Command in 1785 and who demanded the use of officially sealed paper throughout New Spain, recognized that New Mexico represented a special case where absolutism would have to be modified to meet local needs.

Government employees and lay citizens were not the only New Mexicans affected by mail reforms. In March 1785, Rengel informed Anza that Franciscans serving in the colony would have to pay postage on certain types of church correspondence, including reports on ecclesiastical matters, titles of promotion or reassignment, and papal bulls. Pedro Alonso de Allés, the chief treasury officer of the newly created Diocese of Sonora, recommended this change as a means of generating funds that could be used to improve the administration of the missions in the far north.[23]

Jurisdictional Disputes

One reality that surely hampered the communicative process between Santa Fe and Arizpe resulted from the number of commandants general who served during Anza's tenure, as well as the shifting authority over the district between these officers and the viceroys of New Spain. In his ten years as governor, Anza answered to a total of four commandants general. Of these, Croix was the first to recognize the possibility of jurisdictional disputes between his office and the viceregal seat in Mexico City.

In October 1782, Croix informed Anza it had come to his attention that justices in New Mexico were receiving dispatches, orders, and even edicts from Mexico City independent of the commandant general's authority. Anza and his subordinates in New Mexico, in essence, were being called upon to serve two imperial masters, which confused the administrative process. Croix warned Anza that the viceregal government was violating the king's will, and demanded that state officials in New Mexico forward all documents received from the viceroy to Arizpe.[24] Anza complied, and for the moment Croix avoided the turf war he feared would ensue over the

Internal Provinces. Meanwhile, the viceregal court sat back and waited for the right moment to continue its quest for return of the territory it had lost in 1776. Such an opportunity presented itself with Croix's exit from New Spain.

Croix left for Peru early in 1783 and was replaced by Felipe de Neve in August of that year.[25] Neve's term in office, however, was cut short by his untimely death at the Hacienda de Nuestra Señora del Carmen de Peñablanca, Chihuahua, on 21 August 1784.[26] Neve's demise left the administrative future of the General Command in doubt. The territory functioned without a leader for three months; in this period of uncertainty, Viceroy Matías de Gálvez moved to gain control of the northern provinces.

As head of the Audiencia de Guadalajara, Gálvez held the power to nominate a candidate for the office of commandant general. His choice, of course, would fall to an individual willing to fulfill the viceroy's bidding and who would ultimately support the effort to return jurisdiction of the northern provinces to Mexico City. Gálvez's favor went to the highly ambitious José Antonio Rengel.

Rengel had served his king as a lieutenant colonel in the Spanish province of Murcia. He spent most of 1783 preparing to move his family to New Spain, where he would assume the office of commandant inspector of presidios for the Internal Provinces under Felipe de Neve. Rengel arrived in Mexico City in March 1784, and from here he traveled to Arizpe. It was he who first informed Viceroy Gálvez of Neve's death.

Rengel knew how to play the political game well. He proclaimed himself subordinate to the Audiencia de Guadalajara, but once Gálvez submitted his nomination for the office of commandant general, Rengel addressed his correspondence only to the receptive ears of the viceroy.[27] Gálvez, however, died before the Audiencia de Guadalajara could approve Rengel's appointment, and by law the oidores (judges) of the Audiencia de México assumed the viceroy's administrative responsibilities.

Matías Gálvez's death forced Rengel to convince the oidores of the Audiencia de México that he merited the desired promotion. In November 1784, he addressed a letter to this judicial body in the hopes that it would uphold Gálvez's desicion.[28] The oidores in Mexico City agreed to grant Rengel the office of commandant general on an interim basis, but specified that he would have to serve under their direct supervision. Rengel forwarded the Audiencia de México's ruling to Anza in November 1784.[29] Anza, in turn, introduced the new commandant general to the New Mexico community on 12 March 1785.[30]

Rengel's appointment initiated a wave of administrative reshuffling that blurred the lines of power in the Internal Provinces and left residents questioning the hierarchy of leadership in the far north. This atmosphere of bureaucratic confusion spurred among Hispanos new hope that they might finally have Anza removed from the governor's seat in New Mexico and replaced with someone more easy-going. The Franciscans in particular tried to sway the commandant general to this cause, but ultimately failed in their quest to oust the overbearing Sonorense. In large part, Anza's continuance as governor stemmed from the fact that Rengel had received only an interim assignment that ran from November 1784 to August 1786. During his brief tenure, the commandant general saw no legitimate reason to recommend Anza's removal from office.

Ironically, Anza had longed for a new assignment since at least 1781. That year, he asked to be relieved of his command and requested an appointment to any other region of New Spain. When his petition was denied, Anza stoically carried on among the Hispanos, with high hopes that the end of his five-year term in 1783 would afford him a brighter future away from New Mexico.

King Carlos III appointed Manuel de Flon to the governorship of New Mexico in October 1784, but the appointment didn't stick.[31] Flon, who had held the rank of captain of an infantry regiment from Navarre, never took up residency at Santa Fe. Instead, he assumed the administration of Nueva Vizcaya, and soon after accepted the post of intendant for Puebla.[32]

Anza's stay in New Mexico was thus extended for a second five-year term. And although the loyal frontiersman accepted his fate reluctantly, he petitioned the crown once more for a new post in 1786.[33] The king again denied Anza's request, arguing that he needed the seasoned veteran to remain in the colony to preserve the fragile peace he had achieved with the Comanches and to help see the newcomer, Rengel, through his interim command of the Internal Provinces.

Rengel's appointment as interim commandant general in 1784 essentially transferred authority of the General Command back to the viceroy of New Spain. The official subjugation of the district to Mexico City, however, occurred in 1785. That year, Bernardo de Gálvez assumed the office of viceroy once held by his father don Matías. Don Bernardo, nephew of the famed José de Gálvez, had distinguished himself in northern New Spain in the late 1770s and early 1780s. He had fought Apaches in Nueva Vizcaya and received several wounds for his efforts. As governor of Louisiana, Gálvez had rendered military aid to the British Americans during their struggle for independence from England and managed several stunning victories over British forces on the Gulf coast. He had served as governor of Cuba and was ultimately appointed to the viceregal seat of New Spain.[34]

Eager to learn about government and military matters in New Mexico, Gálvez ordered Anza to submit a detailed report regarding the colony's state of affairs in August 1785. The viceroy reminded Anza of the importance of his charge and advised the governor to communicate with him through Rengel.[35] Gálvez's interests in New Mexico stemmed from his need to determine the province's place in a new executive chain of command he planned to impose on the Internal Provinces. The viceroy's administrative program was included in his *Instrucción* (reform policy) of 1786 and it earned a favorable response from his uncle and the king, both of whom now realized that the military district created in 1776 was too vast a territory for one man to manage effectively. Teodoro de Croix had been proven correct.

According to Gálvez's Instructions, the office of commandant general was preserved for the Internal Provinces, but this officer was made subordinate to the viceroy of New Spain. The commandant general was to focus all his energies on the defense of the district. To help him accomplish this primary objective, Viceroy Gálvez divided the northern provinces into three zones of operation and assigned a chief officer to each. On paper, the commandant general remained in charge of military matters in the entire district, so long as his views did not conflict with those of the viceroy. But his direct field command was limited to the provinces of Sonora and the Californias. The two other officers were made subordinate to the commandant general, but were allowed to correspond freely with Gálvez, whose orders superseded all others. One of these two officers was placed in charge of Nueva Vizcaya and New Mexico, while the other saw to the military defense of the eastern provinces.[36]

While Viceroy Gálvez restructured the General Command, Anza continued to serve his king faithfully in New Mexico. Even as the decades of service began to take their toll on the aging and tired governor, grand proclamations were made in Spain and America signaling a perceived rejuvenation of the Bourbon Empire. On 16 February 1786, Rengel informed Anza that José de Gálvez had been granted the title of *Marqués de Sonora,* elevating the common-born inspector general to the titled Spanish nobility.[37] That same month, Anza concluded the crowning achievement of his long career, a peace conference and resulting treaty with the Comanche Indians. In September, Viceroy Gálvez ordered Anza to circulate a royal decree announcing the marriage of the king's granddaughter, doña Carlota, and the heir to the Portuguese crown, Prince Juan.[38] This event symbolized the expansion of empire, and all Spanish subjects were called to a three-day celebration of the union. In October, the governor received more promising news: Pedro Vial had volunteered to carry out an expedition from San Antonio de Béxar to Santa Fe in the hope of increasing contact between Texas and New Mexico. Officials considered Vial's efforts significant because they might improve the economic conditions of these poor colonies and help consolidate the northernmost territory of New Spain.[39]

Anza must have found it difficult to share in celebrating the events of 1786. In August, he received news of the administrative shuffling outlined in the Instructions of 1786 and the appointment of Jacobo Ugarte y Loyola to the office of commandant general.[40] Anza knew that Ugarte y Loyola's installation would not bring political stability to the Internal Provinces, much less to New Mexico. If anything, the shift in authority from Arizpe to Mexico City would only make his job as governor more difficult because he would now have to answer to three masters. At the civic level, he reported to Ugarte y Loyola on bureaucratic matters. Regarding issues of defense, he was required to consult José Rengel, who had been placed in military command of New Mexico and Nueva Vizcaya. Finally, Viceroy Gálvez held supreme authority over all matters pertaining to the General Command, and it was to Gálvez that Anza now turned to for imperial guidance.

The weaknesses inherent in the restructured General Command quickly became apparent. Matters of defense and administration soon pitted Ugarte y Loyola against Viceroy Gálvez and Juan Ugalde, who served as military chief of the region's eastern provinces. To make matters worse, Gálvez died in Mexico City on 30 November 1786, leaving the future of the General Command open to question.[41] In February 1787, Commandant General Ugarte y Loyola regained jurisdiction over the far north, but he told Anza to continue reporting to Rengel regarding inspections and supplies for the Santa Fe garrison. Ugarte y Loyola tried to impress upon Anza the significant role he played as the sole and supreme chief of the General Command.

He demanded that Anza acknowledge him as such, and that Anza continue performing his duties with the exactness, zeal, and ability for which he was known.[42]

By the time Anza received Ugarte y Loyola's order of 9 February 1787, a new viceroy had been chosen for New Spain—Manuel Antonio Flores. As viceroy, Flores reassumed jurisdiction over the far north, but about ten months later, the crown reshaped the three military districts that Gálvez had established. The Internal Provinces were now divided into two separate general commands. Ugarte y Loyola retained control of the western provinces, and Ugalde was assigned to the east. This arrangement did not last long either. In 1792, the northern provinces were once more united under the commandant general, and thus they remained until the end of the colonial era.[43]

The realignment of authority over the General Command between 1787 and 1788 created an atmosphere of mistrust and apathy among officers serving in the district. To a lesser degree, Anza, too, fell victim to the air of uncertainty, but he tried not to allow the constant reshuffling of commanders to interfere with the responsibilities of his command. In the last year of his tenure, Anza spent most of his time preparing to vacate his office and ensuring that the transfer of authority to his successor, Fernando de la Concha, proceeded without a hitch. The crown had bestowed the governorship of New Mexico to Concha in December 1786.[44] Concha, however, did not assume his charge until sometime between mid-August and early-October 1787.[45] In the interim, Anza focused much of his attention on the completion, consolidation, and preservation of the Comanche peace. Anza's peace treaty represented not only the cessation of hostilities between Spaniards and Indians but also one of the few positive achievements in the General Command for several years. As commandants general and viceroys came and went, Anza sealed the treaty with the Comanche Indians at Pecos Pueblo. In so doing, he concluded the final chapter in a long political career, one characterized by personal initiative, talent, and loyalty to the Spanish crown.

Anza's successes and shortcomings as governor cannot be measured in absolute terms, but they do have to be considered from the perspective of the Bourbon Reforms. It was to New Mexico, after all, that the king had sent Anza to achieve that which his predecessor had failed to bring about, a lasting peace between Indians and Spaniards. Anza accomplished this military task. Still, the reconciliation between ethnic groups in the far north would not be permanent; it could not be, because the landscape of the region continued to offer limited resources for which all groups competed.

The ideal of enlightened despotism also proved illusory. During his tenure, Anza did manage to increase the power and efficiency of the state. In so doing, he certainly served as an instrument of royal absolutism. Nevertheless, most of the judicial and administrative reforms espoused by Anza had little effect on the actual process of governance or the legal culture practiced in the colony for centuries. For example, as New Mexico's chief justice, Anza did not alter the legal culture that gave the governor almost absolute power to define the nature of justice in the colony. If anything, Anza preserved these legal traditions, but in so doing he did promote the efficient bureaucracy that the Bourbons considered to be the cornerstone of good government.

Some of the administrative reforms that Spain attempted in New Mexico served as symbolic gestures of royal absolutism. The idea that the powers held by governors could be curtailed and controlled, for example, was impractical. Because of the colony's geographic isolation from the rest of the General Command, New Mexico governors required freedom to make bureaucratic decisions independent of their immediate superiors. The system of communication and mail reform initiated by Anza also demonstrated the need to grant autonomy to New Mexico's governors; in this instance, Anza acted on his own initiative. Even so, by denying Anza the title of captain general, Bourbon officials did address the age-old problem of gubernatorial self-interest. It was the unspoken tradition of administrative autonomy that had allowed earlier New Mexican officials to use their offices for personal gain. There is no evidence to suggest that Anza abused his gubernatorial powers. If he did not so enrich himself, then Anza certainly promoted the ideal of absolutism, for he carried out his charge first and foremost to enhance the power and prestige of his king; in short, Anza never forgot his role as a loyal servant of the Bourbon crown.

Other administrative reforms implemented by Anza did alter the mechanics of governance in New Mexico. His system of communication proved to be the most significant change made in the colony's system of government. By improving the communicative process, Anza increased ties between New Mexico and Arizpe. And although he was not responsible for the creation of the General Command, Anza's participation in the district's administrative chain allowed the crown to make its presence in the colony much more real than it had been in the past. Through the office of commandant general, the governor gained greater and more direct access to his king. This, in turn, reined New Mexico more tightly within the imperial structure, and it allowed the colony to be a more active participant in the maintenance and preservation of the Bourbon world empire.

Part III

The King's Church

CHAPTER NINE

The Failed Mission Ideal

A S AN INSTRUMENT OF BOURBON ABSOLUTISM, Anza had come to Santa Fe to impose the will of his king on the people of New Mexico. In so doing, he incurred the parochial wrath of prominent citizens who had traditionally enjoyed privileges that made them the true masters of the colony. The loudest opposition to Anza's reformist administration, however, did not come from New Mexico's lay population, but from Franciscan missionaries who made up the Custody of the Conversion of Saint Paul. Anza discovered early on that the obstinate friars would not cower easily to his demands, much less to the ideal of enlightened absolutism. Moreover, he learned that Franciscan resistance to secular authority in New Mexico predated his arrival in the colony by some 200 years, and had resulted in a church-state conflict that found its greatest expression in the seventeenth century; a period described as the "Era of Missionary Zeal."[1]

Dissension between secular and church administrators in New Mexico rested on the question of how Spain would subjugate those native people who inhabited the northern fringes of its American empire. In the 1530s, Viceroy Antonio de Mendoza had envisioned a peaceful conquest, one that would counter the violent takeover of central Mexico by Spain's first generation of *conquistadores*. If Hernán Cortés had brought the sword to New Spain, then surely Mendoza could bring the Cross; or so he thought. Regarding the northern frontier, Viceroy Mendoza thus ordered "that the conquest be a Christian apostolic one and not a butchery."[2] But Mendoza's vision of peaceful colonialism dissolved like an ephemeral fantasy soon after Francisco Vázquez de Coronado made first contact with Pueblo Indians in the summer of 1540. Driven by hunger, the Spaniards under Coronado's charge pressed the Zunis of Hawikuh (Cibola) for food, shelter, and obedience. When the Zunis refused their demands, the Spaniards moved into battle formation and attacked. Several months later, the Spaniards again resorted to violence when they faced off against inhabitants of Tiquex Pueblo.[3] As it had at Hawikuh, a landscape of limited resources triggered the call to arms at Tiquex. More important, this environment of want convinced the Spaniards that New Mexico was not worth keeping. In April 1542, Coronado and his entourage of would-be conquerors abandoned the northern frontier.

That same year, the Dominican priest Bartolomé de las Casas traveled to Spain to champion the rights of Native Americans. Las Casas received an enthusiastic audience from King Carlos I who responded by enacting the New Laws. This series of regulations officially recognized the Indians as rational beings worthy of respect and humane treatment and had a long-standing impact on Spain's policy of imperial expansion and the incorporation of natives into the empire.

When King Felipe II decided that Spain would return to New Mexico—fifty-six years after Coronado—he did so with the understanding that colonization of the region would not be one of conquest but of pacification.[4] But how could the king guarantee that his North American subjects would embrace a passive colonialism in the far north when their memories of empire conjured up images of recurring inter-ethnic violence throughout the Americas? The Franciscans believed they had a reasonable answer to this question, and they offered it to Felipe II as their "Mission Ideal."

The friars prefaced their plan for the peaceful colonization of New Mexico by reminding the king that hundreds of Pueblo Indians had been baptized during the Coronado expedition, but cautioning that these children of God had not completed the religious training they needed to enter the kingdom of heaven. The clerics added that Felipe II's failure to order the fulfillment of this education would certainly make the king responsible for condemning the souls of these Native Americans to hell. Perhaps fearing that he might lead the spirits of these lost Pueblos into the fiery depths, the ultra-pious Felipe II agreed to sanction the colonization of New Mexico if the Franciscans convinced him that the occupation could be achieved peacefully. Regarding the king's concerns, the clerics had an answer.

The friars believed that the violence perpetrated in New Mexico during the Coronado expedition had been caused by several factors: a landscape that ultimately led all ethnic groups of the region to compete violently for the few resources it offered; an unwavering desire on the part of local Indians to preserve their culture; a genuine mistrust the natives harbored against the Spaniards; and the belief among Europeans that the usurpation of Native American lands and use of Indians as a cheap source of labor was their manifest destiny. To achieve the peaceful takeover of New Mexico, the Franciscans argued that they would have to wield a heavy hand of power in both the secular and ecclesiastical life of the colony. This they would do from missions that served as the spiritual and economic backbone of New Mexico, as well as centers of learning where the spiritual education of the natives would be fulfilled. Lay officials and colonists would be encouraged to participate in the occupation of the colony, but primarily to help the priests fulfill their evangelical goals. And under no circumstance would colonists be allowed to abuse the Indians, or to confiscate their lands.

As a missionary vanguard on the frontier, the friars would thus serve as educators, indoctrinators, and guardians of the people. According to their mission ideal, they would transform the Native Americans into active parishioners of a Catholic and Spanish world. With this goal achieved, the Franciscans would move on to another "uncivilized" frontier and begin the mission process anew, transforming original mission sites into *doctrinas* (Indian diocesan parishes) administered by the secular clergy—priests not associated with a monastic order.[5]

Armed with state-sponsored powers to extort labor from the Pueblos, as well as to shield them from land-grabbing colonials, the Franciscans followed Juan de Oñate to New Mexico in the 1590s. Here they planted the first Christian vine, and for over 200 years they weeded and fed the colony's spiritual landscape, praying all along that the faith might take root in the hearts and minds of their American flock. But after two centuries of evangelizing on the frontier, it became clear that the clerics had failed to harvest in New Mexico a worthy crop of fully Christianized Indians. Colonials thus questioned the mission ideal and ultimately cast wry aspersions at the good name of the Franciscan order. What irked Hispanos most were the political, social, and economic privileges the friars wielded in the colony, which kept colonists from what they coveted most: the Pueblos' fertile lands.

Throughout the 1600s, the Franciscans countered attacks on their order by redefining how they measured the successes and failures of their mission ideal. Originally, the friars calculated their results by the number of

Native Americans they converted to Christianity. The Pueblos, however, did not embrace the faith as fully as the Spaniards had hoped, so the clerics abandoned the strategy of counting souls as a means of defending their pre-eminent standing in New Mexico. To remain a viable force, the Franciscans adopted the view that the construction of missions justified their continued existence in the colony and should stand as its primary objective. The friars, however, became dependent on Indian labor for their mission-building program, and this reliance on Native American workers resulted in a relationship dynamic that the Spaniards had not anticipated.

The Pueblos understood all too well the vital role they played in the introduction and maintenance of Christianity in their homeland, and as far as they were concerned they had consented to have churches built within their villages. By the sweat of their bodies and the strain of their labor, the Indians stacked brick upon adobe brick until the missions reached high into the heavens. When construction ceased, the Pueblos claimed ownership of the churches and, more important, the right to define what they represented. John L. Kessell has noted that their awareness of agency led the Pueblos to destroy the churches during the revolt of 1680. These were Pueblo homes, and the Franciscans were mere guests in New Mexico. In the end, the friars had no choice but to accept this relationship with the natives. After all, it was the successful mission-building program—more than the true conversion of the Pueblos—that preserved the Custody of the Conversion of Saint Paul in seventeenth-century New Mexico.[6]

Franciscan dependency on Indian labor was carried over into the eighteenth century and expanded beyond the construction of missions. Unlike the Jesuits in Sonora and Baja California, the friars in New Mexico never achieved ownership of Indian lands. Instead, the clerics built churches in preexisting Pueblo communities and relied heavily on the Indians for the food they ate and sold within the colony.[7] In 1764, Vicar and Ecclesiastical Judge Santiago Roybal described the Franciscan's dependency on Indian labor in a report to the bishop of Durango, Pedro Tamarón y Romeral. Roybal wrote:

> The services which the Indians give to the reverend fathers are: They sow for them three fanegas [bushels] of wheat, four almudes [quarts] of maize, two almudes of broad beans, two of vetch; some of them also sow two or three almudes of chick peas and half a fanega of frijoles and

their vegetable or kitchen garden. Throughout the year they never lack firewood, which the Indians who serve weekly bring in carts or on their backs. They have forty [of these Indians who serve for a week at a time], and some have more. They have two sacristans. All the Indians give prompt obedience to the commands of the reverend father missionaries. This is true and is public knowledge in the whole kingdom.[8]

Historian Ross Frank has argued that the Pueblos dominated the production of food in New Mexico well into the 1780s, and that control of the colony's agriculture base allowed them a strong voice in defining Spanish-Indian relations. Frank also suggested that the Pueblos offered "voluntary" tribute to Franciscans and European colonists alike, but only so long as Spanish demands for food, services, and goods remained small and did not upset the natives' ability to control their economies and lives. Colonials accepted this relationship because they did not have the manpower to enforce the tribute systems common to central Mexico.[9]

But why would the Pueblos agree to such a relationship? Frank noted that the total amount of tribute the Indians made available to their Spanish neighbors represented a small portion of their total production. Moreover, he concluded that the Native Americans willingly accommodated both Franciscans and secular authorities with goods and services because the Spaniards helped the Pueblos defend themselves against hostile groups such as the Apaches and Comanches.

This dynamic of mutual accommodation became the cornerstone of Spanish-Pueblo relations in New Mexico between 1750 and 1786. It was a time when raids on Spanish and Indian communities increased in frequency. The 1770s proved to be a period of particularly intense hostilities, so much so that historian Oakah L. Jones, Jr., described it as one of "Defensive Crisis."[10] To survive annihilation at the hands of raiding Indians, both Pueblos and Spaniards recognized the benefits of entering into military, economic, and social alliance.

The spirit of cooperation among Pueblos and Spaniards in the 1700s redefined the role the Franciscans played in New Mexico. By the second half of the century, the crown recognized that the mission ideal in the colony had failed. Most of the Pueblos, at best, had accepted certain aspects of Christianity without fully adopting the faith; they were attracted, for example, to the ceremonialism associated with Catholicism because it enhanced their native religion. In turn, the friars used the incomplete conversion of the Indians as their main excuse to delay secularization of the missions and Indian lands associated with these institutions. Perhaps the friars' greatest failure was their inability to bring Christianity to the region's nomadic Indians. Continued Apache and Comanche raids within New Mexico forced the Bourbons to reevaluate their Indian policy for the region. The crown concluded that the state would now take charge of transforming the colony into a military buffer zone. After 1750, the Spanish monarchy continued to finance New Mexico's missions, but the Franciscans saw their coveted missionary ideal of the 1600s dwindle in importance; the royals were now more concerned with issues of defense.

New Mexico's friars did try to preserve the power they had enjoyed in the seventeenth century. Bourbon kings, especially Carlos III, refused to tolerate this challenge to their royal sovereignty. The absolutist-minded monarchy set out to subordinate the clerics to the state by allowing secular officials a greater degree of authority over the administration of New Mexico's missions. The Franciscans retained their role as educators, but even in this realm of their existence they came under attack by individuals such as Governor Anza.

Anza and the Enlightenment

Like so many of his contemporaries, Anza had scorned the Franciscans. Unlike the veiled greed that marked the rhetoric of other Spanish colonists, however, he believed that the failure to incorporate Indians into mainstream Spanish society had resulted from the efforts of the Custody of the Conversion of Saint Paul in New Mexico to preserve itself as a frontier institution by treating natives as subservient children.[11] The classification of these Americans as wards of the state encouraged the friars to promote themselves as guardians of the Indians, but also hampered the original mission ideals of acculturation and assimilation. Here lay the crux of Anza's argument: as long as the Franciscans were allowed to "guard" the natives from Spanish colonials, there would exist a conscious divide between Spaniards and Indians living in the northern frontier. Anza was not antireligious, and he agreed that the church should determine doctrine. Still, he believed that the political and economic powers that missionaries had enjoyed in America since the 1500s impeded the establishment of a more open society that could bridge the ethnic rift which threatened the very existence of colonies like New Mexico.

What is not clear about Anza is at what point in his life he began to question the mission ideal. As a child, he had enjoyed close ties with the Jesuits. Anza seemed to have developed a father-son relationship with Carlos Roxas, and he expressed dismay at the Jesuit expulsion from Sonora. Jesuit clerics played an instrumental role in his upbringing and education, and they must have influenced his views on religion.[12] Even so, before assuming office in New Mexico, Anza developed a critical view of all missionaries. It is possible that this shift in attitude resulted from exposure to the Enlightenment.[13]

The Enlightenment found a place within the Spanish Empire. Indeed, historians have argued that the essence of Bourbon rule, absolutism, was influenced by the literature of the day because it reinforced the reactionary nature of the dynasty. As historian John Lynch has written:

> The [Bourbon] reform program was informed by a spirit of empiricism and responded to needs rather than ideas. It is true that rulers invoked new theoretical justification for their position, whether it was the contractual theory of Locke, or the theory of "legal despotism" advanced by Physiocrats, who saw monarchy justified by its functions; these were to defend liberty and property, and if the monarchy was to do this effectively it needed strong legislative and executive powers.[14]

Perhaps the greatest proponent of enlightened thought in Spain was the Benedictine monk and professor of theology at the University of Oviedo, Benito Jerónimo Feijóo y Montenegro. Between 1726 and 1759, Feijóo published two separate collections of essays that introduced the Enlightenment to Spain and encouraged his countrymen to adopt reason over superstition.[15] In Spain, ministers such as Pedro Rodríguez, the Conde de Campomanes, and José Moñino, the Conde de Floridablanca, adopted Feijóo's advice.

Campomanes recognized the utility of the Enlightenment and championed the ideal of enlightened despotism by carefully choosing among the views of leading intellectuals. At the same time that he espoused his king's right to rule by the will of God, he rejected clericalism and argued that the church should be subordinate to the state. Campomanes insisted that the state was superior to the individual, and that all Spanish subjects should live to serve it. As a practical man, however, he intended that this Hobbesian model of the social contract counteract anarchical movements initiated in Spain by privileged groups such as the *Mesta* and the Jesuits.[16] The Mesta—a powerful association of sheep ranchers—controlled large tracts of pasture land in Spain; lands that, by law, were not allowed to be used for agriculture. Campomanes attacked this privilege, arguing that reform in the tradition of land use would make more acreage and food available to Spain's growing population.

The creator of the General Command, José de Gálvez, shared Campomanes's views for the most part. Gálvez came from humble origins, yet he managed to raise himself up the imperial ladder and was ultimately appointed Chief Minister of the Council of the Indies—an office in imperial affairs considered second only to that of the king.[17] Gálvez rejected social and economic privilege as a requirement for promotion within the state even though he had acquired the noble rank of *Marqués*. On the issue of bureaucratic promotion, Horst Pietschmann summarized Gálvez's views when he wrote:

[P]ersons of ability should be appointed to all levels of employment in America without taking into consideration, at all, their racial and social origin. He [Gálvez] clearly proposed that Indians and *castas* [people of mixed-race] should also be awarded public office if they possessed the personal talent and merit to deserve such appointments. . . . Man appears here clearly conceived of as an individual, and the politics of the State should be directed at facilitating him with the possibilities to develop himself since in the end, and at last, the general good, or the good of the State, is conceived of as the sum of all individual efforts directed towards its proper well-being.[18]

Officials used this formula for advancement to determine Anza's appointment as governor of New Mexico. One can only speculate to what degree Enlightenment philosophy influenced Anza's rejection of the mission ideal. What is beyond doubt, however, is that his attack on the Franciscans began while he was still living in his native Sonora. As a frontier military officer, Anza made contact with indigenous Americans almost on a daily basis. At such times, when he was not killing them he conversed with Indians. They, in turn, conveyed opinions regarding their refusal to be fully incorporated into the Christian fold. More than once in his career,

Anza reported to his superiors that Sonoran Indians rejected the ideals of acculturation and assimilation at those times when missionary demands for their resources and labor proved excessive. It is probable, then, that interaction with Indians tempered Anza's views about the mission process as much as—perhaps even more than—the enlightened principles his Jesuit friends had introduced into the frontier. Ultimately, Anza concluded that the missionaries had become an obstacle to the goals of incorporation and peaceful coexistence, and he therefore encouraged a dismantling of the mission system: "As for the advancement of these heathens and of those previously reduced, I say the surest way to attain the worthy goals expressed by the fiscal [prosecutor] is to destroy and reform as useless and prejudicial the system up to now observed by the missions."[19]

Anza supported his attack on the missionaries with well-thought-out arguments that targeted specific weaknesses he felt were inherent in the mission ideal. For example, in 1772, while still a captain at Tubac, Anza criticized moving Indians to *reducciones* because they excluded Indians from direct participation in societal functions such as economic activity and the government. Relocated Indians, he argued, were not encouraged to become active citizens of the Spanish empire; this went contrary to the ideal of assimilation that the monarchy had expected missionaries to achieve in the Americas. Anza further noted that the mission policy of servitude led some Indians to violence. Indigenous people rebelled when they felt their European neighbors had violated the spirit of mutual accommodation by making excessive demands of service and refusing to share the products of their labor.

Anza believed that Indians throughout the north rejected Spain because it had tried to impose on them a social order that benefited Europeans at the expense of Native Americans. He stressed this point from Tubac in 1772,when he reported to Viceroy Antonio María Bucareli that in Pimería Alta there had occurred a significant reduction in the mission population. Anza blamed this demographic shift, from thousands to hundreds, on excessive labor demands imposed on the Indians by the previous Jesuit missionaries. The Pimas had fled mission *cabeceras* (head towns) because it was here that they were subjected to the greatest labor demands in ranching and farming. In his report, Anza identified two forms of indigenous flight from missions: some Native Americans reverted to a nomadic lifestyle; others ran away to *pueblos de visita*—mission sites with no resident priest who could make constant labor demands on them. In either case, Anza insisted that indigenous flight ultimately represented the rejection of Spain.[20]

Anza stated that relocation to missions and subsequent indigenous flight locked natives into what he described as their "ancient barbarism." This, he argued, occurred because the Indians were not allowed to participate actively in Spanish society. Anza reminded his superiors that indigenous peoples did not reject all things Spanish. He claimed they were willing to coexist with their European neighbors if the Europeans, in turn, agreed to share natural resources and develop an economy that benefited all. At the time Anza became governor of New Mexico, Spain still had not effectively incorporated these Native Americans into the social and economic fabric of the Provincias Internas.

In a sense, Anza espoused the concept of the community of humankind. He believed that Indians should be granted greater freedom to access and interact with Europeans. Moreover, he encouraged a social policy of cultural immersion for both Indians and Spaniards. He thought that peace and cooperation among ethnic groups would be possible only when Indians learned to believe they were a part of the greater Spanish empire, and when Europeans accepted them as such.

Anza believed Sonora's natives should retain ownership of ancestral lands—as the Pueblos had done in New Mexico—and that they should be allowed to benefit from the fruits of their labor. In addition, he promoted a market economy in which Spaniards and Indians engaged in free trade. Anza insisted that Indians would welcome incorporation into this version of the Spanish social order because it preserved a semblance of their traditional cultures and economic systems.[21]

Anza's views on the mission system reached the attentive ears of the Spanish monarchy as well as secular clerics who shared his evaluation of resident Franciscans stationed in New Mexico. From the 1720s to 1760, bishops from Durango conducted several *visitas* (inspection tours) of the colony that resulted in a consensus highly critical of the friars. After his 1760 tour, for example, Bishop Pedro Tamarón y Romeral concluded that the Indians of New Mexico had learned a few outward signs of Christianity but knew little of what these signs meant. Tamarón added that this nominal acceptance of Catholicism by the Pueblos resulted from the fact that the Franciscans had not bothered to learn native languages and were thus hampered in their efforts at religious instruction.[22] In 1776, one of the Franciscans' own, Francisco Atanasio Domínguez, also criticized the friars and their incomplete conversion of New Mexico's Indians. Of the latter, he wrote: "Even at the end of so many years since their reconquest, the specious title or name of neophytes is still applied to them. This is the reason their condition now is almost the same as it was in the beginning, for generally speaking they have preserved some very indecent, and perhaps superstitious, customs."[23]

Like Tamarón, Domínguez recognized the language barrier that impeded the priests' ability to fulfill their religious duties. Most of the Indians rarely attended confession because they found it difficult to communicate with the friars. Confessions among the Pueblos were more common when the Indians were on their deathbeds; even then, the clerics found it necessary to use translators if they were to absolve the people of their worldly sins.

The Pueblos were attracted to the adornments associated with Christianity. But, as Domínguez noted, their desire to possess medals, crosses, and rosaries stemmed more from their "love of ornament" rather than any sense of devotion to the faith. Likewise, Domínguez reported that the friars had failed to destroy the Pueblos' use of *estufas* (kivas—ceremonial buildings that served as temples), as well as the practice of "bedizening themselves with filthy earths of different colors . . . with which they paint their nakedness from head to foot" in preparation for native dances. Discouraged at what he discovered, Domínguez concluded that the Franciscans had failed in their mission ideal and that the Pueblos, especially those of Picurís and Taos, continued to oppose Christianity: "Under such pretexts they will always be neophytes and minors with the result that our Holy Faith will not take root and their malice will increase. May God our Lord destroy these pretexts so completely that these wretches may become old Catholics and the greatest saints of His Church."[24]

Despite mounting criticism of clerics, the Bourbons decided that the mission ideal could not be abandoned. Yet, with the creation of the General Command in 1776, they insisted that the mendicant orders in the Provincias Internas should be made subordinate to the state. To this end, Governor Anza received orders to support the continued conversion of Indians, but also to bring the Custody of the Conversion of Saint Paul into line with the absolutist ideals of his sovereign.[25]

CHAPTER TEN

The Withering Vine

A NZA ASSUMED OFFICE AS GOVERNOR on good terms with the Franciscans. In 1778, the year he arrived in Santa Fe, the *Convento de San Francisco* in Mexico City received a mission of forty-six peninsular friars—that is, friars who had been born and raised in Spain rather than in Spanish America. From this group of European clerics, sixteen were assigned to the Custody of the Conversion of Saint Paul in New Mexico.[1] Anza assured the Franciscans' superior, Juan Bautista Dosal, that the newly stationed Europeans had been adequately provided for. Dosal thanked Anza for his help in the placement of his brethren, and communicated his belief that Anza and the Franciscans would be able to cooperate for the better service to God and king.[2]

Anza's early efforts to accommodate the friars soon soured. He arrived in New Mexico only to discover a major rift within the Custody of the Conversion of Saint Paul. Anza noted that animosity and division among the friars was playing itself out along ethnic lines and involved the *alternativa*. Established in New Mexico in 1711, the alternativa provided for peninsular and creole (American-born) friars to rotate mission assignments so that neither group could dominate the Custody. The Franciscans deemed this tradition most important when they selected a *custos* (custodial head), particularly because this individual could ally himself with the governor and control the padres.[3] The European missionaries who arrived in New Mexico in 1778 accused their creole brothers of undermining their mission assignments. They complained that the Americanos refused to vacate posts that should go to European friars, and that the Americanos did so only on direct orders from their prelate.[4]

Anza took full advantage of the Franciscan crisis in New Mexico to advance the ideal of enlightened absolutism in the colony. He allied himself with friars already in residence when he took office and continued to subject the order to the will of the crown. Anza justified his attack on the Franciscans by demonstrating that the padres were not living up to certain aspects of the mission ideal. He based some of his criticisms on reports the friars submitted to him themselves. In August 1781, for example, the padres claimed that the reason they neglected the religious instruction of adult Pueblos was the Indians' ignorance. Anza did not accept this excuse. Instead, he ordered the friars to set aside at least two days out of the week for adult education. Moreover, he demanded that the Indians attend mass, as well as learning the *doctrina* (catechism).

Anza warned the Pueblos that their failure to attend these sessions without just cause would result in some form of punishment. For a first offense, unexcused absences would result in eight days of imprisonment and time served in the stocks. Men would serve fifteen days in the Santa Fe prison for second and third offenses, and women would be required to observe fifteen days of daily prayer under the supervision of a *doctrinero* (religious instructor). Anza instructed his magistrates to keep records of attendance and to periodically review the religious instruction offered by the friars.[5]

Education of the Pueblos in Christian doctrine had always been a problem in New Mexico. At the root of this issue was the fact that the Franciscans never mastered the various Pueblo languages. Time and again, bishops from the diocese of Durango, the see to which New Mexico belonged, complained of how the padres had failed in this regard. The friars argued that their inability to communicate with natives—which they said was the Indians' fault for failing to learn Spanish—reduced their effectiveness as educators. It was said that most Pueblo Indians had a rudimentary knowledge of Catholicism, going through the motions of receiving the sacraments without fully understanding what they meant.[6]

Anza kept Commandant General Teodoro de Croix informed of the friars' alleged irresponsibility. As expected, Croix chastised the clerics in a biting letter forwarded to the custos of the Custody of the Conversion of Saint Paul, José Hinojosa, in August 1781. Croix accused the friars of gross negligence regarding the spiritual needs of Zuni Pueblo and demanded the immediate appointment of three padres at the settlement.[7] The friars vacillated on the matter, and in February 1782 Anza informed Croix that his order had not been fulfilled. As a result, Croix reprimanded the clerics yet again and threatened to take serious action against them if the mission seats at Zuni remained vacant.[8]

Fractured relations between New Mexico's American-born and European friars did not end with Croix's reproaches. If anything, the struggle to determine who controlled the Custody of the Conversion of Saint Paul intensified during the early years of Anza's administration. In an effort to settle the point, Anza assumed a more direct involvement in Franciscan affairs. His decision to position himself on the side of the creole friars widened the gap between him and the peninsular clerics, most of whom turned to their fellow European, Diego Muñoz Jurado, for guidance.

Under Muñoz's lead, the European friars campaigned to discredit the governor and curb the state's powers over the Custody of the Conversion of Saint Paul. Time and again, they accused Anza of hating peninsulars and targeting them for discrimination. Moreover, they criticized creole friars who refused to speak out against Anza's tyrannical rule, labeling them as instruments of the state. And in a letter addressed to fray José Pereyro, Muñoz questioned the powers and jurisdiction of Custos Hinojosa, and accused him of thinking that he was omnipotent.[9]

It did not take long for Muñoz to incur Anza's wrath. The haughty friar also earned the fury of the general populace and was soon hated by the very people he was expected to embrace as a servant of God. Citizens of Santa Cruz de la Cañada harbored a virulent resentment towards the friar. They accused him of abusing his responsibilities and of claiming excessive powers to tame and master the people. In 1780, the La Cañada residents petitioned Custos Hinojosa to remove Muñoz from their community. Their request smacked of parochial pride, and at one point the colonists claimed they preferred to live as uncivilized people rather than continue to suffer under Muñoz's tyranny. When Hinojosa balked at their initial request, the citizens of La Cañada brought their case against Muñoz directly to Governor Anza. This move compounded Muñoz's legal trouble because it compromised the option of Custos Hinojosa's intervening on his behalf. Instead, Muñoz now faced the dreaded possibility of having to engage Anza in a court of law.

As a cleric, Muñoz enjoyed the right to be investigated, and possibly tried, by his own brethren. This privilege, which Spain recognized as the ecclesiastical *fuero*, had been a long-standing tradition that applied to all priests within the Spanish empire. As John Lynch noted:

> The Spanish Church enjoyed an immunity from civil jurisdiction which had long since vanished in most other parts of Europe. The personal immunity of the clergy involved two basic privileges, the privilege of *fuero*, which provided exemption from judicial action, prosecution and sentencing by any but ecclesiastical judges, and the privilege of the canon, which protected the priest from any physical violence, arrest, torture and punishment.[10]

Tradition or not, Muñoz lived in an age of reform, when Spanish kings tried to abolish church privileges. He must have wondered if Anza would challenge his right to be investigated under the protection of the ecclesiastical fuero. As chief justice in the province, Anza did hold extreme powers over New Mexico's judicial system and could have used his office to destroy Muñoz.[11] Instead, he extended the privilege of the fuero to Muñoz and asked Custos Hinojosa to handle the case as a gesture of cooperation between himself and the Franciscans. Proceedings (*diligencias*) against Muñoz ran from late 1780 to 30 April 1781; they were initiated by Hinojosa in the name of various people from La Cañada who were represented by one of their own, Juan José Bustos.[12]

Custos Hinojosa initially tried to dismiss the case by claiming that the plaintiffs did not have sufficient cause against Muñoz. In January 1781, however, he informed the European cleric that an investigation would ensue because La Cañada had forwarded a second petition against him that merited review. Hinojosa ordered Muñoz to prepare a testimonial in which he addressed all the accusations made against him. Muñoz prefaced his defense by insisting that he had been defamed as "dishonorable and infamous." He demanded that the custos push to "silence the malicious tongues" of his accusers, which he said they used to bring dishonor upon the order as a whole and the peninsulars in particular.

In their second petition, the La Cañada residents described Muñoz as rash, imprudent, hasty, and inconsiderate toward his flock. They claimed that at one point he excommunicated his entire congregation for no good reason. Muñoz did not deny this charge. Instead, he argued that the plaintiffs deserved excommunication because of their ungodly demeanor. He accused them of claiming they would die before obeying Anza's order to relocate to towns that were easier to defend.[13] He declared that they attended mass and confession only when he threatened to beat them with a stick. When they did visit his mission, they did so as if entering a *caballería* (stable). Moreover, the people refused to make the sign of the cross during mass, "as if they were pagans." They preferred to kneel on one knee and remain covered with their hooded cloaks in the style of the Jews.[14] Worst of all, the people refused to fulfill religious obligations such as paying *diezmos* (tithes) and *primicias* (first fruits). Muñoz, of course, deemed such negligence a major problem because the friars required these collections to cover their annual expenses.

The La Cañada residents also complained that Muñoz overcharged to perform marriages and burials. This, they said contributed to their economic ruin and destruction of New Mexico's *cofradías* (confraternities).[15] Many felt they had paid Muñoz so much that they no longer possessed sufficient wheat or corn to make their daily *atole* (cornmeal mush). Muñoz denied the charge, insisting that his *obvenciones* (fees) were in keeping with the *arancel* (schedule) set by the bishop of Durango.[16] Moreover, he scoffed at the people's alleged impoverishment, claiming that more than half of La Cañada's residents had not paid their first fruits obligation for 1780 even though the amount of goods collected that year for the diezmo proved that food production levels in the alcaldía (district) afforded its people a decent living.

La Cañada settlers had also wearied of Muñoz's relations with women. They suggested that he harassed females during his daily *rondas* (patrols), offering as evidence his custom of referring to women as his *ovejas* (female sheep). Muñoz's disregard for women enraged María Atencio, who testified that he had come to her home one evening and beat her with a stick when she refused to follow him to the mission. During their heated encounter, María grabbed Muñoz by his *capilla* (cowl) and slammed him against a wall. Muñoz admitted he had called María to the mission, but only to ask her to respond to charges of concubinage brought against her by the alcalde mayor of La Cañada. This official had visited María's home on 7 November 1780 and found her, at one in the morning, scandalously engaged with Ventura Cárdenas. The alcalde mayor fled María's home, but not before he dragged Cárdenas from the woman's bed. Muñoz insisted that concubinage was common in the colony, and that it was his responsibility to investigate such affairs. He rejected the notion, however, that he had physically abused María Atencio.

Having answered on the Atencio affair, Muñoz then turned an accusing hand toward the leader of the La Cañada faction, Juan José Bustos. Bustos had served as *mayordomo* (steward) of the mission's *fábrica* (fund collection), giving him easy access to collected tithes, and goods in kind. Muñoz calculated that Bustos had taken goods worth at least sixty-two pesos, probably more, from the mission at La Cañada. He demanded that Bustos surrender the mission's account books, but Bustos refused. Muñoz then called for Bustos's arrest and imprisonment, and he said he would leave La Cañada if Anza ruled in Bustos's favor. Should he win his case, however, Muñoz demanded that his accusers suffer public punishment.[17]

Custos Hinojosa received Muñoz's testimony and immediately proclaimed him innocent of all charges. Because Anza had traveled to Arizpe on official business, the custos directed his report to Interim Governor Manuel de la Azuela. Azuela questioned the La Cañada plaintiffs and discovered that Bustos had forged the signatures of at least sixteen people who had not consented to having their names associated with the case against Muñoz. Azuela, therefore, arrested Bustos on 31 January 1781. When news of Bustos's imprisonment reached La Cañada, other plaintiffs came forward to claim that they too had been tricked into signing the petition and wished to be disassociated from the proceedings.

Anza returned to Santa Fe in March 1781 and upheld Azuela's decision to incarcerate Bustos. From jail, Bustos insisted that the allegations against Muñoz were legitimate. Anza, however, concluded that the case against Muñoz was closed, and on 20 April he informed the friar that the people of La Cañada had been ordered to revere, love, and respect the cleric as was appropriate to his holy ministry. Anza added that Custos Hinojosa was satisfied with the results of the case.

Anza assumed that peace had been restored at La Cañada. The governor's proclamations, however, failed to placate Muñoz. The friar demanded that Bustos receive a public sentencing for his crimes. This, he believed, would restore his honor and that of the peninsular priests.

Muñoz's request altered the nature of his case against Bustos because it focused on the issue of theft, a crime that came under the jurisdiction of the secular courts. Anza tried to undermine Muñoz's further meddling in the Bustos case by referencing laws in the *Recopilación de Leyes* that forbade clerical involvement in legal cases of a secular nature, including theft. These statutes did grant priests the power to represent poor people who worked for the friars, but only if the cleric received a license to do so from his superiors.[18]

In his effort to silence the intrusive friar, Anza proclaimed that Muñoz had not received permission from his superiors to question Anza's decisions in the Bustos case. Custos Hinojosa, however, insisted that he and Vice Custos José de la Prada had warranted Muñoz's efforts to seek justice from Anza. The governor conceded the point. He agreed to grant Muñoz's petition, but only if the friar produced the license he claimed he had been given to pursue the case in secular court. Anza's challenge infuriated Muñoz because it made him look guilty in the eyes of his flock. He lashed out, accusing Anza of attempting to impose a "perpetual silencing" of the Bustos case. Muñoz predicted that Anza's refusal to defend his honor would encourage further accusations, defamations, and debasement of the Custody of the Conversion of Saint Paul. As an example, Muñoz raged that from his prison cell, Bustos was already claiming victory over the padres. Muñoz warned that the peninsular friars would not be silenced until they were exonerated and Bustos was publicly punished, and that there would be no peace in the colony unless Anza submitted to his demands. Finally, Muñoz advised Anza that his reputation as governor was at stake because the entire kingdom was describing the Bustos case as one that state officials were trying to "bury within the earth."

Muñoz's bravado bordered on blackmail but failed to produce its desired results. On 30 April 1781, Anza issued his final decision in the case. He suspended Muñoz's claim against Bustos because neither Muñoz nor his superiors had provided the license Anza had asked to see. Anza informed Muñoz that Custos Hinojosa had, in fact, asked to be released from his responsibility of granting the license. Anza, however, did agree that Juan José Bustos had disturbed the peace in New Mexico long enough; he exiled the troublemaker from the colony.[19]

Although Muñoz and the peninsular friars managed a partial victory against the state through the Bustos case, they refused to curb their attacks on Anza. In May 1782, Muñoz became the center of another legal case. He accused Anza of siding with a *genízaro*—a detribalized Indian incorporated into New Mexico's Spanish society—from Abiquiú who had been charged with disrupting the peace of that pueblo. The Indian, José Domínguez, claimed he had received orders from both Anza and Commandant General Croix to function within Abiquiú as a spy for the governor. The Domínguez case dragged on for four years. In 1786, Domínguez confessed to the charges of disrupting the peace and also to having solicited sexual favors from an elderly woman who was on her deathbed and who had already received last rites.[20]

Anza could not save the wretched Domínguez from the public lashings he received as punishment, nor could he prove that the people of La Cañada were justified in their accusations against Muñoz. What he could and did do, however, was to use the Domínguez and Muñoz cases to inflame animosity that had been building throughout the colony against the peninsular friars. Anza declared the European friars guilty of obstructing justice by meddling in legal cases for which they held no jurisdiction. Moreover, he warned the padres that such interference made them liable for engaging in civil disobedience and preventing the state from fulfilling its charge of maintaining the public peace. Anza's efforts raised doubt among the Hispanos regarding the Franciscans' loyalty to king and country, as well as the intentions and sincerity by which they addressed their spiritual duties.

Anza's intrigues strained church-state relations in New Mexico and left the newly elected custos, José de la Prada, open to criticism from his superior in Mexico City. Provincial Minister Juan Bautista Dosal demanded to know why Prada had allowed the spirit of cooperation between the padres and the governor to deteriorate, perhaps beyond repair. Prada offered no reasonable explanation and soon faced the possibility of being dismissed from his post. Word of Prada's tenuous standing within the Franciscan order reached the governor's office at Santa Fe, and on 20 September 1782 Anza wrote Prada to express concern. Filled with undertones of sarcasm, Anza's letter expressed sentiments of pity and compassion. In it, however, Anza promised to do what he could to end clerical misconduct in the colony and to "conquer" any issues that needed to be addressed, so that Prada could be reconciled with his prelate.[21] Anza had no intention of following through with his offer of support, and without fail Prada was soon voted out of office and replaced as custos by Juan Bermejo.

The Franciscans recognized Anza's veiled attempt to discredit them with his letter of 20 September. They retaliated in 1782 by writing the first of two scathing reports that they believed proved Anza and Bermejo had conspired against the peninsular clerics.[22] They described a series of allegedly prejudiced decisions by Anza—and Custos Bermejo—over a period of time before, during, and after Prada's term as custos.

The friars did not accept Anza's reason for having dismissed Muñoz's petition against Juan José Bustos. Muñoz's failure to secure permission from the custos seemed a petty excuse the governor used to deny Muñoz the justice he had demanded during the case. The padres believed, moreover, that Anza tried to hide behind the law when he cited the *Recopilación de Leyes* to justify his refusal to publicly sentence Bustos as Muñoz demanded. In fact, Anza's authority to render such a sentencing was questionable because he had been ordered to transfer all legal appeals involving ecclesiastics to Arizpe on 26 October 1782.[23] The right to define justice in the Bustos case became the prerogative of the commandant general.

The friars offered witnesses who spoke to Anza's alleged hatred of the Europeans. Fray Francisco de Ozio and the ex-paymaster of the Santa Fe presidio, for example, testified that the governor had threatened the peninsulars when he said, "If I knew where these [European friars] kept their blood, I would take it from them with a knife." They also provided a letter Anza had addressed to fray Sebastián Fernández of Abiquiú, in which he labeled European clerics *ignorantes* (ignorants) who did not know the rules and doctrines of their own order.

Moreover, the friars questioned Anza's use of Indians as *semaneros* (day laborers).[24] New Mexico governors, alcaldes, and even the Franciscans had extracted labor from natives long before Anza assumed his post at Santa Fe. In this capacity, the Indians performed a number of tasks including hauling wood, tending to livestock, cultivating land, and doing household chores. The friars insisted, however, that Anza's demand for Indian labor impeded their religious instruction. They reminded Anza that New Mexico's Indians were not his property to do with as he pleased, and that the Pueblo people were subjects, but of the king not the governor.

The Pueblos did not automatically adopt the Franciscan view on the alleged exploitation of day laborers. One Indian woman from San Felipe, for example, complained to Anza that the resident priest at her pueblo, José Cayetano Bernal, had threatened to beat her because she willingly worked in the governor's house at Santa Fe. Anza consoled the woman, saying that he would intervene against Bernal should the friar carry out his threat.

The Franciscans further accused Anza of meddling in a marriage conducted by Father Santiago Fernández de Sierra at San Juan de los

Caballeros. The governor believed Fernández did not have the authority to marry Diego Antonio Martín to María Guadalupe Armijo because she was a resident of Santa Fe and not a member of Fernández's congregation. Fernández responded that the Council of the Indies had determined that priests could conduct marriages if one of the intendeds was registered within the cleric's jurisdiction, as Martín was. Fernández complained that Anza did not have jurisdiction over the sacraments, insisting that ecclesiastics had sole authority to validate marriages.

The friars further alleged that Anza had demonstrated disdain for the peninsulars when he refused to protect fray Francisco de Ozio from threatening Indians. Ozio had suspected in July 1781 that natives of San Ildefonso Pueblo were conducting a pagan religious ceremony. The friar investigated the matter and confronted the Indians. He tried to stop their dance, but in so doing he attacked one of the Pueblo men. The enraged people hurled verbal insults at Ozio in their native tongue. Ozio took the slurs as a real threat to his person and forwarded news of the incident to Anza and the custos. The Pueblos did likewise, and also sent eight elders to the custos to scorn the friar. Fearing for his life, Ozio abandoned his mission, claiming all along that Anza had refused him protection against Indian attacks because he was European.

That same month, the alcalde mayor of Albuquerque, Francisco Pérez Serrano, took Luis Vallejo into custody for taking part in a sexual affair with his mother-in-law. Vallejo escaped from prison and requested asylum from the friars of Isleta mission. Pérez Serrano then had the accused removed from the church without informing the friars. Custos Prada demanded that Vallejo be returned to the sanctity of the church, alleging that the alcalde mayor had failed to prove the charges against him. When Pérez Serrano refused, Prada threatened excommunication and accused him of hiding behind the office of the governor; Pérez Serrano was Anza's brother-in-law. Prada charged that Anza went out of his way to defend Pérez Serrano because of the family connection, and he expressed outrage when Pérez Serrano forwarded a letter to him in which he claimed the friars had no jurisdiction over the missions of New Mexico. Prada concluded that Pérez Serrano was cut from the same cloth as the other reprobates Anza had brought with him from Sonora, and that such disrespect clearly illustrated the governor's contempt for the peninsular friars.

The minister of La Cañada, Sebastián Antón, also brought charges against Anza and Bermejo—who by now had become Custos. Antón alleged that Anza and Bermejo tried to prevent him from seeking an audience with Commandant General Croix because he planned to denounce them. Antón, it seems, had sought permission from Bermejo to travel. He insisted that Anza had convinced Bermejo to reject the request, and that Anza then refused to let him leave because he had not obtained the required travel permit. Moreover, Antón claimed that Anza tried to lure the Indian governor of Santa Clara Pueblo into his devious plan, encouraging the chief to denounce Antón and demand his removal from office. Anza allegedly turned on the Pueblo leader when he refused to obey and when he professed that the people of Santa Clara Pueblo were content with Antón and wished him no harm.

The friars also accused Anza of attempting to abolish the tradition of Indian servitude for ecclesiastics. If successfully implemented, the abolishment of indigenous service would deprive the clerics of one of their greatest sources of income in New Mexico. In a sarcastic passage, the friars suggested that Anza would gain nothing from depriving them of the tradition, "as if the inconvenience of the padres could result and serve any purpose or peace for his lordship [Anza]." Spain did abolish Indian servitude for the friars in 1784.[25]

Governor Anza and Custos Bermejo were also criticized for unfair treatment of fray Ambrosio Guerra. Guerra had borrowed needed clothing and food from Anza's nephew, Vicente Froncoso. Soon after, the padre was reassigned to the mission at Zuni Pueblo. Before Guerra could assume his new post, Anza and Bermejo accused him of "usurping" items from Ácoma Pueblo. Anza ordered officials at Zuni to confront Guerra and to embargo any goods in his possession. On the road to Zuni, the padre was accosted at Mission San Diego de los Jémez. His fellow clerics soon came to his defense. They argued that the governor and custos should have handled Father Guerra's debt to Froncoso in a manner that did not portray him as a criminal. The friars claimed Anza had no right to make public knowledge of their possessions, and insisted that the governor's attack on Guerra represented yet another example of his campaign to harass and publicly embarrass the Custody of the Conversion of Saint Paul.

In one of the most aggressive allegations against Anza, the friars accused him of acting as if he were the "despotic prelate" of their order. In addition, they criticized former Custos Hinojosa, whom they described

as a "cardboard prelate," and current Custos Bermejo for allowing Anza
to meddle in their affairs. The peninsulars claimed Anza had reneged
on a promise not to abuse his power to determine mission assignments,
adding that in a period of three years, he was responsible for the relocation
or removal from office of clerics in seventy-eight cases. As far as they were
concerned, Anza was a liar who attacked peninsular padres because—unlike
their American-born brethren—they voiced opposition to Anza's rule.

The final case against Anza involved fray Sebastián Fernández. Fernández had been reassigned to Chihuahua and ordered to turn over his mission charge at Abiquiú to Diego Muñoz Jurado. Before taking his leave,
Fernández delivered the mission's *ornamentos* (vestments), *alba* (alb), and
corporales (altar linen) to Father Muñoz. On the day of his departure, he
returned to Abiquiú and removed its best white vestment. The confronta-
tional Muñoz accused Fernández of theft. Fernández, however, claimed
he had bought the item from Diego Borica and then sold it to Clemente
Gutiérrez for one hundred pesos. Muñoz insisted the vestment had been
stolen and demanded that Custos Bermejo take charge of having it returned
to Abiquiú. The custos failed to act, so Muñoz took his case against Fernández before the governor. Anza questioned Gutiérrez, who testified that he
had bought the item from Father Fernández. Gutiérrez added that the purchase did not seem odd when he considered that all the friars engaged in
trade. Bermejo agreed and concluded that the vestment was hopelessly lost.

The peninsulars denounced Gutiérrez and proclaimed that his testimony was a "malicious and venomous" attack on the friars because it insin-
uated that they engaged in the practice of simony—the buying or selling of
church office. Muñoz did not challenge the view that the Franciscans supplemented their annual income through trade. In fact, he believed that the
buying and selling of religious garments was allowed so long as these items
had not already been used to celebrate the mass. Muñoz, however, detected
Anza's hand in Gutiérrez's statement. He suspected that the governor had
dictated the testimony to Gutiérrez and had ordered Custos Bermejo to
approve it. Muñoz could not prove his theory.

The allegations regarding Anza's disregard of and discrimination against
peninsular friars fell on deaf ears. Neither Croix nor Anza seemed willing
to cede to clerical demands for justice, nor to affirm the friars' traditional
privileges and powers. Instead, their thoughts focused more on defense
and a reduction of royal expenditures within the colony. Still, the Francis-

cans proved unwilling to accept a diminished role in New Mexico, so they waited patiently for another time when they could resume their attacks on governor and custos. Such an opportunity presented itself in 1783, at which time Felipe de Neve replaced Croix as commandant general.

In January 1783, the friars forwarded to Neve a *memorial* (petition) they hoped would convince the newly appointed commandant general to champion their cause against Anza.[26] As scathing as they had been in their first report, the padres denounced Anza and Bermejo, declaring them "reprehensible" administrators whose coalition had fueled factionalism within their order.

The Franciscans demanded Custos Bermejo's removal from office, but they insisted that Anza was the catalyst that had caused the deterioration of church-state relations in New Mexico. They accused the governor of dominating and controlling Bermejo through intimidation and bribes, adding that Anza was forwarding "sinister" misinformation to Neve regarding his relations with the peninsulars. The friars pleaded that the commandant general reestablish justice in the colony by confronting those who would impede the missionary work of the Custody of the Conversion of Saint Paul.

The Franciscans did manage to remove Custos Bermejo from his post in February 1783. His replacement, Juan de la Prada, wasted little time in joining the peninsular attack on Anza.[27] Prada informed Anza that the *discretorio* (custodial council) had requested that he be allowed to seek justice in a higher court when Anza ordered him to relocate the custody's office from Taos—where the cleric was stationed when he received the patent of custos—to Zia. Prada made it known that he preferred to serve from Cochití Pueblo because he could better execute the responsibilities of his charge from this location.[28] Anza replied that it was Prada who suggested the custodial office be relocated to Zia, and that the alternate choice of Cochití was Prada's "mistaken effort" to denounce the governor's conduct.

Driven by frustration, Anza refused to accept clerical "ignorance" regarding his authority to determine mission appointments, including Prada's placement at Zia. The governor believed he had always responded favorably to the padres' assignment requests, and would continue to do so. He therefore reached out to Prada by confirming an earlier promise not to abuse the power to remove friars from office unless evidence of misconduct or negligence warranted such action. In an effort to appease Prada, or perhaps to silence him, Anza offered to provide mules that would help carry the custos to his new post in comfort.[29] It seems doubtful that Prada was able, or even willing, to overlook Anza's attempt at sarcasm.

Not wanting to be drawn in by Anza's conciliatory banter, Prada issued a *consulta* (question proposed) to the members of the custodial council in October 1783. This proposal exaggerated the governor's criticism of Prada, asserting that Anza had declared him an "obtrusive and deceitful judge, a disrupter of the peace, an offender of the crown's jurisdiction, and of lacking respect for the office of governor." Prada begged his council to contemplate, without taking into consideration that he was their prelate, but merely in the interest of justice, whether Anza was right in treating him with such contempt. He also asked the council to decide if he was the most appropriate man to direct their order in its mission ideal. Representing the council, Diego Muñoz Jurado declared that the discretorio had unanimously ruled in Prada's favor. The council recognized the custos's jurisdiction in all matters pertaining to the mission ideal and accused Anza of having offended, usurped, and abused his powers as governor.[30]

Try as they might to rally a united front against Anza, the peninsulars failed to discredit him as anticlerical and a hater of Europeans. If anything, by 1784 the European missionaries had become their own worst enemies. It seemed that the more the friars tried to assert their dominance in the colony, the more the crown determined to subdue them to the will of the state.

At the Convento de San Francisco in Mexico City, Franciscan Provincial Minister Juan Bravo had been kept abreast of his brethren's struggle with Governor Anza and Father Bermejo. In March 1784, Bravo conveyed to Custos Prada his concerns over the "lamentable condition" that had led to the breakdown of cooperation between the friars and the governor. Bravo applauded Prada's defense of his jurisdiction as custos and assured him that Bermejo would be reprimanded in writing. Still, he warned Prada to be cautious in continuing his attacks on Governor Anza. He suggested that the custos focus on issues that could be substantiated with evidence and would not be considered controversial. Bravo specifically ordered Prada not to dispute matters of clerical privilege because, at present, this was considered a delicate topic of debate throughout the empire.[31]

Father Bravo offered little sympathy for those padres in New Mexico who had failed to ally themselves with the custos in his struggles with the state. He chastised these friars as men who, "having forgotten their calling, drink inequities as if they were water, and live consumed by every form of vice without fear of God, and without observing the obedience owed to their prelates."[32] Bravo ordered Prada to keep him advised of such clerics so that he could take appropriate measures to remedy their behavior if they did not mend their ways.

Regarding Anza, Bravo stated that he had written to the king to request that the governor be contained within the limits of his jurisdiction. Bravo's petition proved to be too little too late. In 1783, Anza had been sub-delegated royal patronage over the church in New Mexico by the newly appointed commandant general, Felipe de Neve. This grant allowed the governor to control the secular administration of the Custody of the Conversion of Saint Paul. More important, it supported Anza's effort to subordinate the friars to the authority of the state.

In the twilight of the eighteenth century, it became clear that the Custody of the Conversion of Saint Paul would never again enjoy the primacy it had achieved in the past. For the rest of the colonial period, according to John L. Kessell, the colony became a "dumping ground for unruly and depraved friars" who were now considered "the dregs" of society.[33] By 1818, the colony could count five secular priests and twenty-two Franciscans to see to the needs of a population that had grown to an estimated 45,000. Kessell has pointed out that in the Mexican period of 1821 to 1848, this lack of qualified ecclesiastics caused problems regarding the religious life of New Mexico: "Children went unbaptized. . . . Lovers did without the sacrament of marriage and raised families in sin. The sick died without confession and their kin improvised the burial office. Mass was a rare occasion. A priest came only a few times a year, but the collector of tithes never missed."[34]

Juan Bautista de Anza did not live to see the results of his campaign to subordinate the Franciscans to the absolutist will of the Spanish crown. His success as an instrument of this Bourbon ideal, however, sealed the fate of the friars in New Mexico after 1790. Still, Anza cannot be given full credit for the collapse of Franciscan hegemony in the colony. Although he played a pivotal role in completing the subjugation of the Custody of the Conversion of Saint Paul to the state, this was a process that had its roots in the seventeenth century and in the spirit of Spanish imperialism.

In the eighteenth century, the Franciscans made the preservation and maintenance of their existence in the far northern territory the primary focus of their attention. In so doing, the padres sacrificed the mission ideal they had professed from frontier altars in the 1600s. New Mexico's friars did survive secularization into the nineteenth century. By this time, however, the Custody of the Conversion of Saint Paul did not resemble the dynamic, vibrant, and overly zealous order of its youth; instead, as Kessell has suggested, it now gasped for life like a "withering vine."[35]

CHAPTER ELEVEN

Church Reforms

Anza's efforts to subjugate New Mexico's friars to the will of the state could not succeed without the official support he received from his reform-minded monarch, Carlos III. To bring the Franciscans into line with the ideal of absolutism, the king empowered the governor to initiate a series of ecclesiastical reforms in New Mexico designed to create a Spanish American church that functioned primarily for the benefit of the crown. Of these reforms, the most controversial during Anza's tenure involved the powers granted to the state through the *Patronato Real* (royal patronage). The Bourbon effort to implement royal patronage over the church was not a reform measure in itself but a reaffirmation of an imperial tradition older than the Spanish American kingdoms themselves. In New Mexico, the granting of the Patronato Real to Anza proved to be significant: it transferred administrative authority of the missions to the state and empowered the governor to implement policy that defined how the friars conducted day-to-day business of a secular nature. Although the Patronato Real did not allow Anza to alter church doctrine, it did sanction his right to determine the number of missions for the colony, make mission assignments for clerics, control the friars' economic activities, and handle church finances.

The Patronato Real

The Patronato Real found legal expression during the reign of the Catholic Monarchs, Fernando and Isabel. In December 1486, the king and queen convinced Pope Innocent VIII to grant them royal patronage over the church on the Iberian Peninsula; then through papal bulls issued between 1493 and 1508 they acquired secular control of the church in their overseas kingdoms.[1]

Fernando and Isabel believed they had earned the right of patronage over the church for their participation in the expulsion of Moors from Spain in 1492. Having secured the Patronato Real, they used it as a social-political mechanism that laid the groundwork for a unified Spanish empire. Their plan made sense because Catholicism was the one social-cultural trait most Iberians shared. According to historian Charles Gibson, this was especially true after the expulsion of the Moorish and Sephardim communities from Spain:

> In suppressing the non-Christian state in Granada and in forcibly expelling Jews—both acts occurring, with an exaggerated historical coincidence, in the year of Columbus' discovery of America—Ferdinand and Isabella sought to purify Spanish society in a spirit of Christian unity. The acts were militant expressions of religious statehood at the moment of the beginning of American colonization.[2]

The Patronato Real allowed for the nationalization of religion—for the evolution of all church components into the mechanisms that drove the embryonic Spanish state. This polity was designed to unite the Iberian people within a common institutional framework without upsetting the ethnic diversity or class structure of the citizenry. What mattered most to Fernando and Isabel, and their Hapsburg successors, was to make Castile the hub of an expanding Iberian and Catholic world. From the imperial capital, Spanish legal, bureaucratic, economic, religious, artistic, and social traditions were transplanted to the periphery of empire. In this process of state-building, the spiritual and ecumenical ideals of Catholicism were not neglected. Fernando and Isabel thus defined their emerging nation-state as both a secular and a spiritual empire.[3]

The use of the church as a mechanism for state formation was carried over into the eighteenth century, at which time the Bourbon dynasty assumed the Spanish crown. Still, while the Hapsburgs had utilized the Patronato Real to help them solidify and expand their empire, the Bourbons became dependent on it as a means of preserving an imperial structure that was in decline as an international power. In the face of escalating competition from England, France, and Russia, the Bourbons demanded more obedience, loyalty, and service from their priests. More than all others, King Carlos III expected to use his powers over the Spanish church to weed out clerics who challenged the monarchy's right to rule and who had—at least in his eyes—encouraged citizens to engage in civil disobedience. The king, for example, accused the Jesuits of inciting riots in the streets of Madrid in 1766. This led him to expel Loyola's black robes from his empire a year later. If anything, Carlos III demanded that clerics clad in Spanish cloth should encourage their flock to uphold the social order that defined and sustained the fabric of the imperial state. Those who did not would suffer the fate of the Jesuits.

King Carlos III also intended to employ the Patronato Real to gain access to the vast wealth accumulated by the Spanish church, and to use these revenues to help preserve his empire. The Concordat of 1753 allowed Carlos III to achieve this goal; it granted him legal and universal rights to control church appointments, jurisdiction, and revenues in Spain. As such, the accord made it clear that eighteenth-century Spanish priests might swear allegiance to God and pope in their nightly prayers, but during the day they worked for the king.[4]

Anza and the Patronato Real

Governor Anza did not question the issue of ecclesiastical jurisdiction. In his mind, the law was clear. According to historian Jim Norris, papal bulls that granted Spain royal patronage in the Americas,

> most notably Alexander VI, 1493, *Inter c[a]etera* and Jules II, 1508, *Universalis ecclesiae,* acknowledged the rights of the kings to control religious appointments, sites of missions and parishes, their operations, and other matters in exchange for promoting the propagation of the Catholic faith, including the financial responsibilities. In theory, the crown retained ultimate approval for virtually all Church activities.[5]

Anza believed what popes allowed and what the Bourbons ordered—that the Franciscans owed allegiance to the Spanish monarchy and to him as its representative in New Mexico. As an instrument of the Bourbon Reforms, he accepted responsibility for representing the interests of his sovereigns before those of the friars. Anza's first priority in this regard was to enhance the colony's military posture. The ecclesiastical ideal that so characterized seventeenth-century New Mexico became a secondary goal. Historian John L. Kessell has noted that by Anza's time, "friars no longer dictated the affairs of the colony. The primary concerns of the Spanish Bourbon kings and their bureaucracy were defense and revenue, not missions."[6]

Franciscans in New Mexico did not welcome King Carlos III's plan to subordinate their order to the will of the crown. The friars, in fact, had resisted state incursions into their clerical world since the founding of the Custody of the Conversion of Saint Paul in 1616.[7] By the time Anza assumed his office as governor, however, the Custody of the Conversion of Saint Paul was no longer the powerful institution that had once hoped to transform New Mexico into a theocracy. Infighting and a general degeneration in quality of clerics worked against the friars. By 1778, they found themselves struggling to survive among an indigenous people who had never fully accepted them.

In New Spain, the Patronato Real emanated outward from Mexico City. The king delegated patronage to viceroys; the viceroys, in turn, sub-delegated patronage to the governors. With the creation of the General Command in 1776, the commandant general assumed the powers of royal patronage in New Spain's far northern territory. Although it is not clear whether Anza obtained ecclesiastical patronage at the time he assumed the office of governor, he did receive this authority by 1783. On August 19, Commandant General Felipe de Neve informed Anza that he had been granted royal patronage because of the great distances that separated New Mexico from Arizpe, the capital of the Provincias Internas. Neve stated that similar powers had been extended to all the governors of the General Command so that ecclesiastical provisions for these provinces would not be retarded. Neve also informed Anza that the Cathedral Council of Durango had been made aware of this sub-delegation so that it would forward recommendations for mission assignments to the governor in New Mexico.[8]

Anza probably did not receive royal patronage prior to 1783. Even so, it became evident early in his administration that he planned to challenge the autonomy that the friars had enjoyed in the past. In this regard, Anza received support from Spanish officials in America. In April 1779, for example, the assessor general to the Provincias Internas, Pedro Galindo Navarro, forwarded a *dictamen* (opinion) to Commandant General Croix in which he outlined legal precedents that gave the secular clergy specific jurisdictional powers over regular clerics. According to Galindo, laws in the Recopilación de Leyes granted archbishops and bishops the power to investigate and punish clerics for abuses in the administration of the sacraments.[9] Because the Patronato Real granted the state control over the secular church, it essentially empowered Anza to conduct such investigations in New Mexico.

Spain's secular clergy consisted of ordained diocesan priests who owed their primary allegiance to the monarchy. In contrast, regular priests lived by the *regula* (rule) of their religious institution and had to balance the loyalty they owed to the Spanish monarchy with the obedience they extended to the head of their monastic order. The Bourbon kings, especially Carlos III, harbored suspicious sentiments toward the regular clergy, believing that some, like the Jesuits, challenged the ideal of absolutism by downplaying the respect and fidelity they were expected to show the crown. Spanish officials must have embraced Galindo's dictamen of 1779 because it upheld the king's authority to administer the secular affairs of the church through the Patronato Real.

Galindo's dictamen represented an initial step taken by the crown to subordinate the friars to the state during Anza's tenure, and it called on the governor to ensure that statutes pertaining to clerical investigations were obeyed in New Mexico.[10] This in itself did not prove that Anza held the powers of royal patronage. Still, on several occasions prior to 1783 the governor reminded the Franciscans that the Patronato Real was in effect in the colony and rendered the Custody of the Conversion of Saint Paul subordinate to the state. In 1780, for example, he enforced a royal order that required clerics to present the Eucharist to secular officials before receiving the keys to the vessel in which it was housed. This ritual—known as the "mysterious ceremonies" of Holy Thursday and Friday—symbolically affirmed powers granted to lesser officials through the Patronato Real. The tabernacle, after all, was considered a sacred space that stored the most important object used in the Catholic mass—the bread priests transubstantiated into the body of Christ. In both a spiritual and literal sense, secular officials throughout the Spanish empire held the keys to spiritual salvation on at least two days of the religious calendar. For the monarchs, the mysterious ceremonies of Holy Thursday and Friday represented yet another example of their mastery over the Spanish church.[11]

The Franciscans in New Mexico refused to accept that Governor Anza held the powers of the Patronato Real even when, in 1781, Croix ordered

that statutes dealing with royal patronage be strictly observed in the Provincias Internas. The friars argued that these laws were not clear and that
Anza had exaggerated his powers as subpatron of the church. Moreover,
the padres demanded that until the issue of the Patronato Real was settled
in the colony, they should not be subjected to the authority of any secular
official. Specifically, they insisted that Anza not be allowed to claim powers
regarding the placement of priests and that this responsibility remain in the
hands of their custos. The friars also suggested that Anza be held accountable for his actions and that he make public his intentions regarding the
clerics and his use of the Patronato Real. They asked that the division of
powers between the governor and their custos be clarified and set, stating,
"It is unclear . . . who is the true head of the custody [of the Conversion of
Saint Paul]. As things stand, there are now two heads in the order, the governor and the custos."[12]

The weather notwithstanding, the month of March 1784 proved to be one
of the coldest and darkest moments for the Franciscans. On the 10th, Anza
announced that he had been granted full patronage over the church in New
Mexico.[13] That same day, he informed the padres that forced Indian servitude
for clerics had been abolished.[14] The new order of power struck at the very
core of Franciscan consciousness, especially when the priests considered that
the loss of Indian services diminished the labor force they needed to sustain
missions and deprived them of a cherished tradition they relied on to exercise
some control over the lives of indigenous Americans. As the winter season
faded into memory, the spring of 1784 saw the Custody of the Conversion of
Saint Paul almost completely subjected to the will of the state.

Indian Servitude Abolished

Prior to the abolition of servitude, Anza had tried to minimize clerical
demands on the Pueblos by outlining the amount of food the Indians were
expected to set aside to supplement the missions. In 1779, he instructed all
Pueblo communities to plant one field of corn to help feed the friars, and
ordered that this produce be stored in a room for which there should be
multiple keys—one entrusted to the resident padre, and another placed in
the hands of the local justice. Because the Pueblos made corn available on
a weekly basis to aid widows, orphans, and all those legitimately unable to

work, Anza insisted that supplying the missions should not be an added burden for the Indians.[15]

The friars did not take kindly to Anza's meddling in the longstanding labor arrangements they had negotiated with the Pueblos. Throughout the history of the colony, the Franciscans had claimed the right to extract tribute and labor from these Native Americans. Aside from the food they shared with the clerics, the Pueblos also provided the muscle required to construct missions. On a daily basis, they served padres as house servants, cooks, church custodians, wood gatherers, hunters, beekeepers, cloth makers, and aides during Mass and other services.

Anza made a first attempt to abolish Indian servitude for clerics in New Mexico in 1781. That year he declared that the friars could no longer justify their demands for native labor because a smallpox epidemic had decimated the Pueblo population.[16] The governor's position on this issue assumed an air of legality when he claimed to hold powers granted to him through the Patronato Real. The padres retorted that, as of 1781 the Patronato had not been formally extended to Anza and that, therefore, the governor did not have authority to deny them Indian services.[17]

The Franciscans could not make the same argument in 1784. Fully empowered with the Patronato Real, Anza abolished several forms of Indian servitude. These included any labor for the cultivation of land, domestic service as day laborers, the internal and external maintenance of missions, collection of firewood, guarding of livestock, fishing, baking, cooking, milling, spinning, chicken farming, and postal service, unless it served the interests of the crown.

Commandant General Felipe de Neve must have known the friars would challenge the abolishment of Indian servitude in New Mexico because he provided Anza a list of laws included in the Recopilación de Leyes that justified the governor's decree. Codified during the reign of the Catholic Monarchs, Fernando and Isabel, these statutes acknowledged abuses ecclesiastics had inflicted on Native Americans through the practice of servitude, and they had made such exploitation illegal. Neve ordered the governor to ensure the strict enforcement of these statues in New Mexico, keeping constant vigil so that these practices would not continue to the detriment of the Indians. Anza also received authority to deal with any cleric who violated the law.[18]

Felipe de Neve's death late in 1784 stirred the Franciscans yet again to challenge the abolition of Indian servitude.[19] This time around, however, they sent a representative to Arizpe to state their case directly to the newly appointed commandant general, José Antonio Rengel. Fray Santiago Fernández de Sierra asked Rengel to ensure that no mistake had been made regarding the abolition of service. Specifically, he inquired whether Anza's edict included denying clerics access to Indian land, which they needed for their survival, and whether it prohibited the use of sacristans for the ringing of church bells, which called the people to mass. The padre also wondered if the Pueblos would not be required to restore church buildings that had been partially or completely destroyed. He assured Rengel that the Franciscans would obey the edict, but he insisted that the abolition of Indian service for clerics would prove detrimental to the mission ideal in New Mexico. Missions on the western frontier of the colony, including those at Zuni, Ácoma, and Laguna, would suffer most because of the great distances that separated them from Spanish settlements where they procured their supplies.[20]

The Consolidation of Missions

The passive tone of Fernández de Sierra's petition spoke to the profound impact the friars had experienced from Anza's reformist rule, and for the moment the padres surrendered to the governor. Although the future of their spiritual mission seemed lost in the secularizing trend of the day, the clerics did not give up hope of regaining the ideal that originally brought them to the colony. A new light seemed to shine upon their order when Provincial Minister Juan Bravo asked Custos José de la Prada if the Franciscans in New Mexico had initiated the creation of new missions as ordered by the crown.[21]

Prada welcomed Bravo's inquiry but pondered the feasibility of extending New Mexico's mission system when Governor Anza had promoted the opposite. As early as November 1779, Anza suggested that church subsidies (*sínodos*) could be reduced if the colony's missions were consolidated under fewer *cabeceras* (head missions).[22] The governor's plan required that friars serving in settlements with large populations cater to sites with fewer people. Anza's suggestion was not new. Traditionally, cabeceras had provided ecclesiastic services and administration for neighboring villages without priests (*visitas*), with small populations and poor economies.[23]

Anza used the case of Pecos to justify the consolidation of missions. The pueblo had long served as a head mission site in New Mexico's easternmost frontier. A steady decline in Pecos's population, however, forced officials to reclassify it as a visita of Santa Fe.[24]

Anza believed that his consolidation plan of 1779 made economic sense and supported the king's demand for fiscal reform. The Franciscans, however, refused to accept that the Custody of the Conversion of Saint Paul had become a financial burden to the state. Instead, they accused Anza of trying to undermine the ideals of their order because of his contempt for all missionaries. It is likely that Anza harbored little respect for the padres, but he attacked them on economic grounds. Moreover, he argued that the poor quality of services and the degenerate character of clerics did not justify the subsidy paid to all friars who served in the colony. Anza described these subsidies a waste of royal funds.

The economy-minded Croix received Anza's consolidation plan with enthusiasm. Still, he delayed his decision regarding the missions until he received the opinion of his chief legal adviser, Pedro Galindo Navarro. In the meantime, a smallpox epidemic struck New Mexico and ultimately decided the issue of mission consolidations in favor of Governor Anza.

Scholars are uncertain of the origins of the smallpox virus that plagued New Mexico in the spring of 1780. Historian Marc Simmons offers two possibilities. He suggests the virus may have entered the colony from the south, via the Camino Real, after an epidemic hit central New Spain in 1779. Simmons allows, however, that the virus may have originated in the Mississippi Valley. An outbreak struck at the Indians of this region in 1778 and then spread to the upper Missouri, Louisiana, and Texas. In Texas, Lipan Apaches may have transmitted the virus to Comanche bands that, in turn, carried it west to New Mexico.[25]

The smallpox epidemic of 1780–81 ravaged New Mexico's citizenry. It is estimated that more than five thousand people died from the disease, and that this number represented one fourth, or more, of the colony's total population.[26] Among the Spaniards, settlements with the largest populations, such as Albuquerque, were hardest hit. But it was in the Indian pueblos that the virus took its greatest toll.[27]

Anza used the tragic loss of life to call for the reduction of missions in New Mexico, from thirty to twenty sites. As he had done in 1779, Croix delayed any decision on this issue until he received Galindo Navarro's legal analysis in August 1781. The assessor general judged that Anza was the person best qualified to determine the mission situation in New Mexico and agreed that the unfortunate effects of the smallpox epidemic justified the consolidation of missions.[28] Croix thus approved Anza's plan and ordered its fulfillment on 15 September 1781.[29]

The Franciscans knew they could not prevent Anza's mission-consolidation plan, but this did not stop them from stoking the fires of discontent with his superiors. The padres cried out that some of Anza's recommendations might put Franciscan lives in danger. The downgrading of San Ildefonso Mission to a visita of Santa Clara, they insisted, would be especially problematic. This merger required that padres travel long distances—from San Ildefonso to La Cuchilla—in order to minister to the religious needs of their flock. La Cuchilla's location near the confluence of the Chama and Ojo Caliente rivers compounded the risks associated with having to traverse such rugged terrain, especially during the frigid winter months. The friars also expressed great concern over having to chance dangerous rivers during flood season. They accused Anza of not caring whether the padres drowned so long as mission reduction was achieved.[30]

Croix upheld Anza's decision to downgrade San Ildefonso Mission. In 1782, he also permitted the consolidation of Nambe and Tesuque under a single friar at Pojoaque, as well as the transfer of religious duties for Jemez Mission to the minister at Zia and those of Pecos to the friars at Santa Fe.[31] Croix, however, used the San Ildefonso-Santa Clara case to question Anza's reasons for not uniting Santo Domingo and Cochití. Such a combination seemed justified because Santo Domingo and Cochití were closer in distance than Santa Clara and San Ildefonso, and could therefore be better served by one priest.[32] Although Croix's reasoning on this matter reflected Anza's, the reduction of Cochití under Santo Domingo did not occur until 1788. In the meantime, Santa Ana was made a visita of Zia, San Lorenzo was placed under El Paso, and Ácoma was placed under Laguna.[33]

The Spanish crown considered the consolidation of missions under Anza a success, but mostly it welcomed the annual savings of 3,695 pesos that the plan made possible. The governor's efforts in this regard, however, did not last. By 1788, the reform-minded King Carlos III was dead and his successor, Carlos IV, preferred hunting and collecting clocks to the affairs of state. Spain's new monarch fulfilled the outward appearance of his royal station but granted others—his ambitious but scandalous wife, María Luisa de Parma, and her lover, Manuel de Godoy—extensive powers to rule in his name. Unable, or unwilling, to muster the strength of character and mind of his predecessor, Carlos IV assumed his throne with the misperception that all was right in his empire. Historian John Lynch has described Spain's apparent condition as follows:

> The Spain inherited by Carlos IV gave few intimations of instability. Spanish imperial power had never been greater. American trade was free and protected, revenues were high, defences secure. In the peninsula agricultural exports from Andalucía, Catalonia, and even Castile were earning profits for producers and income for Spain. Public works, the construction of industry, textile factories, these and other enterprises were material signs of progress and prosperity.[34]

Underneath this veneer of stability, however, Spain entered into a period of economic decline and social unrest in the 1790s. Out of touch with these problems, Carlos IV allowed a relaxation of the Bourbon ideal of absolutism—a political move perhaps best illustrated by the king's decision in 1790 to allow many Jesuits who had been exiled from the empire in 1767 to return to their home regions. The king's hands-off approach to monarchy found expression in New Mexico. In 1790, a new "band of missionaries" under the sway of Custos Pedro de Laborería forced Anza's successor, Fernando de la Concha, to transform four visitas back to their original status of missions. Laborería also convinced Concha to increase the friars' subsidies.[35]

Clerical Assignments

Beyond his efforts at mission consolidation, Anza also exercised his powers as subpatron of the church to determine clerical assignments in New Mexico. When the governor assumed office in 1778, the friars believed he would respect their right to conduct the placement of priests as prescribed by the *alternativa*—rotating assignments between European- and American-born friars. The Franciscans placed so much faith in Anza that at one point the governor congratulated fray Caetano José Ignacio Bernal for recognizing and supporting his authority to make independent judgments as to affairs of the church.[36]

Franciscan optimism regarding Anza began to fade as the 1780s dawned. In the friars' eyes, the governor's aggressive manipulation of the assignment process interfered with the alternativa tradition. Anza, however, considered the placement of priests a responsibility in keeping with the Bourbon plan to increase the power of the state over the church. This policy was perhaps best manifested by the appointment of Juan Bermejo to the post of *capellán* (presidal chaplain).[37] Although he was one of the peninsular friars who had followed Anza to New Mexico in 1778, Bermejo found favor with the governor because of his willingness to support the subjugation of his order to the state.[38] Anza believed he had found an ally in Bermejo and wasted no time in having the friar appointed to the chaplaincy at Santa Fe.

Anza also played an indirect role in Bermejo's assignment to the post of custos in 1781. The governor had originally intended to leave the selection of a new prelate in the hands of the retiring custos, Juan José Hinojosa. Anza intervened in the alternativa process when Hinojosa announced that José de la Prada would succeed him. Anza feared that he would be unable to mold Prada to his liking because of Prada's authoritarian character. Therefore, Anza insisted that Hinojosa choose another padre as his successor.

Much to Anza's delight, Hinojosa chose Juan Bermejo to replace him as custos. The appointment caused a great stir within the Custody of the Conversion of Saint Paul because the peninsular friars had not championed Bermejo's candidacy for the job. The peninsulars favored Prada, and they moved quickly to have Bermejo removed from office.[39] Bermejo did not serve long at this post, and Prada eventually replaced him in 1782. During his brief tenure, however, Bermejo supported Anza's efforts to subjugate the Franciscans to the state. Time and again, Bermejo failed to question or challenge Anza's mission assignments. More important, he actively subverted the peninsulars' efforts to communicate charges of abuse and corruption by Anza to his superiors. The clerics denounced Bermejo for his alleged conspiracy against them.[40]

Anza's involvement in the assignment of missionaries became a point of contention when Prada assumed the office of custos in 1782. Within months, Prada formally accused the governor of meddling in the process, and yet he mustered enough gumption to request that Anza allow him to make specific appointments. Prada suggested the following assignments: Taos and Picuries to Francisco Martín Bueno; San Juan and Santa Cruz de la Cañada to Ramón Antonio González; Santa Clara and Abiquiú to Francisco de Ozio; San Ildefonso to Lorenzo José de Burgos; Santa Fe and Pecos to José Carral; Santa Ana, Zia, and Jemez to José Vilchez; and La Laguna and Ácoma to Ambrosio Guerra. Prada also asked that San Felipe Mission be reduced to visita status under Santo Domingo, and that the remaining missions be left to their present clerics.[41]

With the exception of Father Burgos, all the nominees mentioned in Prada's petition were included in the peninsular group that accompanied Anza to New Mexico in 1778. It is evident that Prada tried to maneuver key mission assignments in favor of European-born friars. In so doing, he hoped to solidify peninsular control of the Custody of the Conversion of Saint Paul, and perhaps to challenge the state for power. Anza did not care which friars were placed at what missions so long as the padres acknowledged that, as governor, he had final say in the matter. Anza granted Prada his requested assignments in March 1783, but made it a point to note that the decision was his. He also reminded Prada that custom dictated that the custos publicly concede the governor's decision and, upon request, that he do so in writing.[42]

In August 1783, Governor Anza received official patronage power over the church in New Mexico. With the Patronato Real in hand, the question of his right to determine mission assignments ceased to be an issue. Almost overnight, the friars altered their aggressive and demanding posture regarding this matter to an attitude of reluctant submission. The clerics continued to voice concern and criticism of the governor, but they now focused their attacks on matters of relocations, justice, and responsibilities. In one case, Custos Prada wrote to Anza to inquire why he had ordered the relocation of Gabriel de Lago from his assignment at Sandía to the missions of Zuni. Anza replied that the Pueblo governor of Sandía had accused Lago of several undefined infamies. The custos made an unsuccessful attempt to have Anza reverse his order, and Lago remained at the far western region of the colony.[43]

Anza and Prada did not always battle over mission assignments. In April 1784, for example, they agreed on the placement of the ill and aging José Mariano Medrano. Medrano had been stationed at Santo Domingo when Anza transferred Cochití and San Felipe to his jurisdiction. Medrano considered the added responsibility of ministering to an additional two visitas a major burden. He requested that Anza allow him to finish his service in New Mexico strictly at Santo Domingo.[44]

Custos Prada approved of Medrano's petition, but frowned when he learned that Medrano had traveled to Santa Fe to discuss his request with the governor. In so doing, Medrano violated an edict that required citizens to acquire permits to travel within or out of the colony. When Anza discovered the violation, he rejected Medrano's original request and had him relocated to Zuni Pueblo. Shocked at what he considered to be an "acute judgment," Prada asked Anza to reconsider. Prada admitted that Medrano had erred, thus acknowledging Anza's right to punish the friar. The custos, however, reminded Anza that Medrano was close to retirement and would be leaving New Mexico soon. He added that the hardships of travel to Zuni might have negative effects on the friar's already weak health, and that Medrano deserved to finish his stay at Santo Domingo due to his meritorious service record. Prada's emotional plea moved Anza to let the aged padre stay at Santo Domingo.[45]

Having settled the Medrano case, Anza and Prada came to terms on the relocation of other friars in 1784. Custos Prada took over the mission at Pojoaque and Burgos went to Santa Fe. José Carral went to Pecos. Father Vilchez acquired the head mission of Zia and its two visitas of Santa Ana and Jemez. Ambrosio Guerra was assigned to Zuni, but he requested he be relieved of his duties and allowed to travel back to Mexico City in the next conducta (caravan) due to ill health.[46]

Fiscal Reforms: The *Sínodo*

Father Medrano's assignment request is interesting in that it involved the stipend he received for his priestly work. Custos Prada worried that Santo Domingo would lose its state subsidy once Medrano retired. Prada's concerns were not unfounded. He recognized that the governor, like his predecessors, could not escape the issue of funding the clerics while at the same time satisfying Bourbon demands for economic reform. Anza had targeted the subsidy paid to missionaries in his effort to reduce royal expenditures in the colony. The friars questioned this fiscal strategy, arguing that it amounted to a manipulation of church funds and salaries that served the state to the detriment of their order. In the Medrano case, both the friar and the custos demanded that the subsidy for Santo Domingo be preserved even though the cleric's ability to fulfill his charge had been curtailed by his poor health. Whether out of compassion or simply as an effort to appease the troublesome friars, Anza agreed to oblige Medrano's request for his stipend.

The debate over ecclesiastical finances in eighteenth-century Spain, historian Lynch has written, centered on the Bourbon desire to "restore the Spanish monarchy to greatness. The key to power [however] was revenue, and unless the king of Spain could maintain his court, pay his officials, arm his troops, and replace his ships, then administrative reform was mere adornment. Absolutism depended upon resources."[47] For the Bourbons, the quest for greatness went beyond the vast expanse of their territorial empire. Size did matter to these Hispanicized French relatives of Louis XIV, but so too did courtly extravagance. For them, monarchical expressions of power were as much visual affairs as skill in political maneuvering and military might. In short, the Bourbons believed they must "appear" to be wealthy as a monarchy even at times when Iberians took to the streets to protest the people's impoverished state. The monarchy demanded a reduction in state expenditures in order to increase royal revenue. Bourbon economic reform meant royal attacks on the church's wealth and state control of its finances.

The Spanish American church did not escape attacks on its finances by the state. In New Mexico, however, the friars had always depended on royal subsidies to cover the costs of their personal day-to-day needs and the functioning of missions. Moreover, they supplemented their annual pay with revenue collected for administering the sacraments as well as the *diezmo* (tithe), obligations such as *primicias* (first fruits), and goods and services extracted from the Indians. Clerics also supported colleagues assigned to poor parishes, such as Zuni, with *limosnas* (alms) that they donated in the form of goods.

Under Anza, cutbacks in mission subsidies expanded the breach that had characterized church-state relations in New Mexico for generations. Anza openly supported attacks on church funding because he believed the clerics had not lived up to their mission ideal. The governor's "meddling" in ecclesiastical finances, however, was not completely of his own initiative. Commandant General Croix, too, had moved to gain greater control of church finances in the Provincias Internas. In September 1778, he informed the friars that the administration of annual stipends for clerics in New Mexico would be transferred from Mexico City to the treasury of Chihuahua. Croix added that the subsidies would be paid out only after a custodial *síndico* (official) submitted a report in which the friars requesting funding were identified along with their respective mission assignments. Moreover, the governor of New Mexico had to approve the síndico's report.[48]

Anza did not promote a complete abolishment of the stipends, and upon assuming office at Santa Fe in 1778 he supported full payment of ecclesiastical subsidies. That same year, the peninsular friars questioned deductions made to their stipends to cover expenses incurred by fellow priests who had vacated their posts due to death or relocation to other mission sites. The peninsulars argued that this practice was unfair to them since they had not built up the debts of the friars they were replacing. They demanded their full subsidy of 330 pesos without any deductions and concluded, "this solution seems to us to be for the best if we are to live in peace."[49]

Having persuaded Anza to assure that subsidies would be paid in full, the European friars turned their attention to problems in the payment process. A royal order issued in 1773 required that clerics receive their stipends in the field. The padres charged that this edict had not been fulfilled in New Mexico and that their subsidies were first being directed to their provincial head in Mexico City. Here, church officials docked the friars for expenses that the crown had agreed to cover, including travel costs the peninsulars had incurred when they first came to the colony in 1778. Subsidies were "liberated" and transferred to New Mexico only after these deductions were made. Because of this, the friars complained that they had received partial subsidies, and that these always proved inadequate for their annual needs. A short supply of monetary resources, the padres argued, had forced them to demand greater amounts of food, goods, and services from the Pueblo people.

Franciscan concerns over the payout of mission wages forced Croix to enforce the decree of 1773. The commandant general also declared that the trustee responsible for the distribution of subsidies would be held liable, under penalty of law, for fulfilling his charge. In New Mexico, the paymaster of the Santa Fe presidio assumed responsibility for collecting subsidies in Chihuahua and delivering them to the Franciscans.[50]

Although the transfer of subsidy control to the treasury at Chihuahua was well intentioned, the distribution of these funds continued to be a problem. In 1782, the European friars again complained that they were not receiving their stipends in full. Now, however, they accused Anza and Custos Juan Bermejo of manipulating their subsidies. Croix insisted that Bermejo obey the decree of 1773 and reminded Bermejo that stipends granted to ecclesiastics were intended for the sustenance of the individual cleric, and not for the benefit of the Custody of the Conversion of Saint Paul as a whole. Croix streamlined the payout process by having the friars authorize one of their own to collect the stipends in Chihuahua, transfer them to New Mexico, and distribute funds directly to each padre. Moreover, Croix forbade any form of interference in the election of this proctor by the Franciscan provincial in Mexico City or the custos in New Mexico. He added, however, that the friars must grant this individual power of attorney to collect and distribute subsidies in writing.[51]

The internal strife that characterized the Custody of the Conversion of Saint Paul throughout Anza's tenure also hampered the management of church funds in New Mexico. In 1784, the American-born friar Tomás Salvador de Santa Teresa Fernández complained to Commandant General José Antonio Rengel that his peninsular brethren had denied him the alms he was entitled to as supplemental income for his work at Zuni pueblo. As spokesman for the peninsulars, Santiago Fernández de Sierra accused the other Fernández of lying. Thirteen friars from throughout New Mexico's missions, Fernández de Sierra claimed, had donated 260 pesos to Zuni in 1784. The peninsulars insisted that these gifts were coming out of their own subsidies and that Fernández was receiving ninety-five pesos more per year than any other cleric.[52]

The degree to which Anza may have misappropriated ecclesiastical funds, and how, are not clear. This, however, did not prevent the friars from pressing this very issue with the governor's superiors. In 1784, for example, Fernández de Sierra accused Anza of reducing the total allowance for New Mexico by deducting subsidies for missions left vacant by clerics who had been relocated or had died. He charged that by so doing, Anza had violated laws guaranteeing that subsidies designated for such missions would be used to help maintain church buildings and their ornaments. Fernández de Sierra claimed New Mexico was in great need of funds because of the general deterioration of its missions, and he requested that statutes pertaining to this matter be upheld. Moreover, he demanded that Anza ensure the appointment of friars to available missions so that they could collect the stipends assigned to these sites.[53]

Anza's manipulation of church funds did not go undetected. In 1785, fray Sebastián Antón informed Rengel that Anza had approved Alcalde Mayor José Campo Redondo's decision to dock his stipend for a total of forty-four days. Campo Redondo had accused the friar of being absent from his mission at Picurís without just cause and therefore being derelict in his duties;

this, he felt, justified the deductions in Antón's pay. Antón claimed he had been away from his mission from 20 October to 14 November 1784, but only to perform baptisms, funerals, and confessions throughout the jurisdiction of his mission. The friar demanded justice, and the commandant general accommodated him. Rengel ordered Anza to reimburse the value of the subsidy that Antón had been docked and to "recognize" the error he had committed so that such an offense would not occur in the future. Rengel's decision in this matter amounted to an official reprimand of the governor. For Anza, the reproach represented perhaps the first and only time he had been humiliated in the eyes of the friars and the general populace of New Mexico.[54]

Fiscal Reforms: Tithes

Anza's embarrassment at Rengel's hands did not signal a change in the crown's plan to gain greater control of church finances. The friars had already lost their claim to Indian tribute and experienced state interference in the distribution of their subsidies. If this was not enough, the crown decided to attack yet another source of income the clerics depended on, the diezmo. This tithe consisted of a donation all citizens were expected to make in support of the church, theoretically one-tenth of their annual income.

Crafty New Mexicans always found ways to minimize their tithe obligations, usually by reporting less income or undervaluing their assets. Wool producers, for example, reported fewer fleeces than the actual number of sheep in their flock. Likewise, they failed to report the number of fleeces that they gave to others as payment for shearing their animals, or the sheep they killed to eat. The Hispanos made no excuses for condoning such questionable accounting practices, especially when they considered that the tithe represented a donation to padres who held the power to block their usurping of much-coveted Pueblo lands.

Former Custos Bermejo, who was now serving as vicar for the Bishopric of Durango, disagreed. Bermejo believed tithes were obligations to God. He complained that the corruption of New Mexico's sheep farmers deprived the friars of a "true" tenth of wool revenues generated in the colony. Moreover, he believed that the wool producers, not the consumers, should donate diezmos for livestock, and that the value of this tithe should be set at one animal for every ten in the possession of the rancher.[55]

Farmers, too, were expected to support the church with tithes. Known as the *primicia*, this obligation represented a portion of food collected from the first harvest of the year. Like the wool producers, Hispano farmers misrepresented their production levels, usually by failing to report the amount of food they cultivated for personal consumption. As such, farmers normally paid primicias only on the produce they sold. Bermejo insisted that farmers should donate one *media* (half of one hundred) for every six media of food produced—about one-sixth of their crops, or about 50 pounds for every 300 pounds of food—and he held that this quota should hold true even if the farmer cultivated only half his total arable land. If a farmer could not meet the quota, then he should combine his harvest with that of others in the area until together they completed the person's obligation. Bermejo also argued that the primicia should involve not just foodstuffs but also other goods cultivated from the land, such as cotton, and products produced by animals that lived off the land. He included in the last category milk and cheese from cows and goats, and eggs from chickens.[56]

The crown refused to grant New Mexico's friars all that Bermejo had asked regarding the diezmo and primicias. In 1785, however, Carlos III agreed that tithes collected in parishes where priests were absent due to death or retirement would be preserved and used for the benefit of interim clerics that filled these vacated posts. The king asked that these tithes be deposited in royal treasuries from the time a cleric vacated his post until his replacement arrived; it was hoped that this would prevent the monies from falling into the hands of greedy officials.[57] Governor Anza received word of the king's decree from Commandant General Jacobo Ugarte y Loyola in July 1786.[58] This same year, however, the clergy lost control of collecting diezmos when the crown implemented the Ordinance of Intendants in 1786. As a reform measure, the Ordinance reconfigured New Spain into twelve new districts that were presided over by an intendant. These officials were selected by the king and held the power to administer justice, government, finance, and war within their jurisdiction. In the realm of finance, the intendants assumed responsibility for collecting state revenues such as the diezmo.[59]

Confronted by shifting priorities regarding the colony's role within the greater Spanish Empire, the padres found themselves seeking new sources of revenue, as well as audiences to preach to. Having lost access to Indian labor, the Franciscans turned to New Mexico's Spanish population for income and as the primary recipients of their priestly ministrations.[60] Moreover, they continued to push for the expansion of the mission frontier. After the Comanche Peace of 1786, the friars once more focused their evangelical efforts on those natives whom they had thus far been unable to lure to Christianity, including the Hopis, Navajos, and Apaches.[61]

The Franciscans also redoubled their efforts to achieve the complete conversion of the Pueblo Indians. Toward this end, the clerics sought the help of secular officials. Ross Frank has argued that after 1790, the friars urged the state to initiate a campaign that would help them complete aspects of the mission ideal they had failed to achieve. Their demands were not new; they included the suppression of religious practices such as the use of kivas and measures to force the Pueblos to speak Spanish.[62] In an ironic ideological twist, the padres also began to support Hispano encroachment onto Pueblo communal lands. The Franciscans had once argued that the usurpation of these lands was the surest way for Europeans to abuse and exploit Indians.[63] This, however, mattered little to a missionary institution that feared for its very existence in New Mexico. The friars concluded that if their income was now partially dependent on fees colonists paid for sacramental services, then they had to support an economy that ensured greater access to resources for the Hispanic portion of the colony's population.

After Anza left the governorship, the Franciscans made repeated efforts to recoup their loss of funds and personnel. Faced with a state that seemed more concerned with matters of defense, and less interested in their needs, the friars ultimately saw their numbers decline in New Mexico. As such, they found it difficult to oppose renewed efforts to bring their order completely under the jurisdiction of the Bishopric of Durango and a growing demand for the secularization of their missions.

CHAPTER TWELVE

Church Reform and Social Order

CHURCH REFORMS DURING ANZA'S TENURE did not focus solely on clerical appointments and finances, but spoke also to a growing problem of social disorder that had erupted in Spain and was triggered by war costs, inflation, poor harvests, and a significant increase in food prices. Citizens took to the streets of Madrid in 1765, and in December they accosted the queen mother as her coach made its way to the royal palace. The Madrileños begged her to carry news of their plight to her son and ask him to end their suffering. Carlos III refused to be swayed by his starving subjects. He, after all, was the king, and his political will was beyond contest. Instead, the king blamed the crisis on his advisers. He demanded that they fix Spain's ailments and leave him to his favorite pastime of hunting.

Carlos III's response to the social upheavals in Madrid proved disastrous. On 23 March 1766, citizens again swarmed the streets in protest. On the 24th, thirty thousand Madrileños joined in looting and destruction of property that vented their outrage. The demonstrations culminated in a face-off between the rioters and guards at the royal palace. The carnage that followed horrified even the most stalwart of citizens. Both sides suffered casualties, but the guardsmen endured the most violent acts. The mutilated bodies of ten sentries killed during the assault were dragged through the streets, and two were burned as the public cheered on. Mobs roamed the capital for two more days, threatening to continue their assaults on property and troops. At last the king capitulated, and on the 26th of March Carlos III reconciled himself with his subjects by agreeing to address their grievances.[1] In the aftermath of the violence, people from throughout Europe and the Americas contemplated the significance of what had happened in Spain:

"It was a time to remember," historian John Lynch has written. "For four days Madrid was without government, law and order were non-existent, the people ruled, while the Spanish Bourbons, the ultimate in absolutism, looked on bewildered. Spain had experienced the unthinkable. Europe could not believe what it heard."[2]

The Madrid Bread Riots of 1766 shook the royal family to its core. After the uprising, Carlos III ordered an investigation and was conveniently informed that the Jesuits had rallied the insurgents. Public demonstrations soon spread throughout the whole of Spain, but it was the possibility that the Jesuits were plotting to have the king assassinated that ultimately led to their expulsion from the empire.

The Jesuit Expulsion of 1767 did not result in the public order King Carlos III had hoped for. Instead, it fueled public demonstrations in his Spanish American colonies. In New Spain, for example, citizens at San Luis Potosí, Guanajuato, Michoacán, and Colima rioted in protest of the expulsion.[3] Baffled by the support his subjects expressed for the clerics, Carlos III realized that the draconian methods he had thus employed to silence the priests would have to be replaced by more subtle strategies that promoted him as a sovereign acting within the letter of the law. He concluded that such a lofty task could only be achieved by curtailing the spiritual influence the clergy wielded over the faithful.

Knowing that he could not completely subvert the sacred bond shared between a priest and his flock, the king decided instead to use the powers granted to him by the Patronato Real to undermine the clergy's authority to define and administer the sacraments. The strategy bordered on genius because although some of the sacraments existed to help people achieve salvation in heaven, they were also associated with secular and legal issues that affected a person's life from birth to death. The sacrament of baptism, for example, inducted people into the Christian fold and absolved them of sins, but indirectly it also defined their patrimony. A person's birthright determined not only his or her family name but also social standing and the right of inheritance. Such matters fell within the jurisdiction of the king's sovereignty because they dealt with social and legal issues that were rooted in the secular world and affected the lives of people in the here and now rather than in the afterlife. Royal patronage thus allowed the king a great deal of power to determine how clergymen used the sacraments; if such usage challenged or violated secular laws, then the state could claim the right to countermand priestly acts and to reprimand troublesome clerics. As such, King Carlos III recognized that the power he longed to wield over the Spanish clergy was inherent in the Patronato Real, and that it essentially allowed him to use the church as a mechanism for social control.

The social order the king demanded after the Madrid Bread Riots of 1766 now seemed within his grasp. To this end, Carlos III looked to see which of the sacraments he could use to his advantage over the clergy. Of these sacred rites, marriage seemed the most promising because it entailed questions of parental authority to determine socially acceptable partners as well as the lawful patrimony of familial estates.

Marriage and Social Order

Spain's juridical tradition obligated the state to intervene in marriage cases where parents and children quarreled over the qualities of potential suitors, as well as in issues of patrimony. In such cases, the state's actions rested upon its responsibility to foster social order throughout the empire.[4] The intersection of matrimony and symbolic patrimony, however, contrasted with marriage ideals promoted by the church. Ecclesiastical officials had long supported traditions by which parents helped children select suitable partners; they did not agree, however, that people should chose mates to fulfill the economic and/or social designs of their elders. Instead, the clergy argued that individuals should marry for love. The church based this view on the idea that love represented an expression of free will, a power that it considered necessary for individuals to choose good over evil and that was required for salvation of the soul. Clerics proclaimed marriage to be a sacrament that only they could validate through ritual ceremony. Moreover, they marketed the notion that no one could enter the kingdom of heaven without first receiving the sacraments priests monopolized. The church thus concluded that marriages that had resulted from coercion were not only invalid but might be considered sinful. In the 1500s, the clergy cemented its stance on marriage by incorporating it into canon law during the Council of Trent.[5]

Carlos III had questioned the Tridentine codes on marriage that emerged from the Council of Trent because he feared that clerics could use matrimony to promote social unrest by turning children against parents over the issue of choice. The king believed the family served as the social backbone of the empire and that any challenges to parental authority endangered its role as an instrument of socialization and moral guidance. Ultimately, however, Carlos III feared that priest-inspired insubordination within the family might further sway citizens to question his sovereignty as the "father" of all Spaniards, and possibly lead them toward civic disobedience. Such priests represented a paramount threat to his supreme authority and to the absolutist state he represented. Carlos III therefore rejected the Tridentine ideal that individuals should enter into the sacrament of marriage by consent rather than force. He scorned the premise that people should marry for love. Love, after all, represents the personal desires of individuals and a manifestation of their free will, both of which, the king felt, must be sacrificed for the good of the state.

The Royal Pragmatic on Marriage

To enhance his legal position over the clergy, Carlos III promulgated legislation that turned his reformist eye to the institution of marriage. In 1776, the king issued the Royal Pragmatic on Marriages in Spain, and two years later a modified version of this decree found its way to his American colonies. With these marriage laws, the king intended to prevent individuals from marrying outside of their class. Carlos III had expressed great concern regarding unions between social unequals—a practice he believed had become more common in Spain and his overseas domains. The king insisted that such marriages stained the reputation and well-being of families because they disregarded the honor and respect that children owed their parents. With the Pragmatic laws, Carlos III thus demanded that persons under the age of twenty-five obtain permission to marry from their parents; failure to do so could result in the invalidation of a union and even disinheritance. The decrees stated that children over twenty-five could marry without such sanction, but they risked being divested of familial estates if they defied the wishes of their parents.

The marriage laws also cast a disapproving eye toward clerics who encouraged young folk to marry for love and not solely to satisfy the social designs of their parents. As such, the Pragmatic laws suggested that clerical interference in the marriage process was detrimental to the moral fabric of Spanish society and threatened the social order that sustained the empire. In contrast, by reinforcing the rights of parents—namely, those of fathers—

to choose marriage partners for their children, the decrees were aimed at strengthening and perpetuating the patriarchy upon which the empire was built. The laws also minimized priest participation in determining those qualities that defined suitable marriage partners. And finally, the decrees attempted to reduce the church's role in the marriage process to nothing more than a mechanism by which the sacrament was administered and celebrated through ceremony.[6]

Officials implemented the Pragmatic on Marriages in New Mexico on 18 November 1783, at which time Interim Commandant General Felipe de Neve ordered Anza to enforce the laws in the colony.[7] Anza complied, and by 21 April 1784, citizens of New Mexico had been made fully aware of the Pragmatic because the governor ordered it published *a voz de bando* (with the force of a decree) in all settlements of the colony.[8]

New Mexicans did not need to have King Carlos III preach to them about the purpose of matrimony. In truth, the king's views on the institution of marriage had long been the norm in their remote colony. In his book, *When Jesus Came the Corn Mothers Went Away: Marriage, Sexuality, and Power in New Mexico, 1500–1846,* Ramón A. Gutiérrez wrote that the institution of marriage

> was the most important ritual event in the course of life, and it was an occasion when it was necessary for the honor of the family to take precedence over all other considerations. The union of two properties, the joining of two households, the creation of a web of affinal alliances, and the perpetuation of a family's symbolic patrimony—its name and reputation—were of such importance to the honor-status of the group that marriage was hardly a decision to be made by minors. The norm in New Mexico was for parents to arrange nuptials for their children with little or no consideration for their wishes. Filial piety required the acceptance of any union that parents deemed appropriate or advantageous.[9]

According to Gutiérrez, love played little or no role in the matrimonial process. If anything, love was considered "a subversive sentiment, antithetical to the status concerns of a family and to authority relations within the home." Instead, Hispanos were expected to marry within their class. Gutiérrez suggests that this ideal of *igualdad de calidad* (equality in social status) was of special importance to New Mexico's nobles. For members of this group, social status and honor could be enhanced, or tarnished, according to whom one married. Moreover, marriage ensured that familial estates and patrimony would be preserved from one generation to the next.

Parents arranged marriages for their children to assure the perpetuation of their patrimonies, of their honor, and of their good family names. Although strict supervision of adolescent behavior was employed to achieve this aim, particularly among the nobility, and particularly with their women, enough occasions existed in the routine life of the community when normative constraints were weakened. At festivals, dances, and rites of passage, the rigid hierarchies of age, sex, and class were temporarily suspended, and it was then that expressions of love blossomed.[10]

As Gutiérrez has aptly shown, New Mexicans interested in matrimony, especially young ones, also tried to circumvent the wishes of their parents. Here, too, officials believed that priests might be inspiring Hispanos to challenge traditional New Mexican views on marriage. If such was the case, the Franciscans were contributing to the deterioration of acceptable social mores needed for order to prevail in the empire. As he had with the Jesuits, the king decided that clerics, including New Mexico's friars, needed to be reined in and reminded of their place in Spanish society.

Try as he might, King Carlos III could not completely prevent the Franciscans from determining who married whom in New Mexico. Even he conceded that marriage was a sacrament that required compliance with "marital impediments" such as incest, bigamy, and consanguinity—impediments outlined in canons of the Council of Trent—and the friars determined whether such conditions existed in the colony. Through a prenuptial investigatory process known as a *diligencia matrimonial,* the clerics ascertained whether prospective brides and grooms had engaged in any form of unacceptable behavior or if they did not qualify for marriage because of consanguinity. If such was the case, the padres could refuse to marry the supplicants. The Franciscans, however, rarely denied the sacrament of marriage to the New Mexico populace, even in those instances when conduct and/or blood ties proved an issue. In such cases, the friars requested that couples seek a dispensation to marry from diocesan authorities. In contrast, the padres were known to dissolve unions if an impediment was discovered after a marriage had been performed.

In May 1781, fray Sebastián Fernández from Abiquiú informed Vice Custos José de la Prada about such a case.[11] Both Jacinta Trujillo and Antonio

Choño were widowed when they decided to marry. She was an Indian *moza* (maidservant), and Fernández described the groom's relationship with his first wife as "happy." One week after exchanging vows, Jacinta discovered that Antonio could not consummate their union because he was missing his *miembro viril* (penis). She asked to have her marriage dissolved and used the marital impediment of "impotency" to support her request. Father Fernández conducted an investigation, and witnesses supported Jacinta's claim. Not willing to accept blindly the word of possible gossips, Fernández interviewed Antonio himself. Although he did not offer a medical explanation for his condition, Antonio confessed that in previous years his virile member had indeed fallen off in pieces, and he could therefore not consummate his union with Jacinta.

Father Fernández had no choice but to nullify the marriage. According to law, it did not matter that Antonio had treated Jacinta with kindness, sincerity, and the desire to share the rest of his life with her. Jacinta had had other plans. She had agreed to marry Antonio because she wanted to have a baby. Because Antonio could not fulfill his "marital obligation," she opted to find someone who could. Jacinta did identify an individual willing to marry her soon after the annulment, and this man approached Father Fernández to inquire about such a possibility. Fernández saw no reason to prevent this marriage, and claimed that Jacinta and her new partner would be sexually active even if they were not married. The friar deemed such an outcome unacceptable because Jacinta's soul would be damned to hell. Vice Custos Prada agreed to support Fernández's decision.[12]

New Mexico's friars did not oppose marital unions on the basis of canonical impediments alone. On occasion, they refused to recognize specific marriages if a rival cleric had performed them, or if the union involved a question of parish or mission jurisdiction. In 1782, Juan José Llanos challenged a marriage that the peninsular priest of San Juan de los Caballeros, Santiago Fernández de Sierra, had performed in his mission in July 1781. Llanos declared that the union between Diego Antonio Martín and María Guadalupe Armijo was illegal because the bride was a member of his parish at Santa Fe and not Fernández's parish. Llanos asked Governor Anza to order an investigation of this matter, and Anza agreed to do so.

Having been informed that a diligencia was ordered, Fernández went on the offensive. He argued that the Council of the Indies had declared that a priest could conduct marriages if one of the supplicants was a member of his parish. Fernández stated the groom was of his flock, and therefore the marriage was valid. He also proclaimed that Llanos's concerns over this particular marriage had nothing to do with issues of parochial jurisdiction. Instead, Fernández accused Llanos of being more interested in the fees charged for the marriage than its validity. Llanos, it turns out, was known by most of the people in the colony to be greedy when it came to issues of money.

Fernández might have gained Anza's support if his complaint had focused solely on Llanos's avarice. Fernández, however, accused Anza of conspiring against him because he was a peninsular. He charged Anza with meddling in church matters that were outside the scope of the Patronato Real, and he reminded Anza that only ecclesiastics could validate the sacrament of marriage. In an indirect manner, Fernández hinted that the office of the Inquisition might be interested in Anza. The governor's interference in the Armijo-Martín case, he argued, smacked of Protestantism because in that sect marriages were conducted by approval and in the presence of secular magistrates. This suggestion, if proven, would have resulted in serious consequences for Anza. The Inquisition, after all, had made it clear that charges of Protestantism were among the main issues it would investigate.

Anza replied to Fernández's remarks with "thousands of contemptuous reproaches." He charged the cleric with being a false accuser and ordered him to appear before the *Tribunal de la Tierra* (local court). In a fit of rage, Anza said he would be willing to try Fernández in the *Rectísimo Tribunal de Dios* (the most righteous tribunal of God). In an incredible display of self-assurance, the cleric challenged Anza to show his hand. He stated he would present and defend himself in any tribunal of the governor's choosing.

Anza eventually accepted the validity of Fernández's claim regarding the limitation of his powers under the Patronato Real. However, the matter went unresolved until the case was brought before Commandant General Croix. Not wanting to embarrass Anza, or disrupt the governor's efforts to enhance the defensive posture of New Mexico, Croix chose to let the matter cool down. In the end, Anza's attempt to interfere in the sacrament of marriage was unofficially sanctioned by the crown when it implemented the Royal Pragmatic on Marriages in the colony.[13] Although the law did not allow Anza to challenge the validity of marriages—the Franciscans held this power through the diligencias matrimonial—it empowered him to prevent ecclesiastics from using matrimony to disrupt the social order of the province.

Anza found it necessary, on occasion, to support rather than oppose clerical decisions regarding marital unions. This he did in order to preserve peace among the citizenry. In 1781, he upheld the decision of his archrival, Diego Muñoz Jurado, to permit the marriage of Antonia Sánchez and Juan Ignacio Mesta.[14] Antonia's mother, María, had filed suit against Muñoz for coming to her home in the absence of her husband, removing their daughter, and conducting the marriage of Antonia and Juan Ignacio without the consent of Antonia's parents. Muñoz claimed that the couple had come to him to request that he take Antonia away from the "captivity in which she found herself" at her mother's home. Confused, Muñoz decided to visit María and determine whether her daughter's pleas were justified. Muñoz reported that his original impressions of María Sánchez were shattered upon his visit. The woman he thought to be quiet, shy, and a good Christian, turned out to be pernicious, prejudicial, mischievous, and possessing a "venomous and pestilent tongue." He pronounced her an "enemy of the peace."

Through his investigation, Muñoz identified a female Indian servant who had been reared in the Sánchez household. The servant testified that during the tenure of Anza's predecessor, Pedro Fermín de Mendinueta, she had tried to escape the Sánchez home because María and her husband treated her like a slave. The Indian claimed that she wished to live with Antonia and her husband because they treated her with kindness. She threatened to flee to the "heathen" Indians if forced to live with María. Anza decided that ruling against Antonia's parents would best serve the tranquility of New Mexico, regardless of any contempt he felt for Muñoz and his fellow peninsulars. Anza therefore agreed to uphold Antonia and Juan Ignacio's union and ordered that the Indian servant be removed from the Sánchez home.

Women suffered the greatest social and economic setbacks from the reactionary nature of the Royal Pragmatic on Marriages. The law granted men full control over their families while they were alive. Equally important, it redefined traditional rights and powers that women had enjoyed over the family's estates. Women lost all say in choosing marital partners for their children and the right to determine familial heirs, so long as their husbands lived.[15] The Royal Pragmatic stated, in essence, that women surrendered all control of the family's estate to their husbands. Mothers were prohibited from offering any financial aid to disobedient children, even if the mothers had brought these capital assets to their marriages.[16] Carlos III demanded that women recognize their husbands as heads of households. In this light, the law now officially sanctioned the submissive posture of women towards their husbands, a practice that theoretically had not been recognized as tradition.

The Royal Pragmatic on Marriages assigned women the status of second-class citizens on the premise that females were incapable of complex logical reasoning. The Bourbons supported this notion with the argument that men possess superior mental capacities that allow them to better grasp the intricacies of legal and economic matters. The sexism inherent in the law, however, also served as a veiled justification for one of the true goals of the decree, to ensure that men would control the marriage selection process for their children, so that husbands, as heads of households, could be fully empowered over familial estates. The logic of this argument was simple: by eliminating the female voice in the management of estates and questions of inheritance, the crown hoped to reinforce the patriarchy and class structure upon which the empire was built. And this, Carlos III hoped, would restore the social order the king demanded for his empire.

In New Mexico, the sexist tone of the Royal Pragmatic on Marriages found expression in an inheritance case between Juan Ignacio Mesta and Bárbara Baca. Mesta had filed suit against doña Bárbara in 1782 for alleged money and items she had received from her deceased husband, Juan Bautista Durán. Mesta based his suit against doña Bárbara on a clause in his father's last will and testament. This document stated that doña Bárbara's deceased husband had reneged on a business transaction with Mesta's father, Ventura. According to the will, sometime in the 1750s Ventura had granted Durán power of attorney to trade various items in Chihuahua for a share of the profits of any sales. These items included money, livestock, *gamuzas* (buckskins), and textiles. Durán failed to uphold his agreement with Mesta. Instead, he returned to his home at Pajarito with the items and money he had traded for in Chihuahua. In her defense, doña Bárbara claimed she had no knowledge of the goods and money for which she was being sued. She stated that her husband had kept her ignorant of his business dealings, so she knew not how he had acquired the estate she inherited from him.

The case dragged on for two years. In 1784, doña Bárbara's son, José, assumed power of attorney to represent his mother. José brought the case before Governor Anza and demanded justice. He claimed doña Bárbara could not be held liable for his father's affairs because she was a woman, and it was common knowledge that females did not possess the "capacity to understand the business of men."[17] The outcome of this lawsuit is not known, but it is clear that José Baca declared his mother incapable of understanding the intricacies of business and finance in the hope that Mesta would drop the charges against her or that Anza would rule in her favor. It is also likely, however, that José acted in a self-serving manner since he stood to inherit his mother's estate.

King Carlos III included an interesting article in the Pragmatic laws that further increased the state's power over the marital and inheritance processes. The decree stated that grandparents assumed responsibility for naming heirs to estates when children's parents died intestate. Should grandparents not fulfill this legal obligation, then a child's closest next of kin assumed the power to designate heirs. If no relative was available to determine the legal inheritance of a family's estate, then that case was handed over to the state.[18] This clause in the marriage law granted officials like Anza greater control of the inheritance aspect of marriage because they represented the state in cases where the government served as the executor of wills. In so doing, the Pragmatic allowed the crown to expand its control over the private lives of its subjects and thus reinforce the ideal of absolutism.

Anza's copy of the Royal Pragmatic included another clause that made it possible for children to challenge a father's decision regarding marriage partners. The law stated that a father's choice could be overturned if it was proven that his decision was made while he was mentally unstable.[19] This article left open the possibility for all sorts of definitions regarding mental illness, but it allowed suitors to circumvent the possibility of rejection by declaring the father of their beloved crazy.

In at least one instance, the insanity clause in the marriage law was utilized by a New Mexican to seek justice from Governor Anza. In the 1782 Mesta-Baca case, doña Bárbara claimed that her deceased husband had lawfully willed his estate to her. If true, she stood to inherit not only the assets her husband had legally accumulated but also those that he allegedly stole from Mesta's father in the 1750s. Doña Bárbara pleaded that Anza allow her to keep the money and livestock her husband had left her because it was all she owned in the world. Ignacio Mesta challenged the existence of the will and expressed outrage when doña Bárbara claimed that Mesta's father, Ventura, had served as executor of the will. Mesta insisted that doña Bárbara's husband could not have legally executed a will because it was common knowledge in New Mexico that he suffered from dementia. Doña Bárbara herself claimed her husband had been extremely ill and bedridden until his death. Ignacio Mesta thus argued that if doña Bárbara's husband had produced a will, the marriage law rendered it invalid because of his mental condition. On several occasions, Anza ordered doña Bárbara to produce her husband's will, but the fact that she failed to do so suggests that the document never existed.[20] Although the outcome of this case is not known, it nonetheless illustrates how the Royal Pragmatic reinforced the state's involvement in the legalities of marriage and inheritance.

To what degree Anza enforced the Royal Pragmatic on Marriages in New Mexico is uncertain. Whether out of choice, lack of interest, or simply because grounds for his intervention were lacking, Anza avoided marriage cases that dealt with canon law. Instead, he reserved his direct involvement for marital disputes that brought into question secular issues associated with marriage, including patrimony, inheritance, and even mental health. The Royal Pragmatic on Marriages did empower Anza to intervene in such instances because, as governor, he was charged with ensuring that battles between fathers and children, husbands and wives, priests and parishioners would not threaten the social order of the colony.

Enforcement of the Royal Pragmatic on Marriages in New Mexico also raises the question of how often the Franciscans violated the law. Rick Hendricks writes that, given the limited choice of marriage partners, because most New Mexicans were interrelated, the state had little choice but to support clerical decisions regarding prenuptial investigations. Hendricks concludes that the friars retained a great deal of power over the process of matrimony even if "they did lose exclusive control over marriage."[21] For the Bourbons, the appearance of control over marriage and the friars seemed to be more important than their ability to enforce the law. The king accepted a flexible application of the Royal Pragmatic in remote colonies such as New Mexico because, in theory, it reinforced the Bourbons' plan of royal absolutism.

Father Tomás Fernández and the Ácoma Affair

In June of 1787, Anza was several months away from relinquishing his command as governor and military chief of New Mexico. Anza looked back at his tenure in office with satisfaction. But just as he was set to make his triumphant exit from New Mexico, he received a communiqué from the alcalde mayor of Laguna and Ácoma pueblos, Francisco Lobero, which hinted that the modus vivendi he had achieved with the friars might be threatened. In June 1787, Lobero wrote:

> [W]ith the utmost and required respect, and in a manner best suited to satisfy my rights, I appear before my lord [Anza] and state that, having been informed and convinced by Francisco Javier Flores, Esteban Portillo, and Santiago Largo, all three Indians from the Pueblo of Ácoma . . . Cristobal Mascareñas, a resident of Chama, failing to extend the respect due to me, entered into the cited pueblo which is under my jurisdiction . . . and has once again conjured up a complaint against my known conduct in the General Command.[22]

The nature of Mascareñas's complaint is not clear, but it involved an attempt to enlist the Ácoma Indians in a move to discredit Lobero and have him removed from the office of alcalde mayor. Lobero responded by insisting that Mascareñas's attack on his character was an insult to his honor as a citizen and government official. He demanded justice from Anza who, as governor, was obligated to investigate the case. Anza ordered the alcalde mayor of Santa Fe, Antonio José Ortiz, to question all persons with knowledge of Mascareñas's actions and intentions regarding Lobero. Ortiz fulfilled his charge and submitted the diligencias of the case to the governor.

From Ortiz's report, Anza realized that the case was more serious than he had thought. What concerned him was that Mascareñas seemed to be a mere agent for the Franciscan padre Tomás Fernández. According to testimony from the Indians, Fernández hoped to ingratiate himself with the Ácoma people and rally their support against Lobero and the state. As spokesman for the Ácoma witnesses, Javier Flores informed Ortiz that Mascareñas had come to their pueblo on behalf of Father Fernández. He insisted, however, that it was the cleric, and not the Ácomas, who wanted Lobero out of office. All three witnesses firmly concluded that their people refused to support the friar and would reject *malos avisos* (bad or evil advice) from anyone. Baltasar Suytigua also stated that the Ácomas had nothing to request from Governor Anza, and Flores even referred to Father Fernández as a "liar."[23]

In fact, Mascareñas had traveled to Ácoma and met with the pueblo's interpreter, Esteban Portillo, in April 1787. He communicated Fernández's plan and urged Portillo to convince his people that Fernández would support their claims against Lobero and help them rid their pueblo of the alcalde. He relayed Fernández's view that the Ácomas need not fear any reprisals from Anza because the governor would retire from his command in August. He also assured Portillo that Fernández would personally represent their case directly to the custos and to José Antonio Rengel, the Commandant Inspector scheduled to visit the colony in August.

As representative of his people, Portillo rejected Fernández's proposal. He told Mascareñas that the Ácomas had been lied to regarding Lobero, that they had nothing to accuse him of and they had been "unwisely advised to complain" about him. Portillo also denounced Fernández and Mascareñas as troublemakers. He said they could continue their complaints against Lobero, but should leave the Ácomas out of it. Mascareñas departed from Portillo's home, but only after he had accused the Ácomas of being "cowards and crybabies."[24]

Anza recognized that Fernández's role in the Acoma case had reopened the church-state conflict that he thought he had defused while in office. Fernández had displayed great cunning in his plan to challenge the state for power. His choice of the Ácomas as allies was both important and symbolic. Since the era of conquest in the late 1500s, the Ácomas had resisted Spain's presence in New Mexico. In the eighteenth century, they continued to question the Spanish world even as they accepted aspects of it. Fernández also chose the timing of his plan with astuteness. It was common knowledge in the colony that Anza was scheduled to leave office by August 1787. The government, Fernández figured, was always at its weakest during periods of political transition, and he did not hesitate to use this fact to his advantage. He tried to convince the Ácomas that Governor Anza was at the most vulnerable stage of his administration. With Anza out of New Mexico, Fernández claimed that he and the Ácomas could then focus on removing Lobero from office. Fernández's quest for support from the Ácomas did not materialize as he had hoped.

Anza did leave office by August 1787. To the relief of the crown, Fernández's role in the Ácoma affair came to naught. Whether out of respect for the governor or the fact that they had accepted Spain's presence in New Mexico, the Ácomas rejected Fernández. Their bold act reinforced the view that Governor Anza had achieved a clear victory over the Custody of the Conversion of Saint Paul. By subordinating the Franciscans to the will of the crown, Anza had demonstrated that in this remote colony of the Spanish empire, the state now controlled ecclesiastical matters. In New Mexico, after all, it was the king's church.

Conclusion

The King's Governor

IN THE MONTH OF NOVEMBER 1785, delegations of the three main Comanche tribes—the Yupes, Yamparicas, and Cuchanecas—came together at a site on the Río Napestle (Arkansas) known as Casa de Palo. Here, Ecueracapa and Canaquaipe, the two most powerful chiefs of the Cuchanec Comanches, who ranged along the eastern New Mexican frontier and northeastern Texas, made their Yupe and Yamparica cousins feel welcome. The latter groups had traveled from as far as present-day southern Wyoming and northern Colorado to discuss and settle an issue that would have a significant impact on the entire Comanche nation. Six years earlier, the governor of New Mexico, don Juan Bautista de Anza, had killed the war chief Cuerno Verde and demanded a universal peace with all the Comanche tribes. At Casa de Palo, the Horse Lords chose Ecueracapa to represent them in the coming treaty negotiations with Anza and the Spaniards of New Mexico.[1]

The decision to enter into a peace treaty with Spain came in the wake of thirty-five years in which the Comanches supplanted the Eastern Apaches as the most powerful and feared warriors on the western plains of North America. Since at least as early as the 1730s, the Horse Lords had raided Indian and Spanish settlements in New Mexico and Texas as a means of enriching their hunter-gatherer societies. From these sites, the Comanches took quantities of goods they cherished such as European-made weapons, horses, and captives. By 1785, however, the Comanches, like their Pueblo and Spanish neighbors, had grown weary of the constant warfare that pitted these ethnic groups against each other. Violence, especially in the 1770s, and disease had cost many lives all along the hostile frontier. Now,

245

Anza's name reverberated in the minds of all the peoples who inhabited this territory of limited resources. From Santa Fe, the governor's voice rang loud, and his message was clear: all Comanche chiefs must bring their people to the peace table or suffer the fate of Cuerno Verde.

Surely, the Comanches who met at Casa de Palo in 1785 had developed a grudging respect for the Spanish American who had bested Cuerno Verde. Anza, after all, had demonstrated as much skill and cunning on the field of battle as any chief. It is probable that the Comanches' esteem for Anza also stemmed from the vision of reconciliation he proposed to them, a major component, in the Spaniard's mind, of peace by purchase. Since 1779, Anza had promised goods and increased trade to Indians who entered into non-violent coexistence with Spain. The Comanches could not ignore the fact that Anza's plan might prove more profitable and cheaper for them than the previous decades of warfare that had cost so many lives. And so they opted for peace, and the advantages of material culture that came with nonviolence.

In 1779, the Bourbons had made the principle of peace by purchase the cornerstone of their Indian policy for the far north. That year, Minister of the Indies José de Gálvez reasoned that Indians of the region would welcome alliances with Spaniards if the Spaniards ensured the availability of European-made products. Gálvez was even willing to extend the offer of inferior firearms to ensure the assimilation of Native Americans into Spanish society.[2]

In the past, peace by purchase had worked in New Mexico and beyond. In the 1750s, Governor Tomás Vélez Cachupín had emphasized the need for a diplomacy of gifts and trade because these made the Spaniards economically attractive to Native Americans like the Comanches. The governor feared that any deviation from this ideal would further strain Spanish-Indian relations and surely perpetuate the warfare that all New Mexicans dreaded. In response to Vélez Cachupín's concerns, Spanish officials took steps to force Indians to acquire their goods from the nuevomexicanos by closing New Mexico's eastern frontier to aspiring entrepreneurs who followed the earlier example of French traders Pierre and Paul Mallet.[3]

It was in the territory of Louisiana that peace by purchase had proven most effective prior to 1785. From here, Bernardo de Gálvez encouraged his uncle to implement the strategy in the General Command. He had recognized that Spain did not have sufficient troops and resources needed to defend the far north through military means alone. Later on, as viceroy of New Spain, Gálvez included peace by purchase in his Instructions of 1786. Cynically, Gálvez referred to the practice of granting gifts and trade to Indians as a policy of "peace by deceit." In his desire to make Indians dependent on Spain for goods, he went as far as to encourage the sale of liquor to Native Americans so that they might "acquire a taste for it" and forget their warring ways.[4]

Governor Anza disagreed that Spain should promote alcoholism among the natives of the far north. In 1778, he prohibited the sale of liquor to Indians, claiming that the substance always proved detrimental to their physical and social welfare.[5] Like Gálvez, Anza believed in peace by purchase. Unlike the viceroy, however, he did not condone an atmosphere of deception, but rather encouraged the spirit of accommodation. Since his days in Sonora, Anza had urged his king to implement a policy in the north that increased the availability of European-made goods to Indians. More important, he had argued that a lasting peace in the General Command would be achieved only when trade relations between Indians and Spaniards were opened up. Only then, Anza believed, would indigenous peoples be willing to accept their full assimilation into the Spanish world.

It is no surprise that the treaty Anza negotiated with Ecueracapa emphasized economic exchange between Comanches, Spaniards, and Pueblos. On 25 February 1786, the two chiefs met at Santa Fe to discuss the terms of the peace. Here, Ecueracapa requested permission to allow his people to settle near Spanish settlements in New Mexico, to have access to the colony through Pecos, and of course to pursue free trade within the province. In addition, the chief asked Anza to regulate trade at the Pecos and Taos fairs, including fixing currency rates, so that economic abuses committed by nuevomexicanos in the past would no longer tarnish the spirit of accommodation. Finally, Ecueracapa insisted that Spain provide military aid to the Comanches. Anza accepted these recommendations and made demands of his own. He insisted the Comanches make peace with the Utes, uphold their accord with Spain, and extend military aid in the campaigns against the Apaches. Speaking on behalf of his people, Ecueracapa agreed. Having decided the conditions of reconciliation, the Spanish and Comanche chiefs met at Pecos to officially cement their alliance. On 28 February 1786, after exchanging formal greetings, the once contentious parties set on paper the spirit of the peace treaty they had chosen to live by. Afterward, the Indians dug a hole in the ground and quickly filled it to symbolize that the hostility between Spaniards and Comanches was now buried in the earth.[6]

The Comanche Peace represented the crowning achievement of Anza's career as a servant of the Bourbon crown. By negotiating an alliance with the Horse Lords, he had contributed to the preservation of the Spanish empire and given New Mexico a renewed sense of purpose and hope for a prosperous and lasting future. The peace forced most ethnic groups of the region to define the nature of their shared destiny, either reciprocal destruction or mutual accommodation. By choosing the latter in 1786, Indians and Spaniards came to realize that, in at least the economic and material aspects of their respective cultures, they were not as different as they once believed. In this light, the Comanche Peace represented Anza's attempt to reconcile the parochial needs of frontier societies with the imperial demands of his king.

The effects of the Comanche Peace were immediately felt within New Mexico and throughout the General Command. One month after Anza concluded the Pecos treaty, he negotiated a similar pact with the Navajos. A year later, Gila Apaches found themselves pressed against the northern Sonora frontier as a result of military pressure applied by the Comanche, Navajo, Pueblo, and Spanish alliance forged by Anza. Although the peace was not complete, it had altered the social face of the colony by illustrating that the perseverance of human life in this demanding environment depended on the willingness of all its inhabitants to extend a hand of cooperation across the desert landscape.

The trade and military alliances Anza negotiated with nomadic Indians did not assure a permanent peace in the General Command. For the remainder of the colonial era, the Internal Provinces continued their precarious existence on the Spanish-American frontier. And although Anza's reforms proved insufficient to ensure Spain's hold on New Mexico, they were his most lasting contribution in the colony. Administratively, he had improved the efficiency of both the bureaucratic and communicative processes. In so doing, the governor forced New Mexico to take a more active role in the maintenance of the Bourbon empire. Anza's subjugation of the Custody of the Conversion of Saint Paul to the will of the state not only reinforced the ideal of absolutism in the colony but also eliminated the preeminence that the Franciscans had enjoyed in New Mexico. Finally, the defensive reforms Anza initiated in the colony, especially the emphasis he had placed on the use of citizen militias and Indian allies, continued to form the backbone of New Mexico's defenses to the very end of the Mexican Period.

Anza did not live to see the long-term effects that his reformist administration had on the New Mexico colony. He was relieved of his office in 1787, having served for ten years. It is possible that the Bourbons entertained the idea of granting Anza the governor's seat of Texas. Instead, they assigned him the military command of his home province. From there, the crown hoped that Anza would continue to serve its empire as he had in New Mexico. The years of arduous and loyal service, however, had taken their toll, and so the aging frontiersman accepted his new assignment with reserved enthusiasm. Anza left Santa Fe in August 1787 driven by the thought that he would soon be reunited with friends, family, and the lands he had left behind in Sonora. He was going home!

The journey to Sonora, however, proved a difficult undertaking. Anza lumbered along the rugged terrain towards Arizpe and arrived at the capital worn of body and spirit. Anza's health deteriorated throughout 1788, and by 20 December it was apparent that he would not recover from his ailments. Father Miguel Elías González administered confession and last rites, but the flicker of life was drawn from Anza's eyes before he could receive communion. He died that day at Arizpe and was buried in the floor of a side chapel at mission *Nuestra Señora de la Asunción* (Our Lady of the Ascension).[7]

As the citizens of Arizpe gathered to bid him farewell, they must have marveled at the extraordinary life Anza had lived in New Spain's northern frontier. Whether as a military officer, statesman, or friend, he had served them well as a native son of Sonora. But it was in the remote colony of New Mexico where Anza made his most significant contributions to the Spanish empire, and where he had been, in every sense, the King's governor.

Notes

Introduction

1. Since 1973, Juan Bautista de Anza's portrait has generated much controversy regarding its authenticity. Located at the Palace of the Governors in Santa Fe, New Mexico, the painting first came into public view when one of Anza's descendants, James Ainsa, granted Herbert E. Bolton permission to use it for his 1921 book on the Spanish Borderlands. Ownership of the portrait was passed on within Ainsa's family until it was donated to the New Mexico Museum in 1970. In 1973, the Mexican scholar J. Ignacio Rubio Mañe raised doubt that the person depicted in the painting is Anza. Mañe based his view on key features in the portrait, including Anza's beard and the style of his clothing. Mañe argued that neither beards nor the clothes were common to Anza's time. Richard Ahlborn, a curator from the Smithsonian Institution, challenged Mañe's conclusions, claiming that beards were considered fashionable in northern New Spain in the eighteenth century, and that the clothing was probably wardrobe the artist used for the portrait. In 1994, Dr. Michael Weber took Anza's portrait to Mexico City, where it was subjected to x-ray and pigment analysis. The results of these tests suggested inconclusively that the painting might have been produced well after Anza's death, perhaps in the late 1800s or early 1900s. In a phone interview conducted in October 2013, Weber stated that the debate over the validity of Anza's portrait is nowhere near completion. He suggested, however, that the painting is probably a copy of the original that has been lost to time. If Weber is correct, then the man depicted in the portrait could very well be Anza himself, or not. Regarding the debate over Anza's portrait, see the Gallery section in the Internet-based *Web de Anza*, http://anza.uoregon.edu/ and Chávez, *Chasing History*, 121–22.

2. In recent years the tale of Anza's efforts to colonize the San Francisco Bay area has reached a wider audience through the work, among others, of Donald T. Garate and Lynne Anderson-Inman. See Garate, *Basque Explorer.* At the University of Oregon, Anderson-Inman serves as director of *Web de Anza*, an interactive web site dedicated to educating the public about Anza's exploratory and colonizing efforts in Alta California. In 1990, the U.S. Congress established the *Juan Bautista*

de Anza National Historic Trail, thus commemorating important contributions Hispanics have made in the overall history of North America.

3. For a discussion of the impact the Enlightenment had on the Bourbon Reforms, see Lynch, *Bourbon Spain*, 254–61. In this book, Lynch offers a short but useful list of sources relevant to the Enlightenment in Spain on pages 434–36. See also Weber, *Bárbaros*, 2–3, 34–36.

4. Regarding King Carlos III's efforts to eliminate the social privileges of Spanish American criollo elites, see Paquette, *Enlightenment, Governance, and Reform*.

5. Wortman, "Bourbon Reforms," 222–38. See also Cuello, "Economic Impact," 301–23.

6. Teodoro de Croix to Anza, Arizpe, 14 July 1780, SANM II: 800.

7. Lynch, *Bourbon Spain*, 21.

8. Crosby, *Antigua California*, 62.

9. Cutter, *Legal Culture*, 15.

10. Ibid., 73.

11. Regarding Anza's reform measures in the region of El Paso, see Herrera, "Social-Militarization," 501–28.

12. Marc Simmons offers an in-depth analysis of the major military reforms implemented in the province during the colonial era. In part, the present study attempts to elaborate on Simmons's views regarding military reforms during Anza's governorship. See Simmons, *Spanish Government in New Mexico*.

13. The suggestion that Anza profited from corrupt activities at Tubac is included in a report written by the assistant inspector of presidios, Antonio Bonilla, which was addressed to his superior, Hugo O'Conor, on 16 July 1774. This report included Bonilla's views regarding an investigation of corrupt acts committed by the captain of the Terrenate presidio, José Antonio Vildósola. Vildósola—who was married to Anza's niece, María Rosa Tato y Anza—had been dismissed from his command at Terrenate for corruption, but Bonilla insisted that his behavior was common among presidial captains of the region, including Tubac. See Antonio Bonilla to Hugo O'Conor, Chihuahua, 16 July 1774, AGI, Guadalajara, 272:2. See Herrera, "Infidelity and the Presidio Captain," 204–27.

14. See Thomas, *Forgotten Frontiers*.

Chapter One

1. Matson and Fontana, *Before Rebellion*. In the prefatory section of this source there is a wonderful map of Sonora that offers an excellent visual representation of the territory's terrain as well as the way major indigenous groups were dispersed throughout the region. The map is attributed to the Jesuit missionary Juan Nentvig and dated circa 1762.

2. Naylor and Polzer, *Pedro de Rivera*, 2.

3. Radding, *Wandering Peoples*, 1–5.

4. Ibid., 8–12, 25–30.

5. Pupo-Walker, *Castaways*.

6. Radding, *Wandering Peoples*, 32–35. For an excellent analysis regarding the discovery of silver in New Spain and the resultant settlement of the Northern Territory, see Bakewell, *Silver Mining*; and Brading, *Miners and Merchants*.

7. Elliot, *Imperial Spain*, 102. In 1493, King Fernando acquired for Spain exclusive rights to evangelize the New World through the papal bull *Inter caetera*.

8. Kessell, *Mission of Sorrows*, 34.

9. Between 1566 and 1572, the Jesuits evangelized unsuccessfully among North American Indians of the Chesapeake Bay region and in Florida. Although they failed in these endeavors, the Jesuits refused to surrender their call to do mission work. The order turned its sights to New Spain, and in 1591 it assumed pastoral responsibilities in the hostile northwestern territory. For Jesuit activities on New Spain's northern frontier, see Bolton, *Rim of Christendom*; Kessell, *Mission of Sorrows*; and García, *Misiones Jesuitas*.

10. Radding, *Wandering Peoples*, 249.

11. Kessell, *Mission of Sorrows*, 6–9; Radding, *Wandering Peoples*, 35–45.

12. For the dynamics involved in the establishment and breakdown of Spanish-Indian relations in New Spain's northern territory, see Spicer, *Cycles of Conquest*; and Radding, *Wandering Peoples*, 249–301.

13. For the Villasur Expedition of 1720, see Kessell, *Spain in the Southwest*, 208–11; and Weber, *The Spanish Frontier in North America*, 168–71.

14. For an excellent analysis of the Rivera inspection tour of 1724–28, see Naylor and Polzer, *Pedro de Rivera*; Polzer and Sheridan, *The Presidio and Militia*; and Velázquez, *Tres Estudios*.

15. Priestly, *José de Gálvez*, 288.

16. Naylor and Polzer, *Pedro de Rivera*, 2–16.

17. Faulk and Faulk, *Defenders*, 3–9.

18. Ibid.

19. Velazquez, *Tres Estudios*, 3–17. See also Moorhead, *The Presidio*, 31–37.

20. Radding, *Wandering Peoples*, 264–301.

21. Father Carlos Roxas to Father Provincial Andrés Xavier García, Arizpe, 29 December 1748; as cited in Kessell, *Mission of Sorrows*, 91–92; see 91n12. Roxas played a significant role in Anza's youth as a teacher, priest, and perhaps even as a father figure after the young Juan had lost his father.

22. Matson, *Before Rebellion*, xi–xii.

23. The 1751 Pima rebellion and its consequences for northern Sonora are well covered by Kessell, *Mission of Sorrows*, 87–149. In Matson, *Before Rebellion*, are included four translated reports by Father Jacobo Sedelmeyer, who served in Pimería Alta during the revolt, in which he describes Jesuit-Indian relations in the region between January and May of 1751. Sedelmeyer's reports are interesting in that they indicate the Jesuits did not suspect that a Pima rebellion might be brewing in the region. If anything, Father Jacobo expressed a sense of optimism regarding the Jesuits' work in Pimería Alta, as well as the order's desire to expand its

mission field to the Yuma Indians of the Colorado River Valley and perhaps as far north as the Hopi frontier.

24. Kessell, *Friars, Soldiers, and Reformers*, 7.

25. Navarro García, "The North of New Spain," 206–207; Velázquez, *Tres Estudios*, 37, 63–65.

Chapter Two

1. Fray Joseph Abalza, copy of baptismal certificate for Juan Bautista de Anza, Mission San Ygnacio De Guguiarachi, Fronteras, 8 March 1789, AGI, Guadalajara 289:536.

2. In 1728, Pedro de Rivera, who had come to New Spain's far northern territory on an inspection tour of the region's presidial system, allocated 200 *marcas de plata* for the construction of San Ygnacio de Cuguiárachi. The mission was built to serve the spiritual needs of Spanish troops and colonists of the Corodéguachi presidio located several miles to the east and later renamed Fronteras. The money for the mission was transferred to Anza's father, Juan Bautista the Elder, who was charged with overseeing its construction. Anza received the money from his father-in-law, Antonio Bezerra Nieto, who served as captain of the Janos presidio, located in the region of Chihuahua. Juan Bautista de Anza to Viceroy Marqués de Casafuerte, Corodéguachi, 31 October 1728, BNAF caja 12, legajo 200. See also, Smith, *Captain of the Phantom Presidio*.

3. Kessell, "Anza, Indian Fighter," 155.

4. Auttos de visita hechos por el Capitán don Antonio Bezerranieto en la provincia de Sonora y Ostimuri, año 1718, El Archivo de Hidalgo de Parral, fols. 17, 19, 22; as cited by Garate, "Basque Ethnic Connections," 79n41. For a biographical sketch of Antonio Bezerra Nieto, see Almada, *Diccionario de Historia*, 108–109, as cited in Kessell, *Mission of Sorrows*, 34.

5. Garate, "Basque Ethnic Connections," 77–78. No researcher has done more to uncover the Anza family's historical roots than Garate. In his work, he utilized various archives located in Guipúzcoa.

6. Smith, *Captain of the Phantom Presidio*, 33.

7. Garate, "Basque Ethnic Connections," 78.

8. The history of Basque contributions to the exploration, conquest, and colonization of America is well documented. See for example Douglass and Bilbao, *Amerikanuak*; Ispizua, *Los Vascos;* and Ispizua, *Historia de los Vascos.*

9. Garate, "Basque Ethnic Connections," 73–77.

10. Ibid., 79nn41–42.

11. Ibid., 79n43.

12. Kessell, *Spain in the Southwest*, 215–16.

13. Kessell, *Mission of Sorrows*, 38–40.

14. José Patiño to Viceroy Marqués de Cassafuerte, Sevilla, 26 April 1729, AGN, Reales Cédulas, 48, *expediente* 13, ff. 31–33.

15. Smith, *Captain of the Phantom Presidio*, 130. Anza the Elder developed a strong relationship with the Jesuits in Sonora. The missionaries considered him an excellent defender of their order; so much so that in 1734 they appealed to the Viceroy to allow him to travel to Baja California to put down a revolt that had erupted among the Indians located at the southern end of the colony. See Crosby, *Antigua California*, 114–17.

16. Kessell, *Mission of Sorrows*, 40–50.

17. Ibid., 53–60.

18. The story of Antonio Siraumea and the discovery of silver in northern Sonora has been told by several scholars. Among others, for example, Kessell, *Mission of Sorrows*, 61–62; Jones, *Los Paisanos*, 178–79. Garate argued that traditional accounts of this story have perpetuated the myth that the discovery of silver occurred at a *real de minas* called *Arizonac*. He claimed this mining camp never existed and is usually confused with Arizona, a ranch owned by Bernardo de Urrea and located just north of Agua Caliente. Garate attributed the mistaken accounts to the sources most scholars utilized to tell the story—copies of the original depositions given by the people involved in the discovery and resultant silver rush in Sonora, as well as reports filed by government officials who took the testimonies. Collectively, these copies are found in AGI, Guadalajara 185, as well as AGI, Audiencia de México 1256 and 1848A. Through the efforts of Vivian Fisher, retired librarian of the Bancroft Library, the original documents related to the 1736 discovery of silver in Sonora were located at the AGN in Mexico City in 1996. The original documents are now located in AGN, Minería 160, legajos 1 and 2. Based on these sources, Garate concluded that the site of the silver discovery cannot be identified conclusively, but that it must have occurred somewhere between Agua Caliente and the San Luis Valley Spanish settlements in the area of Guevavi and Soamca. Garate, "Arizona," and interview by author, telephone conversation, San Pedro, Calif., 15 January 1999.

19. Kessell, *Mission of Sorrows*, 61.

20. Garate, "Arizona," 6.

21. Ambrosio Melgarejo, copy of a *Relación* (report), Mexico, 21 March 1737, AGI, Audiencia de México 1848A; and Ambrosio Melgarejo, Relación, Mexico, 29 August 1737, AGI, Audiencia de México 1848A.

22. Ambrosio Melgarejo, copy of a Relación, Mexico, 17 September 1737, AGI, Audiencia de México 1848A.

23. Garate, "Arizona," 4–7.

24. Kessell, *Mission of Sorrows*, 74.

25. Jones, *Los Paisanos*, 179.

26. For the Yaqui Rebellion, see Navarro García, *La Sublevación*.

27. Kessell, *Mission of Sorrows*, 69.

28. Garate, "Basque Ethnic Connections," 79n44. Of the six Anza children, only the last two, Josefa Gregoria and Juan Bautista, were born at Fronteras; the others were born at Janos, Chihuahua. See Garate, "Arizona," 16.

29. *Libro de fallecimiento de Castillo-Elejabeitia,* 3 May 1800, *Bizkaiko Elizaren Histori Arkibua Seminario Ikastetxea Derioan,* Derio, Vizcaya, unnumbered pages; as cited in Garate "Basque Ethnic Connections," 80 and 80n51.

30. Juan José Grijalva to juezes asesores de diezmos, San Juan, 13 January 1741, AHAD, microfilm, roll 45, document 1, frames 446–47. It is probable that the location from which Grijalva wrote this document was the mining town of San Juan Bautista, which was located southeast of Arizpe, near Tetuachi where Anza the Elder had operated a mine.

31. Grijalva to asesores de diezmos, San Juan, 22 April 1746, AHAD 49:7.

32. María Rosa Bezerra Nieto to Grijalva, Basochuca, 21 August 1746, AHAD 49:4, 407–408.

33. Grijalva to asesores de diezmos, San Juan, 27 September 1746, AHAD 48:8, 452–53.

34. Grijalva to Captain Francisco Xavier Miranda, San Juan, 25 October 1746, AHAD 49:5, 444–48.

35. Grijalva to asesores de diezmos, San Juan, 5 February 1747, AHAD 49:6, 530–31. Vildósola, an Old World Basque, had been named governor of Sonora in 1741 as a result of his success in putting down the Yaqui rebellion of 1740.

36. Grijalva to asesores de diezmos, Santa María de Baceraca, 20 March 1747, AHAD 49:3, 536–39.

37. Garate, "Basque Ethnic Connections," 82–83.

38. Until documentary evidence proves or disproves that Doña María Bezerra Nieto moved her family from Fronteras to Basochuca sometime after Anza the Elder's death, this argument remains an assumption. There is evidence to suggest that the Anza relocation occurred. Doña María wrote to Capellán Juan José Grijalva in 1746 from Basochuca. Unless she wrote this letter while on a trip—there is no indication that this was the case—then one can assume she was living in Basochuca rather than passing through. Basochuca was located in the environs of Tetuachi, where it is known that Anza the Elder had business ventures and possibly purchased land. Doña María thus may have moved her family to this settlement to take advantage of her husband's holdings. See Garate, "Basque Ethnic Connections," 79, and 79nn41–42.

39. Moorhead, *The Presidio,* 178.

40. Kessell, *Mission of Sorrows,* 155.

Chapter Three

1. Kessell, *Mission of Sorrows,* 140–49.

2. Schröder, "Western Apache External Relations," 12. Schröder was a research fellow at the University of New Mexico History Department from 1997 to 1999.

3. Father Salvador Ignacio de la Peña, "Convite Evangélico á compasión, y Socorro de la Viña del Señor, destrozada, y conculdada con el Alzamiento de la

Pimeria Alta, desde el dia 21 de Noviembre de Año de 1751–1766." Cited in Kessell, *Mission of Sorrows*, 155; and Kessell, "Anza, Indian Fighter," 156n5.

4. Kessell, *Mission of Sorrows*, 155–66.

5. Ibid., 156–57. It is not clear when Juan and Ana met, but it is possible that the encounter took place sometime after 1740, when the Anzas relocated to Basochuca. From here, Juan could have had frequent contact with Ana because she was a resident of Arizpe, as stated by Father Carlos Roxas in the couple's notice of marriage. Juan and Ana met at a young age, perhaps when they were in their teens.

6. Father Felipe Segesser, statement supporting Anza's petition for marriage, Ures, 13 May 1761, AGN, Provincias Internas: 87, f. 388.

7. Miguel Elías González, copy of a marriage certificate for Anza and Pérez Serrano, Arizpe, 5 February 1789, AGI, Guadalajara 289, expediente 526, 4, f. 4. Father Carlos Roxas issued the original certificate of marriage on 24 June 1761.

8. Kessell, *Mission of Sorrows*, 165–66.

9. Radding, *Wandering Peoples*, 252.

10. Kessell, *Mission of Sorrows*, 169.

11. BNAF 38:867, f. 3, 1764; as cited in Radding, *Wandering Peoples*, 253, 349n10.

12. Anza's report to Governor Pineda regarding the 1766 campaign is located in Anza to Pineda, Tubac, 7 March 1766, BNAF 38:855. The report is also discussed in Kessell, "Anza Indian Fighter," and Radding, *Wandering Peoples*, 261–62. Most of the sources that deal with New Spain's military policy for the northern provinces stress the significant role that Indian auxiliaries played in the defense of the region. See for example, Brinckerhoff and Faulk, *Lancers for the King;* Jones, *Nueva Vizcaya;* Moorhead, *Apache Frontier;* and Moorhead, *The Presidio.*

13. Kessell, *Mission of Sorrows*, 173–80. Spain's military reform plan of the late eighteenth century, including Rubí's inspection tour of northern New Spain and his *Reglamento* of 1772, are aptly discussed in Brinkerhoff and Faulk, *Lancers for the King;* Moorhead, *Apache Frontier;* and Weber, *The Spanish Frontier in North America.*

14. Velázquez, *Tres Estudios*, 63–65.

15. For King Carlos III's motivation and decision to expel the Jesuits from the Spanish empire, see Lynch, *Bourbon Spain*, 280–90. For the expulsion of the Jesuits from Sonora, see Kessell, *Mission of Sorrows*, 181–88.

16. For a history of the Jesuit mission front in Baja California, see Crosby, *Antigua California.*

17. Kessell, *Mission of Sorrows*, 182.

18. Anza's orders regarding the Jesuit expulsion of 1767 are located in *Instrucción particular y reservada que devera observar el comisionado del rectorado del Río de Sonora, Don Juan Bautista de Anza, Capitán del presidio de Tubac, para la ejecución de lo resuelto por su magestad en su Real decreto de 27 de Febrero de este año* [1767], BNAF 33:708, ff. 5–7v.

19. Anza to Pineda, place unknown, 4 August 1767, BNAF 236:912, ff. 11–11v. It is possible that Anza wrote this letter to Pineda from Aconchi, because it was there that seventy-one-year-old Father Nicolás Perera lay ill and unable to ride south to Mátape.

20. Father Perera did not survive the Jesuit expulsion of 1767; he died en route to Mexico City, at Ixtlan del Río in Nayarit, on 29 August 1768. See Zelis, *Catálogo de los Sugetos*, 32, 167.

21. Anza to Pineda, Arizpe, 15 August 1767, BNAF 39:886, quoted in Kessell, *Friars, Soldiers, and Reformers*, 14.

22. The increase of Apache raids into northern Sonora in the late 1760s and the initiation of the Seri Wars are aptly covered in Kessell, *Friars, Soldiers, and Reformers*, 21–49.

23. The story of the Catalán troops who served in the Seri wars is well documented in Sanchez, *Spanish Bluecoats*.

24. Kessell, *Friars, Soldiers, and Reformers*, 56–57.

25. Pedro de Corbalán to Viceroy Antonio María Bucareli y Ursua, Álamos, 24 December 1771, AGI, Guadalajara 512:227.

26. Kessell, *Friars, Soldiers, and Reformers*, 54–62.

27. Viceroy Marqués de Croix to Julián de Arriaga, Mexico, 29 April 1770, AGN, Correspondencias de Virreyes Marqués de Croix y Marqués de Branciforte, 14, f. 432. Other documents regarding Anza's request for promotion to the rank of captain of the cavalry are located in AGI, Guadalajara 512.

28. Anza to the King, 1770, AGN, Correspondencia de Virreyes Croix y Branciforte 13, f. 433; and AGI, Guadalajara 512.

29. Viceroy Marqués de Croix to Julián de Arriaga, Mexico, 25 January 1771, AGN, Correspondencia de Virreyes Croix y Branciforte 14, f. 74.

30. Kessell, *Friars, Soldiers, and Reformers*, 51–52.

31. Ibid., 39.

32. For Anza's views regarding Indians and the failed mission system of the far north, see Kessell, "Anza Damns the Missions."

33. Kessell, "Anza Damns the Missions," 58.

34. Radding, *Wandering Peoples*, 35.

35. Kessell, "Anza Damns the Missions," 59–60.

36. Juan Rodríguez Cabrillo opened up Alta California for Spain in 1542, at which time he sailed into the waters off the coast at Point Loma. From 1602 to 1603, Sebastián Vizcaíno mapped and gave Alta California its place names, most of which continue to be used to this day. With the latter expedition, Spain made a first attempt to seek a suitable location for a permanent settlement in California. Vizcaíno's work coincided with Juan de Oñate's colonizing campaign in New Mexico. Spain desired that Oñate explore the lands west of New Mexico in the hope that he could find the elusive Northwest Passage, a water route that would allow vessels to sail from the Atlantic to the Pacific Ocean. The settlement of Alta California was also considered important because of privateering activities carried

out by infamous sailors such as Sir Francis Drake, who plundered Spanish vessels along the Pacific Coast in the 1570s as an agent of Queen Elizabeth I of England. In 1587, off the coast of Baja California, another British privateer, Thomas Cavendish, took as his prize a Spanish galleon en route to Mexico from the Philippines. See Weber, *The Spanish Frontier in North America*, 40–42, 82–84.

37. Ibid., 165–71, 181–83, 198–203.

38. For the Portolá and Serra colonizing expedition of Alta California, see Rolle, *California: A History,* 54–64; and Weber, *The Spanish Frontier in North America,* 244–46.

39. Sánchez, *Spanish Bluecoats,* 32–70.

40. Juan Bautista de Anza, Muster Roll of 1774 Expedition From Sonora to Monterrey, Presidio de Altar, 18 January 1774, AGI, Guadalajara 513:1389.

41. Juan Bautista de Anza to Viceroy Antonio Bucareli Y Ursua, San Dionisio, 9 February 1774, AGI, Guadalajara 513:1389.

42. Anza's 1774 and 1775 trips to Alta California are well documented in Bolton, *Anza's California Expeditions.* The first of these five volumes was issued in narrative form as *Outpost of Empire: The Story of the Founding of San Francisco.* See also Pourade, *Anza Conquers the Desert*; Martí, *Juan Bautista de Anza: Diario;* Kessell, *Friars, Soldiers, and Reformers,* 93–121; and Weber, *The Spanish Frontier in North America,* 251–58.

43. Antonio Bonilla to Hugo O'Conor, Chihuahua, 16 July 1774, AGI, Guadalajara 272:2. For Vildósola and Bonilla's inspection of Terrenate, see Herrera, "Infidelity and the Presidio Captain," 219.

44. Teodoro de Croix to José de Gálvez, Arispe, 23 April 1780, AGI, Guadalajara 277:517; and Croix to Gálvez, Arispe, 23 April 1780, AGI, Guadalajara 517. For the José Antonio Vildósola and María Tato y Anza affair, see Herrera, "Infidelity and the Presidio Captain."

45. Juan Bautista de Anza to Viceroy Antonio Bucareli y Ursua, Terrenate, 8 June 1774, AGI, Guadalajara 513:1489.

46. Antonio Bucareli y Ursua to Julián de Arriaga, Mexico, 27 August 1774, AGI, Guadalajara 513:1489.

47. Kessell, *Friars, Soldiers, and Reformers,* 99–100.

48. Cutter, "*The Defense of Northern New Spain,*" 20–21. O'Conor had fled Ireland for Spain in 1751 as a result of a failed rebellion against the British. He travelled to New Spain in 1763 as part of a wave of officers ordered to New Spain to help professionalize Spain's overseas military. O'Conor served in the far north at Nueva Vizcaya and Texas, eventually rising to the office of governor in the latter province.

49. Kessell, *Friars, Soldiers, and Reformers,* 103–10.

50. Fray Francisco Garcés to Zuni Ministers, Oraibi, 3 July 1776, AGN, Historia 25, parte 3, f. 260. See also Kessell, *Friars, Soldiers, and Reformers,* 119–20; and Weber, *The Spanish Frontier in North America,* 253–56.

51. Documents regarding Anza's trip to Hopi country in 1780 are located in *Cartas reservadas de Anza a Croix sobre la reconquista de la Provincia de Moqui y*

la reducción de sus moradores en los Pueblos de Sandía, Sabinal, y otros, 1779–1780, BNAF 31:633, ff. 1–14. A copy of Anza's Hopi diary is in AGN, Historia 25, ff. 288–318v.

52. Herrera, "Before the Waters," 23. For an excellent description of Anza's California Expeditions, see Guerrero, *The Anza Trail.*

53. Gálvez to the Viceroy of New Spain, Madrid, 24 December 1776, AGN, Reales Cédulas 109, expediente 181.

54. Weber, *The Spanish Frontier in North America,* 257–58. For the Yuma Revolt of 1781, see also Forbes, *Warriors of the Colorado;* and Santiago, *Massacre at the Yuma Crossing.*

55. Kessell, *Friars, Soldiers, and Reformers,* 122–32.

Chapter Four

1. Mendinueta assumed the office of governor in New Mexico in March 1767; he was of noble rank, from the Iberian province of Navarre. Service record, Pedro Fermín de Mendinueta to Julián de Arriaga, Santa Fe, 17 March 1767, AGI, Guadalajara 300. This copy of Mendinueta's service record was included in a letter from Viceroy Antonio Bucareli y Ursua to Arriaga in which Mendinueta was recommended for promotion to the rank of brigadier. Bucareli to Arriaga, México, 27 December 1775, AGI, Guadalajara 515, as cited in Thomas, "Governor Mendinueta's Proposals."

2. Teodoro de Croix to Mendinueta, Arizpe, 11 February 1778, SANM II: 720.

3. What happened to Mendinueta after his retirement is not clear. He and his family, however, were living in Havana, Cuba, by 1786. That year, Mendinueta was appointed sub-inspector of royal troops in New Spain. He served at this post until June 1789, at which time the king ordered him to travel to Spain. A total of nineteen documents dealing with Mendinueta's appointment as sub-inspector of royal troops are located in Mendinueta, New Spain, 4 January 1786 to 11 June 1790, AGI, Audiencia de México 3172.

4. Herrera, "Social-Militarization," 502. See also, Frank, "*Settler to Citizen,*" 30–37.

5. Mendinueta to Croix, Santa Fe, 3 November 1777, AGI, Guadalajara 276, as cited in Thomas, "Governor Mendinueta's Proposals," 35–36.

6. Weber, *The Spanish Frontier in North America,* 221.

7. Thomas, *Teodoro de Croix and the Northern Frontier,* 24. See also Archer, *The Army in Bourbon Mexico,* 1–2.

8. For a history of New Spain's silver-producing region, see Bakewell, *Silver Mining and Society;* and Brading, *Miners and Merchants.*

9. Thomas, *Teodoro de Croix and the Northern Frontier,* 21.

10. Royal Title of Appointment for Juan Bautista de Anza, Aranjuez, 19 May 1777, AGI, Audiencia de México 1216. An English version of this document appears in Thomas, *Forgotten Frontiers,* 115–19.

11. Anza to José Antonio Arrieta, Chihuahua, 8 June 1778, CJMA, microfilm (second printing), roll 10, book 1, frame 597; and SANM II: 720, 724, 734, and 751.

12. For the *bastón de justicia*, see Simmons, *Spanish Government in New Mexico*, 57, 179, 219; and Scholes, "Civil Government," 75.

13. Sections of this chapter were originally published in Herrera, "Social-Militarization."

14. Thomas, *Forgotten Frontiers*, 5–9. In Sonora's Pimería Alta region, colonists experienced intense attacks by the Western Apaches between 1775 and 1776, a period in which the Tubac garrison had been dismantled and relocated to Tucson.

15. Ibid., 10–15.

16. For Anza's views regarding warfare and economic relations between Indians and Europeans, see Kessell, "Anza Damns the Missions;" and Herrera, "Social-Militarization," 502–503.

17. The military strategy for the General Command adopted by Spain at the 1778 Chihuahua council of war is aptly discussed in Thomas, *Forgotten Frontiers*; and Thomas, *Teodoro de Croix and the Northern Frontier*. See also Weber, *Bárbaros*, 6–9.

18. Schröder, "Western Apache External Relations," 17.

19. For an excellent discussion of Spain's military reform policy under Charles III, see Lynch, *Bourbon Spain*, 306–17.

20. Archer, *The Army in Bourbon Mexico*, 4–8.

21. For a detailed discussion of the military reforms Anza implemented at El Paso, see Herrera, "Social-Militarization."

22. Ibid., 504. For the establishment of Spanish El Paso, see Sonnichsen, *Pass of the North*, 19–24; and Cruz, *Let There Be Towns*, 36–51.

23. The king to the viceroy of New Spain, Conde de Paredes, Madrid, 4 September 1683, AGI, Audiencia de México 1117. See also Moorhead, *The Presidio*, 20–21; and Navarro García, *Don José de Gálvez*, 26.

24. Herrera, "Social-Militarization," 505; and Simmons, *Spanish Government in New Mexico*, 113–15.

25. Warner, "Frontier Defense," 5.

26. Archer, *The Army in Bourbon Mexico*, 9.

27. Anza to Lieutenant Governor José Antonio Arrieta, El Paso, 19 September 1778, CJMA, roll 10, book 1, 1774, frame 598.

28. Anza to Arrieta, El Paso, 12 September 1778, CJMA, roll 10, book 1, 1774, frames 604–605. See also Herrera, "Social-Militarization," 505–506.

29. Herrera, "Social-Militarization," 505–506; Anza to Arrieta, El Paso, 12 September 1778, CJMA, roll 10, book 1, 1774, frames 604–605; and Anza to Arrieta, El Paso, 4 November 1778, CJMA, roll 13, book 1, 1791, frame 164.

30. Croix to José de Gálvez, Mexico City, 26 July 1777, AGI, Guadalajara 516.

31. Croix to Gálvez, Arizpe, 23 December 1780, AGI, Guadalajara 277:581; Croix to Gálvez, Chihuahua, 23 October 1778, AGI, Guadalajara 267:298; and Navarro García, *Don José de Gálvez*, 335.

32. Noyes, *Los Comanches,* xxiv.

33. Anza to Arrieta, El Paso, 12 September 1778, CJMA, roll 10, book 1, 1774, frames 604–605. See also, Navarro García, *Don José de Gálvez,* 335; and Herrera, "Social-Militarization," 506–508.

34. Herrera, "Social-Militarization," 517; and Sonnichsen, *Pass of the North,* 33.

35. Croix to King Carlos III, Chihuahua, 27 July 1778, AGI, Guadalajara 267:236.

36. Anza to Arrieta, 4 November 1778, CJMA, roll 13, book 1, 1791, frame 164. See also Frank, *From Settler to Citizen,* 65–82. Translations of documents related to the establishment of a route between New Mexico and Sonora are included in Thomas, *Forgotten Frontiers,* 171–221.

37. Anza to Croix, El Paso, 30 November 1778, AGI, Guadalajara 267; and Croix to Gálvez, Chihuahua, 28 December 1778, AGI, Guadalajara 275:332.

38. Anza to Arrieta, El Paso, 5 October 1778, CJMA, roll 13, book 1, 1791, frames 152–55.

39. Anza, copy of Croix's instructions regarding the reorganization of militias in El Paso, El Paso, 3 November 1778, CJMA, roll 13, book 1, 1791, frames 156–63.

40. Lynch, *Bourbon Spain,* 308–10.

41. Herrera, "Social-Militarization," 509.

42. Simmons, *Spanish Government in New Mexico,* 117.

43. Herrera, "Social-Militarization," 510; Anza, El Paso, 3 November 1778, CJMA, roll 13, book 1, 1791, frames 156–63.

44. Croix to Arrieta, Chihuahua, 8 December 1778, CJMA, roll 10, book 1, 1774, frames 550–551.

45. Croix to Anza, Arizpe, 28 July 1780, SANM II: 803.

46. Croix to Anza, Arizpe, 17 September 1780, SANM II: 807.

47. José Antonio Rengel, Chihuahua, 9 December 1784, SANM II: 900.

48. Anza, El Paso, 3 November 1778, CJMA, roll 13, book 1, 1791, frames 156–63.

49. Anza to Arrieta, El Paso, 26 November 1778, CJMA, roll 13, 1791, frames 177–78.

50. Navarro García, *Don José de Gálvez,* 335.

51. Anza, El Paso, 3 November 1778, CJMA, roll 13, book 1, 1791, frames 156–63.

52. Navarro García, *Don José de Gálvez,* 335.

53. Thomas, *Teodoro de Croix,* 40–42.

54. Anza, edict, El Paso, 19 November 1778, CJMA, roll 10, book 1, 1774, frames 607–609.

55. The citizens of El Paso to Croix, Arizpe, 20 July 1780, SANM II: 793.

56. Moorhead, *The Presidio,* 65.

57. Croix to Arrieta, Chihuahua, 20 March 1779, CJMA, roll 11, book 1, 1774, frames 195–96.

58. Thomas, *Teodoro de Croix,* 43.

59. Croix to Nicolas Soler, Nombre de Dios, June 1779, CJMA, roll 11, part 2, book 1, frames 193–94.

60. Navarro García, *Don José de Gálvez*, 335–36.

61. Frank, *From Settler to Citizen*, 119–25.

Chapter Five

1. Hämäläinen, *Comanche Empire*, 23. See also Noyes, *Los Comanches*, xix–xxix.

2. Hämäläinen, *Comanche Empire*, 2–6; and Noyes, *Los Comanches*, 11–39.

3. Noyes, *Los Comanches*, 37; and John, *Storms Brewed*, 310. Both Noyes and John argue that the Comanches considered vengeance an obligation, a social ideal second in importance only to the display of courage in battle and in everyday life.

4. Noyes, *Los Comanches*, 5–10; and John, *Storms Brewed*, 321. John suggests that the Comanches who surrendered to Governor Vélez did so because they feared drowning in the water hole more than dying in battle. She writes that the Comanches considered drowning to be an ignominious death that trapped the spirit of the deceased in its corpse, making it impossible for the soul to ascend into the afterlife.

5. Noyes, *Los Comanches*, 49–59.

6. Ibid., 60–68.

7. *Extracto*, Viceroy Marqués de Croix, Mexico City, 30 January 1769, AGI, Guadalajara 512. The information included in this extract comes from campaign reports Pedro Fermín de Medinueta submitted to the viceroy, which were dated 17 September and 9 November 1768. In these documents, Mendinueta described military actions he ordered against the Comanches during the summer and fall of 1768.

8. Ibid.

9. The name of the second Cuerno Verde, Tabico Narityante, is mentioned by Pedro Bautista Pino in *Exposition*, 47. In 1940, Alfred Barnaby Thomas argued that the Cuerno Verde who led the attack on Ojo Caliente in 1768 was the same individual Anza killed during his campaign against the Comanches in 1779. Most historians today, however, agree that Tabico Narityante was the son of Cuerno Verde, and that he recovered the chief's green-horned headdress to avenge his slain father and carry on his legacy of all-out war against the Spaniards. Regarding the identity of Tabico Narityante see Thomas, *The Plains Indians*, 167n68; John, *Storms Brewed*, 468–69; Noyes, *Los Comanches*, 323n2; Hämäläinen, *Comanche Empire*, 104; and Kessell, "Juan Bautista de Anza: Father and Son" 29–58.

10. Frank, *From Settler to Citizen*, 30–37; John, *Storms Brewed*, 474–80.

11. John, *Storms Brewed*, 474–75.

12. Mendinueta to Croix, Santa Fe, 3 November 1777, AGI, Guadalajara:276.

13. John, *Storms Brewed*, 469–70.

14. A translation of Anza's Comanche Campaign diary is in Thomas, *Forgotten Frontiers*, 122–39. An excellent narrative of the expedition is Noyes, *Los Comanches*, 74–81.

15. Thomas, *Forgotten Frontiers*, 134.

16. Anza also took the headdress of Narityante's second-in-command, Jumping Eagle, which he forwarded to Croix as a trophy of war. Anza mentions that he sent Cuerno Verde's headdress to Commandant General Croix in a letter dated 1 November 1779, of which there is a translation in Thomas, *Forgotten Frontiers*, 141–42.

17. Ibid.

18. For the Awatovi massacre, see Kessell, *Spain in the Southwest*, 189–91; and Simmons, "Trail Dust."

19. Fray Damián Martínez to Hugo O'Conor, Zuñi, 1 April 1775, AGN, Historia: 52, expediente 9; as cited in Adams, "Fray Silvestre," 97. This article does an excellent job of describing Vélez de Escalante's relations with the Hopis and includes a translation of the diary the cleric kept during his 1775 visit to their pueblos.

20. Adams, "Fray Silvestre," 107.

21. Anza to Croix, Santa Fe, 1 November 1779, BNAF 31, 633, document 1. A translation is located in Thomas, *Forgotten Frontiers*, 145–48.

22. Anza to Croix, Santa Fe, 1 November 1779, BNAF 31, 633, document 2. Translation in Thomas, *Forgotten Frontiers*, 148–50.

23. Fray Andrés García to Anza, Zuni, 3 November 1779, BNAF 31, 633, document 4. Translation of a copy in Thomas, *Forgotten Frontiers*, 168–69.

24. Anza to Croix, Santa Fe, 13 November 1779, BNAF 31, 633, document 3. Translation in Thomas, *Forgotten Frontiers*, 166–68.

25. Croix to Anza, Arizpe, 31 December 1779, BNAF 31, 633, document 7. Translation in Thomas, *Forgotten Frontiers*, 169–71.

26. Thomas, *Forgotten Frontiers*, 222–24.

27. Anza's Hopi diary is located in AGN, Historia 25, parte 3. Translation in Thomas, *Forgotten Frontiers*, 227–39.

28. Thomas, *Forgotten Frontiers*, 236–37.

29. See for example Croix's order of 1782, in which he insisted that Anza continue to see to the reduction of the Hopis "suavemente" (gently). Croix to Anza, Arizpe, SANM II: 835.

30. Thomas, *Forgotten Frontiers*, 45.

31. Croix to Anza, Arizpe, 25 March 1781, SANM II: 819.

32. In May 1780, Anza received complaints from the Franciscans regarding Navajo thefts of livestock from settlements in the colony, including the settlement of Cerrillos. The governor reminded the padres of the crown's demand for the use of peaceful persuasion, rather than force, when dealing with such activities. He ordered the friars to be patient with the Indians, but agreed that armed retaliation would be condoned if the Navajos continued their raiding forays into the colony. See Anza, Santa Fe, 28 May 1780, AASF, Loose Documents, Missions, 52, 1780:1.

33. For Spain's 1784–86 military offensive against the Gila Apaches, as well as Anza's efforts to sever the Gila-Navajo alliance and renegotiate a peace agreement with the Navajos, see Thomas, *Forgotten Frontiers*, 41–56, 245–91, and 343–63.

34. Ugarte y Loyola to Anza, Chihuahua, 5 October 1786, SANM II: 942. Translation in Thomas, *Forgotten Frontiers*, 351–57.

35. Rengel to Anza, Paso del Norte, 10 August 1787, SANM II: 961a.

36. Thomas, *Forgotten Frontiers*, 55–56.

Chapter Six

1. A translation of Mendinueta's 1772 report to Viceroy Antonio María Bucareli regarding forced relocation of citizens to centralized towns is located in Thomas, "Governor Mendinueta's Proposals," 26–31.

2. Ibid., 29.

3. Mendinueta, Mission report, Santa Fe, 8 January 1773, AGN, Provincias Internas 152. See also Navarro García, *Don José de Gálvez*, 334.

4. For the Francisco Atanasio Domínguez–Silvestre Vélez de Escalante expedition, see Warner, *The Domínguez-Escalante Journal*.

5. Miera y Pacheco hailed from the *Montañas de Burgos* (mountains of Burgos) in northern Spain, and had settled his family at El Paso in 1743. Here, he served in the local presidial garrison as an engineer and developed a reputation as a skilled cartographer. Miera y Pachecho relocated to Santa Fe in 1754, and for the next thirty years he produced for various governors sketches of the New Mexico landscape. Moreover, he lent his artistic abilities as a santero to many mission churches in the colony. See Kessell, *Miera y Pacheco*.

6. Don Bernardo Miera y Pacheco, as cited in Adams and Chávez, *Missions of New Mexico*, 4. For an excellent discussion of settlement patterns in colonial New Mexico, see Simmons, "Settlement Patterns," 54–68.

7. Simmons, "Settlement Patterns," 58–61.

8. Anza to Arrieta, Santa Fe, 3 November 1779, CJMA, roll 13, book 1, 1788, frames 350–53.

9. Citizens of Santa Fe to Croix, Arizpe, 22 June 1780, BNAF 31: 634.

10. Fray Juan Agustín de Morfi, *Descripción geográfica del Nuevo México*, 1782, AGN, Historia: 25. A translation of Morfi's description is located in Thomas, *Forgotten Frontiers*, 87–114. According to Morfi, the population of Analco was augmented by an influx of refugees from the peripheral frontier that surrounded Santa Fe and which had been under constant attack by raiding Indians.

11. Lieutenant Manuel de Azuela listed José María Cordero as habilitado for the Santa Fe garrison in a presidial review for February 1781. See Azuela, Extract of presidio review, Santa Fe, 1 February 1781, SANM II: 817.

12. Citizens of Santa Fe to Croix, Arizpe, 22 June 1780, BNAF 31: 634.

13. Croix to Anza, Arizpe, 21 June 1780, SANM II: 795. The permits mentioned by Croix and Vigil reflected a concern on the part of Spanish officials regarding the growing problem of banditry on the king's highways of the far north. In 1783, Commandant General Felipe de Neve informed Anza that the number of *facineros* (highwaymen) in colonies such as New Mexico was on the rise. Neve wrote that

it had become difficult for local justices to recognize bandits due to the fact that people moving about the colonies did so without documentation that identified their destination and reasons for travelling. Neve expressed concern that many of these rogues were being recruited from indigenous communities. For this reason, he ordered the governor and custos of New Mexico to inform all citizens that travel-permit edicts would be enforced in the colony and that violators would be arrested and punished accordingly. Anza fulfilled Neve's demand by 15 April 1784. It is possible that the edicts had little effect on the problem of banditry, because by November 1786 the governor once again issued a bando that called on New Mexicans to acquire travel permits. See Neve to Anza, Arizpe, 10 December 1783, SANM II: 871 and 871a; Neve to the custos of New Mexico, Arizpe, 10 December 1783, AASF, Loose Documents, Missions, 1783, documents 1 and 2. See also, Anza, edict, Santa Fe, 15 April 1784, SANM II: 887a; and Anza to Lieutenant Governor Eugenio Fernández, Santa Fe, 21 November 1786, CJMA, roll 12, book 1, 1786, frame 300.

14. Anza had suggested that the Analco residents should be forcibly relocated to the frontier between Santa Fe and Albuquerque. Thomas, *Forgotten Frontiers*, 92, and 379–80n59.

15. Thomas, "Governor Mendinueta's Proposals," 29–30.

16. Enrique R. Lamadrid supports the idea that New Mexicans of the 1770s felt animosity toward Anza because he was not a "native son" of the colony. He suggests that the Hispanos may have expressed their malice by excluding the governor's significant role from a popular play of that era, *Los Comanches*, in which the nuevomexicanos commemorated the final defeat of Cuerno Verde and the end of the Spanish-Comanche wars. Lamadrid, "Los Comanches," 173–88.

17. For Spain's involvement in the American Revolution, see Weber, *The Spanish Frontier in North America*, 265–70; Chávez, *Spain and the Independence of the United States;* and Broughton, "Francisco Rendón."

18. For the Spanish-British War of 1779–1783, see Lynch, *Bourbon Spain*, 320–21.

19. Croix to Anza, Arizpe, 11 February 1780, SANM II: 785.

20. Croix to Anza, Arizpe, 12 August 1781, SANM II: 825; and Croix to Anza, Arizpe, 12 August 1781, SANM II: 827.

21. Croix to Anza, Arizpe, 16 January 1783, SANM II: 850a.

22. Croix to the custos of New Mexico, Arizpe, 12 August 1781, AASF, Loose Documents, Missions, 52, 1781:4. See also Croix to the custos of New Mexico, Arizpe, 12 August 1781, AASF, Loose Documents, Missions, 52, 1781:8.

23. Croix to Anza, Arizpe, 22 January 1783, SANM II: 850b.

24. Felipe de Neve to Anza, Arizpe, 14 January 1784, SANM II: 875.

25. Anza, edict, Santa Fe, 13 March 1784, SANM II: 885. See also Anza to Fernández, Santa Fe, 26 November 1784, CJMA, part 2, roll 11, book 1, 1783, frames 99–101.

26. Simmons, *Spanish Government in New Mexico*, 113.

27. Croix to Anza, Arizpe, 14 July 1780, SANM II: 800.

28. Gerónimo de la Rocha y Figueróa, Instructions for the construction of presidios, Arizpe, 19 January 1781, SANM II: 814.

29. Moorhead, *The Presidio*, 172–77.

30. Croix to Anza, Arizpe, 1 May 1780, SANM II: 788. Both Moorhead and Simmons offer detailed analyses of military fiscal corruption and reform measures pertinent to New Mexico in the second half of the eighteenth century. See Moorhead, *The Presidio*; and Simmons, *Spanish Government in New Mexico*, 112–56.

31. Croix to Anza, Arizpe, 4 September 1781, SANM II: 830.

32. Simmons, *Spanish Government in New Mexico*, 122.

33. Croix to Anza, *Intrucción sobre la cobranza de situados, su inversión y manejo*, Arizpe, 23 June 1780, SANM II: 794. See also Simmons, *Spanish Government in New Mexico*, 134–39.

34. SANM II: 794.

35. Croix to Anza, Arizpe, 19 July 1780, SANM II: 801.

36. Croix to Anza, Arizpe, 20 January 1781, SANM II: 815.

37. Paymaster José María Cordero was listed as being on active duty in several monthly presidial reviews conducted for the Santa Fe garrison in 1781. See Manuel de Azuela, Presidio review, Santa Fe, 31 January 1781, SANM II: 816a; Anza, Presidio review, Santa Fe, 1 April 1781, SANM II: 820; and Manuel de Azuela, Presidio review, Santa Fe, September 1780 to December 1781, SANM II: 833a. Anza listed Cordero as being at Chihuahua in Anza, Presidio review, Santa Fe, 1 August 1781, SANM II: 826.

38. The effects of the 1781 smallpox epidemic on the Santa Fe garrison, including the number of illnesses and deaths caused by the virus, are included in Manuel de Azuela, Presidio review, Santa Fe, 28 February 1781, SANM II: 817a; Manuel de Azuela, Extract of a presidio review, Santa Fe, 1 March 1781, SANM II: 818; Anza, Presidio review, Santa Fe, 1 April 1781, SANM II: 820; Anza, Presidio review, Santa Fe, 1 May 1781, SANM II: 822; and Anza, Presidio review, Santa Fe, 1 June 1781, SANM II: 823.

39. Croix to Anza, Arizpe, 16 July 1781, SANM II: 825.

40. Commandant General Jacobo Ugarte y Loyola had contracted Guizarnótegui to supply all the presidios of Nueva Vizcaya and New Mexico. Simmons, *Spanish Government in New Mexico*, 137; and Moorhead, *The Presidio*, 201–21.

41. Moorhead, *The Presidio*, 218.

42. Commandant General Jacobo Ugarte y Loyola to Anza, Chihuahua, 25 August 1786, SANM II: 938. Ugarte y Loyola refers to Anza's letter of 14 July 1786 in this document.

43. Although the exact date of Maldonado's reappointment to the office of habilitado is not clear, he is mentioned as serving in this capacity in a document written by Anza and dated 15 May 1787. See Anza, Santa Fe, 15 May 1787, SANM II: 952.

44. Moorhead, *The Presidio*, 218.

45. Anza to Arrieta, El Paso, 4 November 1778, CJMA, roll 13, book 1, 1791,

frames 182–83. Translations of documents pertaining to the establishment of a New Mexico–Sonora road are located in Thomas, *Forgotten Frontiers*, 171–221.

46. For information on fray Miguel de Menchero, see Jones, *Los Paisanos*, 120–23.

47. Mendinueta, Copy of an *informe* (report) dated 9 November 1775, México, 20 March 1777, AGN, Provincias Internas 169, parte 6, ff. 1–6.

48. Fray Francisco Garcés, Oraibi, 3 July 1776, AGN, Historia 25, parte 3, ff. 260–260v.

49. Anza to Arrieta, El Paso, 26 November 1778, CJMA, roll 13, book 1, 1791, frames 179–81.

50. Correspondence between Croix and Anza regarding the establishment of a route between New Mexico and Sonora is located in *Extractos de auxilios y providencias pedidas por Anza para unificar la apertura del Camino del Norte de Nuevo México a Sonora*, México, 1779–80, BNAF 31, 629. Translations of these sources, including Anza's diary of the New Mexico–Sonora expedition, appear in Thomas, *Forgotten Frontiers*, 171–221.

51. Although the Spaniards failed to establish a New Mexico–Sonora route with Anza's 1780 expedition, they did not give up hope. Between October and November 1788, the captain from Santa Cruz presidio in Sonora, Manuel de Echeagaray, explored the territory north of Tucson and the region of the Río San Francisco, which Father Menchero had written about in the 1740s. Echeagaray's forces managed to discover a pass that led from the river to Zuni Pueblo, but they failed to reach this westernmost settlement of New Mexico. It was not until 1795 that the captain from Tucson presidio, José de Zúñiga, made a successful trip from northern Sonora to Zuni. For the Echeagaray and Zúñiga expeditions, see Hammond, "Zúñiga Journal," 40–65.

52. Thomas, *Forgotten Frontiers*, 188.

53. Croix to Anza, Arizpe, 23 October 1780, SANM II: 809.

54. BNAF 31, 629. Translations of José Antonio Vildósola's and Francisco Martinez's campaign diaries are in Thomas, *Forgotten Frontiers*, 207–21.

55. Pino's views regarding the defense of New Mexico, including the use of militias, presidios, and trade between Indians and Spaniards, are discussed in Pino, *Exposition*, 17–28.

Chapter Seven

1. Kessell, *Remote Beyond Compare.*

2. Regarding the role municipal governments played in Spain's Bourbon Reform program of the eighteenth century, see Cuello, "Economic Impact," 301–23.

3. Simmons, *Spanish Government in New Mexico*, xiii. For more on the institutional makeup of government in Spanish New Mexico, see Scholes, "Civil Government," 71–111.

4. Lynch, *Bourbon Spain*, 84.

5. Ibid., 291–98.

6. Thomas, *Teodoro de Croix*, 17–21.

7. For the settlement of Alta California by Spain, see Rolle, *California: A History*, 54–66.

8. For the French presence in Texas, see Chipman, *Spanish Texas*, 70–85.

9. Jones, *Provincial Development in Russia*, 1–11.

10. Croix to Anza, Chihuahua, 24 August 1778, SANM II: 738.

11. Although Croix's main concern involved the defense of the Internal Provinces, the Bourbons insisted that the commandant general continue to see to the religious conversion of indigenous groups, as well as the expansion of the imperial frontier. Thomas, *Teodoro de Croix*, 19.

12. Simmons, *Spanish Government in New Mexico*, 21–23.

13. Ibid., 26–27.

14. Hugo O'Conor to Croix, *Papel Instructivo*, Mexico, 22 July 1777, AGI, Guadalajara 516, as cited and translated in Cutter, *Defense of Northern New Spain*, 34–45. Cutter offers a brief but informative biography of O'Conor and explains don Hugo's relationship with Croix.

15. Thomas, *Forgotten Frontiers*, 13; and Weber, *The Spanish Frontier in North America*, 224.

16. Anza to Croix, San Miguel de Horcasitas, 1 September 1777, AGI, Guadalajara 516:1.

17. Thomas, *Teodoro de Croix*, 28–32.

18. Thomas, *Forgotten Frontiers*, ix.

19. Anza to Croix, San Miguel de Horcasitas, 1 September 1777, AGI, Guadalajara 516:1.

20. Croix to Anza, Hacienda del Avinito, 16 October 1777, AGI, Guadalajara 516:2.

21. El Rey, AGI, Audiencia de México: 1216.

22. Simmons, *Spanish Government in New Mexico*, 59–60.

23. El Rey, AGI, Audiencia de México: 1216, as translated in Thomas, *Forgotten Frontiers*, 116.

24. Priestley, *José de Gálvez*, 334.

25. Thomas, *Forgotten Frontiers*, 117–19.

26. Simmons, *Spanish Government in New Mexico*, 57–58.

27. Priestley, *José de Gálvez*, 334.

28. Simmons, *Spanish Government in New Mexico*, 58, see 58n16.

29. Commandant General José Antonio Rengel to Anza, Arizpe, 20 June 1787, SANM II: 951; and Rengel to Anza, Paso del Norte, 12 July 1787, SANM II: 961.

30. The responsibilities of the governor in New Mexico are well covered in Simmons, *Spanish Government in New Mexico*, 54–55.

31. Anza, edict, Santa Fe, 31 May 1782, SANM II: 840. Spanish law required the governors of New Mexico to conduct one general inspection of the colony during

their tenure. See *Recopilación de leyes de las Indias*, law 11, title 2, book v; and Simmons, *Spanish Government in New Mexico*, 65.

32. Anza, general inspection report and edict, Santa Fe, 27 August 1782, SANM II: 843.

33. Anza to Arrieta, El Paso, 4 and 26 November 1778, CJMA, roll 13, book 1, frames 164, 177–78.

34. For a discussion of New Mexico's judicial system, see Simmons, *Spanish Government in New Mexico*, 17–20, 66–68, and 161–66.

35. Ibid., 17; and Cutter, *Legal Culture*, 59–63.

36. Croix to Anza, Arizpe, 21 February 1782, SANM II: 837; Anza to Lieutenant Governor Eugenio Fernández, Santa Fe, 27 December 1782, CJMA, roll 11, book 1, frames 88–89; and Fernández to Anza, El Paso, 28 January 1783, CJMA, roll 11, book 1, frame 90.

37. AGI, Guadalajara 268, "Instrucción formada en virtud de Real Orden de S.M., que se dirige al Señor Comandante General de Provincias Internas don Jacobo Ugarte y Loyola para gobierno y puntual observancia de este Superíor Gefe y de sus inmediatos Subalternos." México, 26 August 1786, as cited in Cutter, *Legal Culture*, 56 and 167n42.

38. Cutter, *Legal Culture*, 35–38.

39. Ibid., 31–34.

40. Ibid., 39–41.

41. Ibid., 107–109.

42. Croix to Anza, Arizpe, 10 February 1780, SANM II: 784.

43. Croix to Anza, Arizpe, 19 July 1780, SANM II: 802.

44. Anza to the alcaldes mayores of Taos, la Cañada, Queres, Alameda, Albuquerque, and Laguna, Santa Fe, 24 April 1784, SANM II: 890.

45. Marcos Sánchez and Juan Maya to the alcalde of Isleta, Tomé, August 1782, with Anza's response, Belén, 25 August 1782, AASF, Loose Documents, Missions, 1782: 6.

46. The case between the community of Las Truchas and the alcaldes, José Sánchez and José Campo Redondo, is located in SANM II: 856.

Chapter Eight

1. For the mechanics of government in eighteenth-century New Mexico, see Simmons, *Spanish Government in New Mexico*, 159–213.

2. Anza to Fernández, Santa Fe, 16 November 1785, CJMA, roll 13, book 1, frame 90.

3. See Croix to Anza, Arizpe, 12 January 1780, SANM II: 782; Croix to Anza, Arizpe, 25 June 1783, SANM II: 864; and Simmons, *Spanish Government in New Mexico*, 23.

4. Navarro García, *Don José de Gálvez*, 318–21; and Simmons, *Spanish Government in New Mexico*, 101–107.

5. Croix to Anza, Arizpe, 18 April 1781, SANM II: 821.

6. Simmons, *Spanish Government in New Mexico*, 102n50.

7. Documents regarding Roybal's case include Croix to Anza, Arizpe, 3 January 1782, SANM II: 833b; and Croix to Anza, Arizpe, 15 January 1784, SANM II: 813.

8. Croix to Anza, Arizpe, 15 July 1782, SANM II: 842.

9. Croix to Anza, Arizpe, 10 December 1782, SANM II: 848.

10. Croix to Anza, Arizpe, 10 December 1782, SANM II: 848.

11. Felipe de Neve to Anza, Arizpe, 18 December 1783, SANM II: 872.

12. Simmons, *Spanish Government in New Mexico*, 103.

13. Neve to Anza, Arizpe, 17 March 1784, SANM II: 886.

14. Navarro García, *Don José de Gálvez*, 430.

15. Neve to Anza, Arizpe, 18 December 1783, SANM II: 873.

16. See, for example, Anza's edict announcing the governor's inspection tour of New Mexico, Santa Fe, 31 May 1782, SANM II: 840.

17. Examples of the cordilleras Governor Anza indicated on the margins of state documents can be found in SANM II: 840; Anza, report on his inspection tour of New Mexico, Santa Fe, 27 August 1782, SANM II: 843; Anza to New Mexico's justices, edict regarding the publication and archiving of a royal notice announcing the birth of the infante, Fernando María, Santa Fe, 6 August 1785, SANM II: 917; Anza, regarding the conferral of the title of "Marqués de Sonora" on José de Gálvez, Santa Fe, 30 September 1786, SANM II: 941.

18. Neve to Anza, Arizpe, 18 December 1783, SANM II: 873; and Simmons, *Spanish Government in New Mexico*, 104.

19. Simmons, *Spanish Government in New Mexico*, 104–106.

20. José Antonio Rengel to Anza, Chihuahua, 8 March 1785, SANM II: 909.

21. See for example Croix to Anza, proclamation announcing the designation of Arizpe as the seat of government for the General Command, Arizpe, 25 June 1783, SANM II: 864.

22. See Anza, edict, Santa Fe, 19 August 1786, SANM II: 937.

23. Rengel to Anza, Chihuahua, 17 March 1785, SANM II: 910.

24. Anza to Fernández, El Paso, 2 January 1783, CJMA, roll 11, book 1, frames 91–93.

25. Regarding Neve's appointment, see José de Gálvez to Neve, copy of royal appointment, El Pardo, 15 February 1783, SANM II: 857a; Neve to Custos of New Mexico, Arizpe, 12 August 1783, AASF, Loose Documents, Missions, 1783: 3; and Anza, edict, Santa Fe, 10 March 1784, SANM II: 882.

26. Simmons, *Spanish Government in New Mexico*, 27n7; and Navarro García, *Don José de Gálvez*, 430, 443.

27. Navarro García, *Don José de Gálvez*, 443–44.

28. Rengel to Anza, Chihuahua, 30 November 1784, SANM II: 898.

29. Ibid., 898

30. Anza to the justices of New Mexico, Santa Fe, 12 March 1785, SANM II: 911.

31. El rey, royal appointment for don Manuel de Flon, San Lorenzo, 28 October 1784, AGI, Audiencia de México 1216.

32. Navarro García, *Don José de Gálvez*, 506n225.

33. Ibid., 506.

34. Weber, *The Spanish Frontier in North America*, 227–29, 265–70.

35. El Conde de Gálvez to Anza, México, 10 August 1785, SANM II: 916.

36. Simmons, *Spanish Government in New Mexico*, 27–29; and Navarro García, *Don José de Gálvez*, 452–55.

37. Rengel to Anza, Chihuahua, 16 February 1786, SANM II: 933.

38. Anza, royal cédula, Santa Fe, 2 September 1786, SANM II: 940.

39. Jacobo Ugarte y Loyola to Anza, Chihuahua, 20 October 1786, SANM II: 944.

40. Anza, cédula announcing Jacobo Ugarte y Loyola's appointment to the office of commandant general, Santa Fe, 14 August 1786, SANM II: 936.

41. Boeta, *Bernardo de Gálvez*, 120–21.

42. Ugarte y Loyola to Anza, Chihuahua, 9 February 1787, SANM II: 949.

43. Simmons, *Spanish Government in New Mexico*, 29–31.

44. El rey, cédula regarding the appointment of Fernando de la Concha to the office of governor for New Mexico, Madrid, 10 December 1786, AGI, Audiencia de México 1216.

45. Rengel to Anza, Paso del Norte, 10 August 1787, SANM II: 961a; and Concha, Santa Fe, 2 October 1787, SANM II: 957.

Chapter Nine

1. Scholes, "Civil Government," 80.

2. Agapito Rey, "Missionary Aspects," 22–31.

3. For the Coronado Expedition of 1540, see Bolton, *Coronado*; Flint, *Great Cruelties*; and Kessell, *Spain in the Southwest*, 29–55.

4. Kessell, *Spain in the Southwest*, 71–73.

5. Although it has been criticized, Bolton's essay "The Mission as a Frontier Institution" does offer a concise explanation of the mission ideal in Spanish America. Bolton's essay was criticized in part for assuming that Spanish law required the missions to remain active in a specific region for only ten years. After this, the mission was to be secularized. Although Bolton's assumption has been proven wrong regarding the law, historians seem to agree that the mission was supposed to be a temporary and transitional institution that laid the groundwork for secular parishes. See Bolton, "The Mission," 49–65. See also Weber, *The Spanish Frontier in North America*, 92–95; and Norris, "Franciscan Hegemony."

6. Kessell, *Missions of New Mexico*, 8–11. Kessell argues that Spaniards and friars serving in seventeenth-century New Mexico were too few to use coercion as a means. He suggests that the friars convinced the Pueblo people to first build smaller structures such as conventos. At the same time, the friars worked at devel-

oping relationships of understanding and cooperation with the Pueblos in the hope that the Indians would accept them and Christianity. This done, the friars would then convince the Indians to provide the labor for construction of larger mission structures.

7. Ibid., 10–11, 11n8.

8. Vicar and Ecclesiastical Judge don Santiago Roybal to the Bishop of Durango, Pedro Tamarón y Romeral, Santa Fe, 6 April 1764. Quoted by Felipe Cantador in a copy of Tamarón's 1760 report on New Mexico, Nombre de Dios, 11 July 1765, translated in Adams, *Bishop Tamarón's Visitation,* 78.

9. Frank, *From Settler to Citizen,* 13–30. Frank's argument is supported if looked at in a historical context regarding Spanish-Indian relations. In the winter of 1540–41, Spaniards under the leadership of Francisco Vázquez de Coronado tried to impose forced levies of food, blankets, women, and an entire Tiguex pueblo on the Tiwas. The Indians responded to these excessive demands with violent resistance. In another example, similar Spanish demands on the Pueblos during the 1660s and 1670s resulted in the Pueblo Revolt of 1680. See Kessell, *Kiva, Cross, and Crown,* 18–19 and chapter 6.

10. Jones, Jr. *Pueblo Warriors,* chapters 5–6, 131–69.

11. Kessell, "Anza Damns the Missions," 53–63.

12. Anza's family's relations with the Jesuits in Sonora were so strong that in the 1730s the order appealed to the viceroy to allow his father to travel to Baja California to put down a rebellion which had erupted at the southern end of the colony. For more on Anza the Elder, see Smith, *Captain of the Phantom Presidio,* 109, 129, 135; Garate, *Basque Explorer*; and Kessell, *Mission of Sorrows,* 38, 69. For the Baja California rebellion, see Crosby, *Antigua California,* 114–17.

13. To date, the nature of Anza's education is not clear, but it is possible that he received some formal training in Mexico City where Enlightenment literature did find a receptive audience.

14. Lynch, *Bourbon Spain,* 254. For the Spanish Enlightenment, see also Kern, *Historical Dictionary,* 188–94; and Herr, *Revolution in Spain.*

15. Kern, *Historical Dictionary,* 205–206. Feijóo's intellectual interests included subjects such as medicine, politics, aesthetics, pedagogy, social criticism, literature, natural sciences, astronomy, philosophy, and superstitions. His essays on these themes were collected in his works, *Teatro Crítico Universal* (1726–1739) and *Cartas eruditas* (1742–1760).

16. Lynch, *Bourbon Spain,* 258–61. The *Mesta* was an official association of individuals and organizations that owned large flocks of sheep and that, since the time of Ferdinand and Isabela, had acquired virtual control of pasturelands in Spain through the right of *posesión.* In the eighteenth century, the Mesta came under attack by a general populace that was going hungry due to the association's virtual monopoly over arable land it did not use to produce food. As a result, officials such as Campomanes and Floridablanca initiated agricultural reform measures to increase the amount of land available to the peasant masses, and thus reverse

the food production crisis. During Anza's time, King Carlos III tried to reduce the hereditary power of the Mesta to control pasturelands. He hoped to open up these lands to peasants so that they might farm it and thus contribute to the failing Spanish economy. See Herr, *Revolution in Spain*, 111–18.

17. Gálvez's personal and political life are well discussed in Priestly, *José de Gálvez*.

18. Translated from Pietschmann's "Protoliberalismo" in Vázquez, *Interpretaciones*, 31–32.

19. Anza to Viceroy Antonio María Bucareli, Tubac, 15 December 1772, AGN, Provincias Internas 152; translated in Kessell, "Friars versus Bureaucrats," 151–62.

20. Anza outlined his criticisms of the mission system in his 15 December 1772 report to Viceroy Bucareli. Translated in Kessell, "Anza Damns the Missions," 53–63.

21. Ibid., 59–60. For issues regarding land usage, resource allocation, spatial identity, trade, and group relations in Sonora, see Radding, *Wandering Peoples*.

22. Adams, *Bishop Tamarón's Visitation*, 31.

23. Adams and Chávez, *Missions of New Mexico*, 254.

24. Ibid., 258.

25. Thomas, *Teodoro de Croix*, 19.

Chapter Ten

1. Documents relating to the assignment of peninsular friars in New Spain and New Mexico in 1778 are located in AGI, Audiencia de México, 2730, 2732, and 2734. See also Kessell, *Kiva, Cross, and Crown*, 348; and Hendricks, "Church-State Relations, 24–42.

2. Anza to Provincial Juan Bautista Dosal, Santa Fe, 20 February 1779; and Dosal to Anza, Mexico City, 21 April 1779, BNAF 31: 632.

3. Kessell, *Kiva, Cross, and Crown*, 351–52; and Hendricks, "Church-State Relations," 38–39.

4. BNAF 31: 632.

5. Copy of an edict, Juan Bautista de Anza, Santa Fe, 25 August 1781, AASF, Loose Documents, Missions, 52, 1781: 5.

6. For the issue of Pueblo education in Christian doctrine, see Adams, *Bishop Tamarrón's Visitation of New Mexico*, 31, 48; and Adams and Chávez, *Missions of New Mexico*, xx, 255.

7. Teodoro de Croix to the Custos of New Mexico, Arizpe, 10 August 1781, AASF, Loose Documents, Missions, 52, 1781: 3. Croix deemed the appointment of clerics to Zuni Pueblo as vital for his plan to bring the Hopi Indians into alliance with Spain. Zuni was the westernmost Pueblo settlement in New Mexico, and it was the closest to the Hopi homeland. Between 1779 and 1780, Governor Anza had studied the possibility of moving the Hopis to settlements that were allied with Spain; Zuni, being the closest, was the obvious first choice. The Hopis were in dire

need of help. For several years, they had experienced a series of droughts that left them on the verge of starvation. In 1780, Anza traveled to the western pueblos and managed to relocate some of the Hopis to settlements along the Río Grande such as Sabinal and Sandía. Anza's Hopi diary and correspondence regarding the plight of the Hopis are located in AGN, Historia 25, 288–318v; BNAF 31: 633; and a translation in Thomas, *Forgotten Frontiers*, 227–41.

8. Croix to Custos José de la Prada, Arizpe, 5 February 1782, AASF, Loose Documents, Missions, 52, 1782: 11. Appointing a minister to Zuni Pueblo proved problematic throughout Anza's tenure. The settlement's isolation from the Río Grande valley made it difficult to protect and provide for the friars, who always ran a risk of harm from surrounding Indian groups and from within Zuni itself. See Commandant General Jacobo Ugarte y Loyola to Anza, Chihuahua, 10 February 1787, SANM II: 950.

9. Fray Diego Muñoz Jurado to fray José Pereyro, Santa Clara, n.d., AASF, Loose Documents, Missions, 52, 1781: 11.

10. Lynch, *Bourbon Spain*, 271–72.

11. The judicial powers enjoyed by Spanish governors serving in peripheral colonies like New Mexico are aptly discussed in Cutter, *Legal Culture*, 69–73.

12. The people of La Cañada to Custos Hinojosa, La Cañada, no date, AASF, Loose Documents, Missions, 52, 1781: 10. The *diligencias* in the case against fray Diego Muñoz Jurado are located in SANM II: 812. The case is also discussed in brief by Gutiérrez, *When Jesus Came*, 312–13.

13. Anza had experienced similar resistance from the citizens of Santa Fe when they appealed to Commandant General Croix and managed to acquire a restraining order forbidding the governor to relocate the capital to the south side of the Santa Fe River. See Simmons, *Spanish Government in New Mexico*, 77.

14. Gutiérrez, *When Jesus Came*, 313.

15. Ibid., 312. Gutiérrez writes that this claim by the people of La Cañada was completely unwarranted. He does add that after 1781, the friars became stricter in their demand of payment for church services. The Franciscans did this because the state had initiated a movement to abolish the tradition of requiring Indians to pay fees for marriages and burials, as well as of providing labor.

16. In New Mexico, fees for church services were set in both *pesos reales*, which corresponded to actual currency, and *pesos de la tierra*, which represented the value of a commodity in pesos reales. Normally, two pesos de la tierra were the equivalent of one peso real. Most people in the colony paid for services in kind, usually in food products, but also in leather, livestock, candles, wax, and textiles. In his testimony, Muñoz mentions that one individual paid for services with an old *anquera* (horse's rump cover) and an *espadín* (rapier).

17. Diligencias in the case between fray Diego Muñoz Jurado and Juan José Bustos, New Mexico, 1781, AASF, Loose Documents, Missions, 52, 1781:7.

18. Laws 80 and 93, title 14, book 1, *Recopilación de leyes de los reynos de las Indias*, 1681.

19. AASF, Loose Documents, Missions, 52, 1781:2.

20. *Diligencias* in the case against José Domínguez, AASF, Loose Documents, Missions, 52, 1782: 5.

21. Anza to Custos José de la Prada, Santa Fe, 20 September 1782, AASF, Loose Documents, Missions, 52, 1782: 10. In his letter, Anza does not identify the friars, nor does he define the nature of their disobedience. Fray Angélico Chávez described the friars as having a "disobedient attitude," thus suggesting that they were not actually acting out their opposition to the state. See Chávez, *Archive*, 43.

22. The report the peninsular friars wrote regarding Anza's treatment of them is located in AASF, Loose Documents, Missions, 52, 1782: 12. The author of the report is not stated, but fray Angélico Chávez suggests that fray Diego Muñoz Jurado wrote it. Chávez, *Archive*, 43. To whom the report was written is also not stated, but it is possible that Commandant General Croix was the intended recipient because he was Anza's immediate superior. The peninsular friars identify Muñoz as the author in a second report; this one was directed to a new commandant general, Felipe de Neve. Friars to Neve, Arizpe, 14 January 1783, AASF, Loose Documents, Missions, 52, 1783: 4. It is interesting to note that in the first report the friars occasionally described Anza as having "good will and affection" towards them. This, however, was done in a sarcastic tone that tries to exaggerate what they believed to be the governor's actual hatred of them.

23. Croix's order to Anza regarding the transmittal of judicial cases to Arizpe is mentioned in Anza to Lieutenant Governor Eugenio Fernández, El Paso, 2 and 28 January 1783, CJMA, roll 11, book 1, frames 90–93.

24. Indians assigned to work for secular officials for one-week periods were referred to as *semaneros*. Indian *fiscales* handled the assignment of semaneros to secular officials. Their goal was to meet Spanish demands for labor without disrupting the Indians' ability to provide for their own needs. See Frank, *From Settler to Citizen*, 28–30.

25. SANM II: 883.

26. Peninsular friars to Commandant General Felipe de Neve, 14 January 1783, Arizpe, AASF, Loose Documents, Missions, 52, 1783: 4. Felipe de Neve was appointed commandant general of the Provincias Internas by royal cédula of 15 February 1782. He took possession of his office on 12 August 1783. See AASF, Loose Documents, Missions, 52, 1783: 3.

27. Custos José de la Prada to Governor Anza, Zia, 14 February 1783, AASF, Loose Documents, Missions, 52, 1783: 7.

28. Custos Prada to the Custodial Council, Zia, 5 October 1783, AASF, Loose Documents, Missions, 52, 1783: 5. Since the founding of the New Mexico colony in the late 1500s, the Franciscans had utilized a strategy of opposition to the state by relocating the custodial office away from the governor's place of residence. Perhaps the most notorious example of this strategy occurred in 1613 when the self-appointed custos, fray Isidro Ordóñez, relocated the custodial office to Santo

Domingo during his struggles with Governor Pedro de Peralta. See Kessell, *Kiva, Cross, and Crown*, 93–98.

29. Governor Anza to Custos Prada, 15 March 1783, AASF, Loose Documents, Missions, 52, 1783: 9.

30. AASF, Loose Documents, Missions, 52, 1783: 5.

31. Provincial Minister fray Juan Bravo to Custos Prada, Mexico City, 10 March 1784, AASF, Loose Documents, Missions, 52, 1784: 2.

32. Ibid.

33. Kessell, *Missions of New Mexico*, 14.

34. Ibid., 14–15.

35. Ibid., 5. Kessell utilizes the concept of a "withering vine" to metaphorically describe the degeneration and decline of the Custody of the Conversion of Saint Paul in New Mexico throughout the eighteenth century.

Chapter Eleven

1. For a discussion of the Bourbon view regarding absolutism and the church during Anza's time, see Lynch, *Bourbon Spain*.

2. Gibson, *Spain in America*, 68–69.

3. Elliot, *Spain and its World*, 7–9. For more on the idea of Spain as an emerging nation-state, see Lynch, *Spain under the Habsburgs*, vol. 1, 1–12.

4. Lynch, *Bourbon Spain*, 269–80.

5. Norris, "Franciscan Hegemony," 25.

6. Kessell, *Kiva, Cross, and Crown*, 301.

7. For the founding of the Custody of the Conversion of Saint Paul and the early struggles between friars and secular authorities in New Mexico, see Kessell, *Kiva, Cross, and Crown*, 93–103.

8. Neve had replaced the first commandant general, Teodoro de Croix, when the latter was reassigned to the office of viceroy for Peru in 1783. Neve to Anza, Arizpe, 19 August 1783, SANM II: 866.

9. Galindo Navarro cited laws 28, 29, and 31, title 15, book 1 of the *Recopilación* to support his opinion. Pedro Galindo Navarro to Commandant General Teodoro de Croix, Chihuahua, 19 and 20 April 1779, AASF, Loose Documents, Missions, 52, 1779: 4.

10. For a discussion of the struggles between New Mexico's regular and secular clergies, see Adams, *Bishop Tamarrón's Visitation;* Adams and Chávez, *Missions of New Mexico*; and Norris, "Franciscan Hegemony," 128–52.

11. Croix to Anza, Arizpe, 26 June 1780, SANM II: 797.

12. Report by the Franciscans to the commandant general, New Mexico, 1782, AASF, Loose Documents, Missions, 52, 1782: 12.

13. Anza, edict, Santa Fe, 10 March 1784, SANM II: 881.

14. Ibid., 883; and AASF, Loose Documents, Missions, 52, 1784: 1.

15. Anza to Pueblo Governors, Santa Fe, 16 March 1779, AASF, Loose Documents, Missions, 52, 1779: 1.

16. See Kessell, *Missions of New Mexico*, 14; and Frank, *From Settler to Citizen*, 198. Frank states that the Pueblo population never exceeded more than nine thousand to ten thousand after the smallpox epidemic and for the rest of the colonial era.

17. AASF, Loose Documents, Missions, 52, 1782: 12.

18. Governor Anza, edict regarding the abolishment of personal Indian service for ecclesiastics, Santa Fe, 10 March 1784, AASF, Loose Documents, Missions, 52, 1784: 1. See also SANM II: 883. The statutes that Neve cited included laws 23, book 1, title 13; law 87, book 1, title 14; laws 1, 2, 8, 9, 23, book 6, title 1; and laws 6, 43, book 6, title 12.

19. Felipe de Neve died late in 1784 and was replaced by Rengel, who served as interim commandant general. Rengel informed Governor Anza of his appointment, issued by the Audiencia de México and dated 20 November 1784. José Antonio Rengel to Anza, Chihuahua, 30 November 1784, SANM II: 898.

20. Fray Santiago Fernández de Sierra to Commandant General José Antonio Rengel, El Paso del Norte, May–June 1784, AASF, Loose Documents, Missions, 52, 1784: 4.

21. Provincial Minister fray Juan Bravo to Custos José de la Prada, Mexico City, 10 March 1784, AASF, Loose Documents, Missions, 52, 1784: 2.

22. Kessell notes that Anza first suggested the reduction of missions from an economic perspective. Kessell, *Kiva, Cross, and Crown*, 543n61. Anza's report regarding his suggestion is mentioned in Navarro to Croix, Arizpe, 6 August 1781, SANM II: 832; and Croix to Anza, Arizpe, 15 September 1781, SANM II: 831.

23. In an ecclesiastical sense, the term *visita* referred to a "church without a resident priest, but which is regularly 'visited' by a priest who conducts services." It should not be confused with an inspection, civil or ecclesiastical. The use of the term *cabecera* to identify head missions was borrowed from Spanish tradition regarding civic administration. In the latter dynamic, a cabecera was the head town of an *alcaldía mayor* (major district). See Simmons, *Spanish Government in New Mexico*, 167n24, 219, 223.

24. Regarding Anza's mission consolidation plan and the case of Pecos, see Kessell, *Kiva, Cross, and Crown*, 348–50.

25. Simmons, "New Mexico's Smallpox Epidemic," 319–26.

26. Scholars who have investigated the smallpox epidemic of 1780–81 utilized burial records for New Mexico located in the Archive of the Archdiocese of Santa Fe. These included: AASF, Bur-3, Albuquerque, Box 2; AASF, Bur-25, San Felipe, Box 13; AASF, Bur-49, Santa Fe, Box 27; AASF, Bur-51, Santa Fe Castrense, Box 28; AASF, Bur-46, Sandia, Box 10; AASF, Bur-37, Santo Domingo, Box 31; AASF, Bur-8, Cochiti, Box 6; AASF, Bur-30, Santa Clara, Box 20. Although these documents are incomplete and unclear regarding the exact number of deaths from smallpox, researchers agree that the total exceeded five thousand. See Simmons, "New

Mexico's Smallpox Epidemic;" Hendricks, "Church-State Relations," 24–42; and Kessell, *Kiva, Cross, and Crown*, 348.

27. Simmons, "New Mexico's Smallpox Epidemic," 321–22.

28. Galindo Navarro to Croix, Arizpe, 6 August 1781, SANM II: 832.

29. Croix to Anza, Arizpe, 15 September 1781, SANM II: 831.

30. Franciscan report to Croix, New Mexico, 1782, AASF, Loose Documents, Missions, 52, 1782: 12.

31. Kessell writes that the reduction of Pecos to visita status in 1782 "was merely a clerical matter," and that Pecos had been treated as a charge of the capital for two decades even though it held the status of "mission." Kessell, *Kiva, Cross, and Crown*, 349.

32. Croix to Anza, Arizpe, 27 January 1783, SANM II: 854.

33. For a table that illustrates the consolidation of missions carried out by Anza between 1782 and 1788, see Hendricks, "Church-State Relations," 27.

34. Lynch, *Bourbon Spain*, 374

35. Kessell, *Kiva, Cross, and Crown*, 352–53.

36. Anza to fray Caetano José Ignacio Bernal, Santa Fe, 19 December 1779, AASF, Loose Documents, Missions, 52, 1779: 4.

37. Fray Juan Bermejo served as capellán of the Santa Fe presidio until 30 April 1781, at which time fray Juan José Llanos replaced him. Llanos was a logical replacement for Bermejo because he had served as capellán for the expedition that Anza led to Sonora in 1780. See Anza, Presidial Review, Santa Fe, 1 May 1781, SANM II: 822; and fray Juan José Llanos, Death certificate for Corporal Bartolo Gutiérrez, Paso del Norte, 12 January 1781, SANM II: 820.

38. In 1779, Croix informed Anza that the assistant inspector of the province of Coahuila, Captain Luis Cazorla, had presented him with a report in which he expressed concern and doubts regarding recent appointments of presidial chaplains. The crown, it seemed, equated the abilities of a capellán with the degree of loyalty he expressed towards the state. On 17 April 1782, Galindo Navarro submitted a dictamen on this issue to Croix. In his opinion, the assessor general argued that capellanes in the far northern territory must be dependent on their captains and the commandant general rather than on the custodial head. In addition, the assessor claimed that the commandant general and his governors held sole power to make capellán appointments. In this light, it can be argued that Father Bermejo was chosen to fill the presidio chaplaincy of New Mexico because he appeared to be more loyal to the monarchy than to his own custody. See Croix to Anza, Arizpe, 24 April 1782, SANM II: 838.

39. Franciscan report, New Mexico, 1782, AASF, Loose Documents, Missions, 52, 1782: 12.

40. Peninsular friars to Neve, Arizpe, 14 January 1783, AASF, Loose Documents, Missions, 52, 1783: 4. See also AASF, Loose Documents, Missions, 52, 1782: 12.

41. Prada to Anza, Zia, 14 February 1783, AASF, Loose Documents, Missions, 52, 1783: 7.

42. Anza to Prada, 15 March 1783, AASF, Loose Documents, Missions, 52, 1783: 9.

43. Prada, Consulta, Zia, 5 October 1783, AASF, Loose Documents, Missions, 52, 1783: 5.

44. Anza to Prada, Santa Fe, 26 April 1784, AASF, Loose Documents, Missions, 52, 1784: 3.

45. Ibid.

46. Ibid.

47. Lynch, *Bourbon Spain*, 109.

48. Croix to fray Juan José de Hinojosa, Villa de Chihuahua, 20 September 1778, BNAF 31, 629.

49. Franciscan replacements to Croix, Chihuahua, 4 February 1779, BNAF 31, 632.

50. The correspondence between Croix, Custos Hinojosa, and the Franciscans regarding payment of the sínodo is located in AASF, Loose Documents, Missions, 52, 1779: 2.

51. Croix to Bermejo, Arizpe, 22 January 1782, AASF, Loose Documents, Missions, 52, 1782: 4.

52. Peninsular friars, Representación to Commandant General José Antonio Rengel, Paso del Norte, May-June 1784, AASF, Loose Documents, Missions, 52, 1784: 4.

53. Ibid.

54. Fray Sebastián Antón to Rengel, Chihuahua, 3 March 1785, SANM II: 908; Rengel to Anza, Chihuahua, 3 March 1785, SANM II: 908.

55. Fray Juan Bermejo to Custos Prada, New Mexico, 1783, AASF, Loose Documents, Missions, 52, 1783: 10.

56. One *media* was equal to about one half of a hundredweight, or about 50 pounds for every 100 pounds.

57. The king to all secular and ecclesiastical officials of his kingdoms of the Indies and the Philippines, San Lorenzo, 19 November 1785, SANM II: 922.

58. Commandant General Jacobo Ugarte y Loyola to Anza, Chihuahua, 22 July 1786, SANM II: 935.

59. Brading, *Church and State*, 8. For a discussion of the intendant system and New Mexico, see Simmons, *Spanish Government in New Mexico*, 33–41.

60. Kessell, *Missions of New Mexico*, 11.

61. Primary documents related to Franciscan missionary efforts among the Navajos, Zunis, and the Hopis respectively include AGN, Provincias Internas 152, ff. 118–26; Anza, Documents regarding vestments, tools, and furniture of the failed Navajo missions, April 1782, Santa Fe, AASF, Loose Documents, Missions, 52, 1782: 2 and 1782: 3; various documents regarding religious ornaments for missions among the Navajos, September 1781–82, SANM II: 829; Croix to Anza regarding Navajo missions, Arizpe, 24 January 1783, SANM II: 853; Croix regarding Zuni Mission, Arizpe, 10 August 1781, AASF, Loose Documents, Missions, 52,

1781: 3, and 1782: 11; Neve to Anza regarding Zuni Mission, Arizpe, 7 January 1784, SANM II: 874; Ugarte to Anza regarding Zuni Mission, Chihuahua, 10 February 1787, SANM II: 950; Vice-Custos fray Mariano Rodríguez de la Torre regarding his 1755 expedition to Hopi country, Santo Domingo, 11 June 1776, AGN, Historia 25, ff. 261–67; fray Francisco Garcés to Zuni minister regarding his letter from the Hopi pueblos, Oraibi, 3 July 1776, AGN, Historia: 25, f. 260; Anza, Hopi Diary, 1779–80, BNAF 31: 633; and AGN, Historia 25, ff. 288–315; Croix to Anza regarding reduction of the Hopis, Arizpe, 24 January 1782, SANM II: 835.

62. Frank, *From Settler to Citizen*, 196–209.

63. See, for example, the debate carried on between José de Gálvez and the Franciscans of Sonora in the 1770s regarding Gálvez's plan to transform the province's missions into "profitable collective farms." Like Anza, Gálvez believed that the missions in the far northern territory had evolved into "stagnant, government subsidized, and semi-autonomous concentration camps." He believed that by returning ownership of land to Indians, these people would become "emancipated and integrated citizens working their own lands and paying their fair share." Kessell, *Friars, Soldiers, and Reformers*, 152.

Chapter Twelve

1. Lynch, *Bourbon Spain*, 261–62.

2. Ibid., 263.

3. Brading, *Church and State*, 3–5.

4. Lavrin writes that Spain's legal code, the Siete Partidas, granted parents the power to disinherit daughters who married against their wishes. Lavrin, *Sexuality and Marriage*, 4–6.

5. Seed, *To Love, Honor, and Obey*, 32–48.

6. A transcribed version of the 1776 Pragmatic on Marriages can be found in Konetzke, *Colección de documentos*, vol. 3, tomo 1, pp. 406–413. For discussion of the 1778 Pragmatic, see Hendricks, "Church-State Relations," 29–31. See also Boyer, *Lives of the Bigamists*, 63–65; and Gutiérrez, *When Jesus Came*, 315.

7. Neve to Anza, Arizpe, 18 November 1783, SANM II: 870. See also Anza to Lieutenant Governor Eugenio Fernández de Leyba, Santa Fe, 27 November 1783, CJMA, roll 12, book 1, frame 87; and Local Justices, Laguna and Zuni, 20 April 1784 and 26 April 1784, SANM II: 903.

8. SANM II: 862, 888.

9. Gutiérrez, *When Jesus Came*, 227.

10. Ibid., 240. For a discussion of class and marriage, see Gutiérrez, *When Jesus Came*, 225–40.

11. Fray Sebastián Fernández to Prada, Abiquiú, 22 May 1781, AASF, Loose Documents, Missions, 52, 1781: 1.

12. Prada to the Franciscans, Santa Ana, 30 May 1781, AASF, Loose Documents, Missions, 52, 1781: 6. It is interesting to note that Prada's report to the friars

regarding the Jacinta Trujillo-Antonio Choño case was written almost entirely in Latin. Why Prada did so is not certain, but it is possible that he used Latin in order to keep Governor Anza ignorant of its content.

13. The marriage case between Diego Antonio Martín and María Guadalupe Armijo is located in AASF, Loose Documents, Missions, 52, 1782: 12.

14. The marriage case between Antonia Sánchez and Juan Ignacio Mesta is located in the diligencias against fray Diego Muñoz Jurado by members of the parish of Santa Cruz de la Cañada, New Mexico, 1781, SANM II: 812.

15. CJMA, roll 12, book 1, frames 414–36.

16. SANM II: 862.

17. Diligencias in an inheritance case between Lieutenant Juan Ignacio Mestas and Bárbara Baca, New Mexico, 1782–84, SANM II: 845.

18. SANM II: 862; and CJMA 12: 1, ff. 414–36.

19. SANM II: 888.

20. SANM II: 845.

21. Hendricks, "Church-State Relations," 30–31.

22. Francisco Lobero to Juan Bautista de Anza, Santa Fe, June 1787, SANM II: 956.

23. Testimony from Francisco Javier Flores, Santiago Largo, and Baltasar Suytigua, Santa Fe, 23 June 1787, SANM II: 956.

24. Testimony of Esteban Portillo, Santa Fe, 9 July 1787, SANM II: 956.

Conclusion

1. For Anza's efforts to bring the Comanche tribes into a peace agreement, and the resultant Comanche Peace of 1786, see Thomas, *Forgotten Frontier*, 71–83, 292–342.

2. Weber, *The Spanish Frontier in North America*, 227.

3. Ibid., 196–98.

4. Ibid., 227–30.

5. Anza, edict, El Paso, 19 September 1778, CJMA, roll 19, book 1, 1774, frames 593–95.

6. Thomas, *Forgotten Frontier*, 76–77, 329–32.

7. AGI, Audiencia de Guadalajara 289.

Bibliography

Primary Sources/Archives

AASF: Archive of the Archdiocese of Santa Fe, Albuquerque, New Mexico
  Loose Documents, Missions: 52 (1779, 1780, 1781, 1782, 1783, 1784).
  Burials: 3, 8, 25, 30, 37, 46, 49, 51.
AGI: Archivo General de Indias, Seville, Spain
  Audiencia de Guadalajara: 82, 185, 276, 278, 281 pt. 7, 289, 300.
  Audiencia de México: 25, 1117, 1216, 1256, 1848A, 2730, 2732, 2734, 3172.
  Patronato: 20.
AGN: Archivo General de la Nación, Mexico City, Mexico
  Californias: 12, 29, 36 pts. 3–5, 39.
  Correspondencias de Virreyes Marqués de Croix y Marqués de Branciforte: 13,
    14.
  Historia: 24, 25 pt. 3.
  Minería: 160.
  Provincias Internas: 30, 87, 141, 152, 154, 169, 237.
  Reales Cédulas: 48, 109.
AHAD: Archivo Históricos del Arzobispado de Durango, Durango, Mexico
  Microfilm, rolls: 45, 48, 49.
BNAF: Biblioteca Nacional de México, Archivo Franciscano, Mexico City, Mexico
  Cajas: 12, 31, 33, 36, 39, 236.
CJMA: Ciudad Juárez Municipal Archive, Ciudad Juárez, Mexico
  Microfilm, Second Printing, rolls: 10, 11, 12, 13.
SANM II: Spanish Archive of New Mexico, Series II, New Mexico State Archive
    and Records Center, Santa Fe, New Mexico
  Microfilm, rolls: 10, 11, 12, 13, 15, 21, 22.

Secondary Sources

Adams, Eleanor B. *Bishop Tamarón's Visitation of New Mexico, 1760.* Albuquerque:
  Historical Society of New Mexico, 1954.

——. "Fray Silvestre and the Obstinate Hopi." *New Mexico Historical Review* 38 (April 1963): 97–138.

Adams, Eleanor B., and Fray Angélico Chávez, eds. and trans. *The Missions of New Mexico, 1776: A Description by Fray Francisco Atanasio Domínguez with Other Contemporary Documents*. Albuquerque: University of New Mexico Press, 1956.

Almada, Francisco R. *Diccionario de Historia, Geografía, y Biografía Sonorense*. Chihuahua: Ruíz Sandoval, 1952.

Archer, Criston. *The Army in Bourbon Mexico, 1760–1810*. Albuquerque: University of New Mexico Press, 1977.

Bakewell, Peter J. *Silver Mining and Society in Colonial Mexico, Zacatecas 1546–1700*. Cambridge: Cambridge University Press, 1971.

Bancroft, Hubert Howe, *History of California*. Vol. 1, *1542–1800*. San Francisco: The History Company, 1886.

——. *History of Arizona and New Mexico, 1530–1888*. San Francisco: The History Company, 1889.

Boeta, José Rudolfo. *Bernardo de Gálvez*. Madrid: Publicaciones Españolas, 1976.

Bolton, Herbert Eugene. *Anza's California Expeditions*. 5 vols. Berkeley: University of California Press, 1930.

——. *Coronado on the Turquoise Trail: Knight of Pueblos and Plains*. Albuquerque: University of New Mexico Press, 1949.

——. *Outpost of Empire: The Story of the Founding of San Francisco*. New York: Alfred A. Knopf, 1931.

——. *Rim of Christendom, a Biography of Eusebio Francisco Kino, Pacific Coast Pioneer*. New York: Macmillan, 1936. Reprint. Tucson: University of Arizona Press, 1984.

——. "The Epic of Greater America." *American Historical Review* 38, no. 3 (April 1933).

——. "The Mission as a Frontier Institution in the Spanish-American Colonies." In *New Spain's Far Northern Frontier: Essays on Spain in the American West, 1540–1821*. Edited by David J. Weber, 49–65. Dallas: Southern Methodist University Press, 1979.

——. *The Spanish Borderlands: A Chronicle of Old Florida and the Southwest*. New Haven: Yale University Press, 1921.

Bowman, J. N., and Robert F. Heizer. *Anza and the Northwest Frontier of New Spain*. Los Angeles: Southwest Museum, 1967.

Boyer, Richard. *Lives of the Bigamists: Marriage, Family, and Community in Colonial Mexico*. Albuquerque: University of New Mexico Press, 1995.

Brading, David A. *Church and State in Bourbon Mexico: The Diocese of Michoacán, 1749–1810*. Cambridge: Cambridge University Press, 1994.

——. *Miners and Merchants in Bourbon Mexico, 1763–1810*. Cambridge: Cambridge University Press, 1971.

Brinckerhoff, Sidney B., and Odie B. Faulk. *Lancers for the King: A Study of the Frontier Military System of Northern New Spain with a Translation of the Royal Reglamento of 1772*. Phoenix: Arizona Historical Foundation, 1965.

Broughton, William H. "Francisco Rendón: Spanish Agent in Philadelphia, 1779–1786, Intendent of Spanish Louisiana, 1793–1796," Ph.D. diss., University of New Mexico, 1994.

Chávez, fray Angélico. *Archive of the Archdiocese of Santa Fe, 1678–1900*. Washington, D.C.: Academy of American Franciscan History, 1957.

Chávez, Thomas E. *Chasing History: Quixotic Quests for Artifact, Art, and Heritage*. Santa Fe: Sunstone Press, 2013.

———. *Spain and the Independence of the United States: An Intrinsic Gift*. Albuquerque: University of New Mexico Press, 2002.

Chipman, Donald. *Spanish Texas, 1519–1821*. Austin: University of Texas Press, 1992.

Crosby, Harry W. *Antigua California: Mission and Colony on the Peninsular Frontier, 1697–1768*. Albuquerque: University of New Mexico Press, 1994.

Cruz, Gilbert R. *Let There Be Towns: Spanish Municipal Origins in the American Southwest, 1610–1810*. College Station: Texas A&M University Press, 1988.

Cuello, José. "The Economic Impact of the Bourbon Reforms and the Late Colonial Crisis of Empire at the Local Level: The Case of Saltillo, 1777–1817." *The Americas* 44, no. 3 (January 1988): 301–23.

Cutter, Charles R. *The Legal Culture of Northern New Spain, 1700–1810*. Albuquerque: University of New Mexico Press, 1995.

Cutter, Donald C., ed. *The Defense of Northern New Spain: Hugo O'Conor's Report to Teodoro de Croix, July 22, 1777*. Dallas: Southern Methodist University Press, DeGolyer Library, 1994.

Douglass, William A., and Jon Bilbao. *Amerikanuak: Basques in the New World*. Reno: University of Nevada Press, 1975.

Elliott, J. H. *Imperial Spain, 1469–1716*. London: Penguin Books, 1963.

———. *Spain and Its World, 1500–1700*. New Haven: Yale University Press, 1989.

Faulk, Odie B., and Laura Faulk. *Defenders of the Interior Provinces: Presidial Soldiers on the Northern Frontier of New Spain*. Albuquerque: Albuquerque Museum, 1988.

Flint, Richard. *Great Cruelties Have Been Reported: The 1544 Investigation of the Coronado Expedition*. Dallas: Southern Methodist University Press, 2002.

Forbes, Jack D. *Warriors of the Colorado: The Yumas of the Quechan Nation and Their Neighbors*. Norman: University of Oklahoma Press, 1965.

Frank, Ross. *From Settler to Citizen: New Mexican Economic Development and the Creation of Vecino Society, 1750–1820*. Berkeley: University of California Press, 2000.

Franklin, Ida Luisa. *Bride for a Silver King*. Denver: Three Rivers Press, 1980.

García, Ricardo León. *Misiones Jesuitas en la Tarahumara, Siglo XVIII.* Juarez: Universidad Autónoma de Ciudad Juárez, 1992.

Garate, Donald T. "Arizona: The Basque Connection." Paper presented at the Joint Meeting of the Arizona and New Mexico Historical Societies, Santa Fe, April 1–3, 1998.

———. "Basque Ethnic Connections and the Expeditions of Juan Bautista de Anza to Alta California." *Colonial Latin American Historical Review* 4 (Winter 1995): 71–93.

———. *Juan Bautista de Anza: Basque Explorer in the New World, 1693–1740.* Reno: University of Nevada Press, 2005.

Gibson, Charles. *Spain in America.* New York: Harper & Row, 1966.

Gonzalez-Berry, Herlinda, and David R. Maciel, eds. *The Contested Homeland: A Chicano History of New Mexico.* Albuquerque: University of New Mexico Press, 2000.

Gray, Genevieve. *Fair Laughs the Morn: A Historical Romance of the Anza Expedition to California, 1775-76.* Santa Fe: Sunstone Press, 1994.

Guerrero, Vladimir. *The Anza Trail and the Settling of California.* Berkeley: Heyday Books, 2006.

Gutiérrez, Ramón A., and Elliot Young. "Transnationalizing Borderlands History." *The Western Historical Quarterly* 41, no. 1 (Spring 2010): 26–53.

———. *When Jesus Came, The Corn Mothers Went Away: Marriage, Sexuality, and Power in New Mexico, 1500–1846.* Stanford: Stanford University Press, 1991.

Hämäläinen, Pekka. *The Comanche Empire.* New Haven: Yale University Press, 2009.

Hammond, George P., ed. "The Zúñiga Journal: Tucson to Santa Fe: The Opening of a Spanish Trade Route, 1788–1795." *New Mexico Historical Review* 6 (January 1931): 40–65.

Hendricks, Rick. "Church-State Relations in Anza's New Mexico, 1777–1787." *Catholic Southwest: A Journal of History and Culture* 9 (1998): 25–42.

Herr, Richard. *The Eighteenth-Century Revolution in Spain.* Princeton: Princeton University Press, 1958.

Herrera, Carlos R. "Before the Waters . . . The Desert: An Early History of the Imperial Valley." In *Imperial-Mexicali Valleys: Development and Environment of the U.S.-Mexican Border Region.* Edited by Kimberly Collins, Paul Ganster, Cheryl Mason, Eduardo Sánchez López, and Margarito Quintero-Nuñez. San Diego: San Diego State University Press, 2004.

———. "Infidelity and the Presidio Captain: Adultery and Honor in the Lives of María Rosa Tato y Anza and José Antonio Vildósola, Sonora, New Spain, 1769–1783." *Journal of the History of Sexuality* 15, no. 2 (May 2006): 204–27.

———. "Juan Bautista de Anza and the Social-Militarization of Bourbon El Paso: 1778–1788." *Journal of the Southwest* 46, no. 3 (Autumn 2004): 501–28.

———. "New Mexico Resistance to U.S. Occupation during the Mexican-American War of 1846–1848." In *The Contested Homeland: A Chicano History of New Mexico*. Edited by Erlinda Gonzalez-Berry and David R. Maciel. Albuquerque: University of New Mexico Press, 2000.

———. "The King's Governor: Juan Bautista de Anza and Bourbon New Mexico in the Era of Imperial Reform, 1778–1788." Ph.D. diss., University of New Mexico, 2000.

Hurtado, Albert L. "Herbert E. Bolton, Racism, and American History." *Pacific Historical Review* 62, no. 2 (May 1993).

———. "Parkmanizing the Spanish Borderlands: Bolton, Turner, and the Historian's World." *Western Historical Quarterly* 26, no. 2 (Summer 1995).

———. "Romancing the West in the Twentieth Century: The Politics of History in a Contested Region." *Western Historial Quarterly* 32, no. 4 (Winter 2001): 417–35.

———. "The Spanish Borderlands." *OAH Magazine of History* 10, no. 2 (Winter 1996, Latinos in the United States): 12–13.

Ispizua, Segundo de. *Historia de los Vascos en el Descubrimiento, Conquista y Civilización de América*, 6 vols. Bilbao, Spain: J. A. Lerchundi, 1914–1919. San Sebastián: Ediciones Vascas, 1979.

———. *Los Vascos en América: México*. Madrid: Ediciones Vascas, 1918.

Jackson, Robert H., and Edward Castillo. *Indians, Franciscans, and Spanish Colonization: The Impact of the Mission System on California Indians*. Albuquerque: University of New Mexico Press, 1995.

John, Elizabeth A.H. *Storms Brewed in Other Men's Worlds: The Confrontation of Indians, Spanish, and French in the Southwest, 1540–1795*. Norman: University of Oklahoma Press, 1975.

Jones, Oakah L., Jr. *Los Paisanos: Spanish Settlers on the Northern Frontier of New Spain*. Norman: University of Oklahoma Press, 1979.

———. *Nueva Vizcaya: Heartland of the Spanish Frontier*. Albuquerque: University of New Mexico Press, 1988.

———. *Pueblo Warriors and Spanish Conquest*. Norman: University of Oklahoma Press, 1966.

Jones, Robert E. *Provincial Development in Russia: Catherine II and Jakob Sievers*. New Brunswick: Rutgers University Press, 1984.

Kern, Robert W. *Historical Dictionary of Modern Spain, 1700–1988*. Westport, Conn.: Greenwood Press, 1990.

Kessell, John L. "Anza Damns the Missions: A Spanish Soldier's Criticism of Indian Policy, 1772." *Journal of Arizona History* 13 (1972): 53–63.

———. "Anza, Indian Fighter: The Spring Campaign of 1766." *Journal of Arizona History* 9 (1968): 155–62.

———. *Friars, Soldiers, and Reformers: Hispanic Arizona and the Sonora Mission Frontier, 1767–1856*. Tucson: University of Arizona Press, 1976.

———. "Friars versus Bureaucrats: The Mission as a Threatened Institution on the

Arizona-Sonora Frontier, 1767–1842." *Western Historical Quarterly* 5 (April 1974): 151–62.

———. "Juan Bautista de Anza: Father and Son—Pillars of New Spain's Far North." In *Western Lives: A Biographical History of the American West.* Edited by Richard Eutalain, 29–58. Albuquerque: University of New Mexico Press, 2004.

———. *Kiva, Cross, and Crown: The Pecos Indians and New Mexico, 1540–1840.* Tucson: Southwest Parks and Monuments Association, 1987.

———. *Miera y Pacheco: A Renaissance Spaniard in Eighteenth-Century New Mexico.* Norman: University of Oklahoma Press, 2013.

———. *Mission of Sorrows: Jesuit Guevavi and the Pimas, 1691–1767.* Tucson: University of Arizona Press, 1970.

———, ed. *Remote Beyond Compare: Letters of Don Diego de Vargas to His Family From New Spain and New Mexico, 1675–1706.* Albuquerque: University of New Mexico Press, 1989.

———. *The Missions of New Mexico Since 1776.* Albuquerque: University of New Mexico Press, 1980.

———. *Spain in the Southwest: A Narrative History of Colonial New Mexico, Arizona, Texas, and California.* Norman: University of Oklahoma Press, 2002.

Konetzke, Richard. *Colección de documentos para la Historia de la Formación Social de Hispanoamérica 1493–1810.* Madrid: Consejo Superior de Investigaciones Científicas, 1962.

Lamadrid, Enrique R. "Los Comanches: Text, Performance, and Transculturation in an 18th Century New Mexican Folk Drama." In *Recovering the U.S. Hispanic Literary Heritage*, vol. 3. Houston: Arte Público Press, 2000.

Lavrin, Asunción, ed. *Sexuality and Marriage in Colonial Latin America.* Lincoln: University of Nebraska Press, 1989.

Lynch, John. *Bourbon Spain, 1700–1808.* Oxford: Basil Blackwell, 1989.

———. *Spain under the Habsburgs.* Vol. 1, *Empire and Absolutism, 1516–1598.* New York: New York University Press, 1984.

Martí, Julio César Montañé. *Juan Bautista de Anza: Diario del Primer Viaje a la California, 1774.* Hermosillo, Sonora, Mexico: Sociedad Sonorense de Historia, en coedición con Reprográfica, S.A., 1989.

Martínez, Wilfred. *Anza and Cuerno Verde: Decisive Battle.* Pueblo, Colo.: El Escritorio Press, 2001.

Matson, Daniel S., and Bernard L. Fontana, eds. *Before Rebellion: Letter & Reports of Jacobo Sedelmayr, S.J.* Tucson: Arizona Historical Society, 1996.

Moorhead, Max L. *The Apache Frontier: Jacobo Ugarte and Spanish-Indian Relations in Northern New Spain, 1769–1791.* Norman: University of Oklahoma Press, 1968.

———. *The Presidio: Bastion of the Spanish Borderlands.* Norman: University of Oklahoma Press, 1975.

Navarro García, Luis. *Don José de Gálvez y la Comandancia General de las Pro-*

vincias Internas del Norte de la Nueva España. Seville: Escuela de Estudios Hispano-Americanos de Sevilla, 1964.

———. *La Sublevación Yaqui de 1740.* Seville: Escuela de Estudios Hispano-Americanos de Sevilla, 1966.

———. "The North of New Spain as a Political Problem in the Eighteenth Century." Translated by Elizabeth Gard and David J. Weber. In *New Spain's Far Northern Frontier: Essays on Spain in the American West, 1540–1821.* Edited by David J. Weber, 206–207. Albuquerque: University of New Mexico Press, 1979.

Naylor, Thomas H., and Charles W. Polzer, eds. *Pedro de Rivera and the Military Regulations for Northern New Spain, 1724–1729: A Documentary History of His Frontier Inspection and the Reglamento de 1729.* Tucson: University of Arizona Press, 1988.

Nieto-Phillips, John M. "When Tourists Came, The Mestizos Went Away: Hispanophilia and the Racial Whitening of New Mexico, 1880s-1940s." In *Interpreting Spanish Colonialism: Empires, Nations, and Legends.* Edited by Christopher Schmidt-Nowara and John M. Nieto-Phillips. Albuquerque: University of New Mexico Press, 2005.

Norris, Jim. *After "The Year Eighty": The Demise of Franciscan Power in Spanish New Mexico.* Albuquerque: University of New Mexico Press, 2000.

———. "The Breakdown of Franciscan Hegemony in the Kingdom of New Mexico, 1692–1752." Ph.D. diss., Tulane University, 1994.

Noyes, Stanley. *Los Comanches: The Horse People, 1751–1845.* Albuquerque: University of New Mexico Press, 1993.

Padilla, Genaro. *My History, Not Yours: The Formation of Mexican American Autobiography.* Madison: University of Wisconsin Press, 1993.

Paquette, Gabriel B. *Enlightenment, Governance, and Reform in Spain and Its Empire, 1759–1808.* Basingstoke: Palgrave Macmillan, 2008.

Pietschmann, Horst. "Protoliberalismo, Reformas Borbónicas y Revolución: La Nueva España en el Ultimo Tercio del Siglo XVIII." In Josefina Zoraida Vázquez, *Interpretatciones del Siglo XVIII Mexicano: El Impacto de las Reformas Borbónicas,* 31–32. Mexico City: Nueva Imagen, 1992.

Pino, Don Pedro Bautista. *The Exposition of the Province of New Mexico, 1812.* Translated and edited by Adrian Bustamante and Marc Simmons. Santa Fe and Albuquerque: El Rancho de las Golondrinas and University of New Mexico Press, 1995.

Polzer, Charles W., and Thomas Sheridan. *The Presidio and Militia on the Northern Frontier of New Spain: A Documentary History.* Vol. 2, pt. 1, *The Californias and Sinaloa-Sonora, 1700–1765.* Tucson: University of Arizona Press, 1997.

Pourade, Richard. *Anza Conquers the Desert.* San Diego: Union-Tribune Publishing, 1971.

Priestly, Herbert Ingram. *José de Gálvez: Visitor General of New Spain, 1765–1771.* Berkeley: University of California Press, 1916.

Pupo-Walker, Enrique, ed. *Castaways: The Narrative of Alvar Núñez Cabeza de Vaca*. Berkeley: University of California Press, 1993.

Radding, Cynthia. *Wandering Peoples: Colonialism, Ethnic Spaces, and Ecological Frontiers in Northwestern Mexico, 1700–1850*. Durham: Duke University Press, 1997.

Recopilación de leyes de los reynos de las Indias, 1681. Reprint. Madrid: Ediciones Cultura Hispánica, 1773.

Rey, Agapito. "Missionary Aspects of the Founding of New Mexico." *New Mexico Historical Review* 23 (January 1948): 22–31.

Rolle, Andrew F. *California: A History*. Arlington Heights, Ill.: AHM Publishing, 1978.

Romero, José Luis. *Latinoamérica: las ciudades y las ideas*. Buenos Aires: Siglo Veintiuno Editores, 1976.

Sánchez, Joseph P. *Spanish Bluecoats: The Catalonian Volunteers in Northwestern New Spain, 1767–1810*. Albuquerque: University of New Mexico Press, 1990.

Sandos, James A. "From 'Boltonlands' to 'Weberlands': The Borderlands Enter American History." *American Quarterly* 46, no. 4 (December, 1994): 595–604.

Santiago, Mark. *Massacre at the Yuma Crossing: Spanish Relations with the Quechan, 1779–1782*. Tucson: University of Arizona Press, 1998.

Schmidt-Nowara, Christopher, and John M. Nieto-Phillips, eds. *Interpreting Spanish Colonialism: Empires, Nations, and Legends*. Albuquerque: University of New Mexico Press, 2005.

Scholes, France V. "Civil Government and Society in New Mexico in the Seventeenth Century." *New Mexico Historical Review* 10 (April 1935): 71–111.

Schröder, Ingo W. "Western Apache External Relations during Spanish Colonial Times." Unpublished article, University of New Mexico.

Seed, Patricia. *To Love, Honor, and Obey in Colonial Mexico: Conflicts over Marriage Choice, 1574–1821*. Stanford: Stanford University Press, 1988.

Simmons, Marc. "New Mexico's Smallpox Epidemic of 1780–1781." *New Mexico Historical Review* 41 (October 1966): 319–26.

———. "Settlement Patterns and Village Plans in Colonial New Mexico." In *The Spanish Borderlands: A First Reader*. Edited by Oakah L. Jones, Jr., 54–68. Los Angeles: Lorrin L. Morrison, 1974.

———. *Spanish Government in New Mexico*. Albuquerque: University of New Mexico Press, 1968.

———. "Trail Dust: Massacre at Awatovi is Little Known Act of Genocide," *Santa Fe New Mexican*, August 2, 2013.

Smith, Fay Jackson. *Captain of the Phantom Presidio: A History of the Presidio of Fronteras, New Spain, 1686-1735*. Spokane: Arthur Clark, 1993.

Sonnichsen, C. L. *Pass of the North: Four Centuries on the Rio Grande*. El Paso: Texas Western Press, 1968.

Spicer, Edward H. *Cycles of Conquest: The Impact of Spain, Mexico, and the United*

States on the Indians of the Southwest, 1533–1960. Tucson: University of Arizona Press, 1962.

Thomas, Alfred Barnaby. *Forgotten Frontiers: A Study of the Spanish Indian Policy of Don Juan Bautista de Anza, Governor of New Mexico, 1777–1787*. Norman: University of Oklahoma Press, 1932.

———. "Governor Mendinueta's Proposals for the Defense of New Mexico, 1772–1778." *New Mexico Historical Review* 6 (January 1931): 21–39.

———. *Teodoro de Croix and the Northern Frontier of New Spain, 1776–1783*. Norman: University of Oklahoma Press, 1941.

———. *The Plains Indians and New Mexico, 1751–1778: A Collection of Documents Illustrative of the History of the Eastern Frontier of New Mexico*. Albuquerque: University of New Mexico Press, 1940.

Thomas, David Hurst. "Cubist Perspectives on the Spanish Borderlands: Past, Present, and Future." In *Columbian Consequences*. Vol. 3, *The Spanish Borderlands in Pan-American Perspective*. Edited by David Hurst Thomas. Washington, D.C.: Smithsonian Institution Press, 1991.

Truett, Samuel. "Epics of Greater America: Herbert Eugene Bolton's Quest for a Transnational American History." In *Interpreting Spanish Colonialism: Empires, Nations, and Legends*. Edited by Christopher Schmidt-Nowara and John M. Nieto-Phillips, 215. Albuquerque: University of New Mexico Press, 2005.

———. *Fugitive Landscapes: The Forgotten History of the U.S.-Mexico Borderlands*. New Haven: Yale University Press, 2006.

Turner, Frederick Jackson. *The Frontier in American History*. New York: Henry Holt, 1921.

Vázquez, Josefina Zoraida, Coordinadora. *Interpretaciones del Siglo XVIII Mexicano: El Impacto de las Reformas Borbónicas*. Mexico City: Nueva Imagen, 1992.

Velázquez, María del Carmen. *Tres Estudios Sobre Las Provincias Internas de Nueva España*. Mexico City: El Colegio de México, 1979.

Warner, Ted J. "Frontier Defense." *New Mexico Historical Review* 41 (January 1966): 5–19.

Warner, Ted J., ed., fray Angélico Chávez, trans. *The Domínguez-Escalante Journal: Their Expedition Through Colorado, Utah, Arizona, and New Mexico in 1776*. Salt Lake City: University of Utah Press, 1995.

Weber, David J. *Bárbaros: Spaniards and Their Savages in the Age of Enlightenment*. New Haven: Yale University Press, 2005.

———. *New Spain's Far Northern Frontier: Essays on Spain in the American West, 1540–1821*. Albuquerque: University of New Mexico Press, 1979.

———. "The Idea of the Spanish Borderlands," in *Columbian Consequences*. Vol. 3, *The Spanish Borderlands in Pan-American Perspective*. Edited by David Hurst Thomas, 3–20. Washington D.C.: Smithsonian Institution Press, 1991.

——. "The Spanish Borderlands of North America: A Historiography." *OAH Magazine of History* 14, no. 4 (Summer 2000): 5–11.

——. "The Spanish Borderlands, Historiography Redux." *The History Teacher* 39, no. 1 (November 2005): 43–56.

——. "The Spanish Legacy in North America and the Historical Imagination." *Western Historical Quarterly* 23, no. 1 (February 1992): 4–24.

——. *The Spanish Frontier in North America*. New Haven: Yale University Press, 1992.

——. "Turner, The Boltonians, and the Borderlands." *American Historical Review* 91, no. 1 (February 1986) 66–81.

Wortman, Miles. "Bourbon Reforms in Central America." *The Americas* 32, no. 2 (October 1975): 222–38.

Zelis, Raphael. *Catálogo de los Sugetos de la Compañía de Jesús que formaban la Provincia de México el día del arresto, 25 de Junio de 1767*. Mexico City: Imprenta de I. Escalante, 1871.

Index

military career, Anza's: Anza's fame
among Comanches, 246; approval
of, 51–52; California expeditions,
60–68; Comanche campaign,
105–6, *107*, 108–10; Comanche peace,
175, 176–77, 248; Cuerno Verde,
104–105; early training, 43, 45; Hopi
resistance and relocation, 110–17;
Indian incorporation strategy, 58–59;
leadership analyzed, 104–105; martial
readiness of New Mexico, 156–57;
Navajo alliance, 117–20; New Mexico
arms edict, 156–57; overview, 3, 56;
promotions, 46, 56, 64, 68; refusal to
be perceived as a coward, 108–109;
relationship with father, 104–105;
significance of Sonora experience, 2;
strategies analyzed, 105–106, 108–109;
tactics in Sonora, 50; trips to Mexico
City, 63, 64, 68, 70
military reforms, 252n12; finances
and corruption, 133–37; military
selection/conscription, 88, 90; New
Mexico, 248–49; Prussian model,
81–82; uniforms, 82, 84, 88
military training in northern
garrisons, 43
military troops: Anza's reforms, 12,
132–33; extra pay, 89–90; pensions,
134, 167; use of uniforms, 82, 84, 88
Mimbreño Apaches, 81, 119, 137–38, 139
Mimbres Mountains, 138, 139–40
mission ideal: Anza on, 12, 113, 186–87,
194, 211–12; Bolton on, 272n5;
consolidation, 216; defense of, 183–84;
dependence on Indian labor, 184;
described, 182–83; expansion, 216;
as Franciscan notion, 182; greatest
failure, 186; later campaign, 228;
limited success, 13, 185–86; results
among Pueblos, 185–86; sacrifice
of, 207–208; Spanish colonists
questioning, 183

mission ideal in Sonora: Anza I's
support, 35; Anza on, 57–59, 190;
failure of, 56–59; Jesuits in Sonora,
27, 35
missions: *alternativa* rotation, 193;
consolidation of, 216–19; criticized,
190–91; deterioration, 225; financial
reforms, 57; pueblos de visita
preferred, 189–90. *See also individual
missions by name*
Mixtón War, 20
Morfi, Juan Agustín de, 265n10
Muñoz Jurado, Diego, 195–200, 204,
206, 237, 276n22
mutual accommodation policies, 70,
71, 99

Nambe mission, 218
Narityante, Tabico, 102, 263n9. *See also*
Cuerno Verde
Navajo Indians: alliance with Anza,
117–20; broken ties with Spain,
119–20; Franciscan efforts, 228;
intermarriage with Pueblos, 119;
peace alliance, 119; peace pact,
248; punitive expeditions against,
103; raids, 77; social-militarization
program, 79; thefts of livestock,
264n32; uprising of 1796, 120
Navajo raids: attacks on Hopis, 114, 115,
116, 118; environmental crisis, 102;
Franciscans on, 264n32; on Hopis,
115, 116
Navarro, Francisco Trébol, 79
Neve, Felipe de: on acordada, 160;
appointment, 205, 276n26; on
banditry, 265–66n13; death, 172, 216,
278n19; Indian servitude abolished,
215; mail service reforms, 168–70;
marriage laws, 233; reputation, 168;
royal patronage to Anza, 207, 212;
war tax, 131
New Laws, 182